Research on
Effective
Models
for
Teacher
Education

Teacher Education Yearbook

Volume 8 *Founded in 1991*

Editors

D. John McIntyre, *Southern Illinois University, Carbondale*

David M. Byrd, *University of Rhode Island, Kingston*

Association of Teacher Educators

Research on
Effective
Models
for
Teacher
Education

Teacher Education Yearbook VIII

Editors

D. John McIntyre • David M. Byrd

CORWIN PRESS, INC.
A Sage Publications Company
Thousand Oaks, California

For information address:

Corwin Press, Inc.
A Sage Publications Company
2455 Teller Road
Thousand Oaks, California 91320
E-mail: order@corwinpress.com

Sage Publications Ltd.
6 Bonhill Street
London EC2A 4PU
United Kingdom

Sage Publications India Pvt. Ltd.
M-32 Market
Greater Kailash I
New Delhi 110 048 India

Printed in the United States of America

Library of Congress Cataloging-in-Publication Data

ISSN: 1078-2265
ISBN: 0-7619-7615-9 (Cloth)
ISBN: 0-7619-7616-7 (Paper)

This book is printed on acid-free paper.

00   01   02   03   04   05   06   7   6   5   4   3   2   1

Editorial Assistant: Catherine Kantor
Production Editor: Diana E. Axelsen
Editorial Assistant: Victoria Cheng
Typesetter: Lynn Miyata
Cover Designer: Tracy E. Miller

Contents

foster active inquiry in their classrooms?

base their instruction on knowledge of subject matter, students, the community, and curriculum goals?

reflect on their teaching in order to improve it?

Of course, the ways in which different researchers choose to address those questions vary widely, but this phenomenon provides us with good information about the efficacy of particular research methods for answering particular questions. If many teacher education researchers used a common framework for research, we could develop programs of research that build on each other and inform what we all do, not just what we do in our individual programs. Meta-analysis might yield more and deeper understandings about effective teacher education.

Earlier, I stated that assessing the impact on teachers was the easier part of teacher education research. Assessing the impact on their students is an almost overwhelming task. Yet, student growth and learning are the ultimate goals of all education, and it is becoming increasingly clear that teacher education program accountability will include this component.

Many variables affect student learning other than teacher education and teacher performance: Morale, climate, and school support; resources available; parental support; teacher autonomy and professionalism; political environment; professional development opportunities for teachers; teacher salaries; school structure; and money spent directly on teachers and instruction are some of these factors. Obviously, teacher education can be effective but teachers ineffective because of the effects of these variables. Also, the most common measures of student learning, standardized tests, are not necessarily compatible with the goals of teacher education programs based on INTASC or other standards. These facts should not make teacher educators disclaim accountability for student learning, but rather should make us careful about the nature of what we are willing to be accountable for.

Teacher education can be accountable for making connections between teacher performance and student learning. If research shows that certain teacher behaviors and knowledge lead to increased student learning, and if we then show that our programs develop that knowledge and performance, we can assume that the teachers are having a positive effect on their students. We can develop teachers who are willing and able to inquire into the effects of their teaching on student learning (action research) and use the results of the inquiry to support teacher education effects on student learning. Not only can we conduct studies such as that done by the National Commission on Teaching and America's Future (NCTAF), in which programs that prepare teachers who are successful at teaching diverse learners are identified, but we can also determine the common features of those powerful programs (NCTAF, 1997). We can and must attend to the connections between what we do in teacher education and how and whether students learn and grow.

The chapters in this yearbook are examples of ways in which to study the power of teacher education. They describe practices of teacher education based on theory, research, and experience and then assess influences of these practices. These research findings become part of the knowledge base on good teacher education. They are one of the layers, one of the dolls. This book can inform the development of teacher education programs and be part of programs of teacher education research devoted to inquiry about impacts of teacher education programs on teachers and on those teachers' students.

Reference

National Commission on Teaching and America's Future (NCTAF). (1997). *Doing what matters most: Investing in quality teaching.* New York: Author.

DIVISION I

Models for Enhancing
the Professional Development
of Teachers

OVERVIEW AND FRAMEWORK

Frances K. Kochan

Frances K. Kochan is Director of the Truman Pierce Institute in the College of Education at Auburn University and Associate Professor in the Department of Educational Foundations, Leadership, and Technology. She has served as a teacher, principal, and superintendent in the public schools. Her current research interests include creating collaborative environments and relationships, beliefs and their relationship to practice, and leadership, with a particular focus on the principalship and issues of gender. She serves as a Board Member of the Holmes Partnership. She is coeditor of a book on school leadership, has authored numerous book chapters, and has published in a variety of journals, including *Theory Into Practice, Planning and Changing,* and *Journal of Teacher Education.*

Overview

The authors in Division I share models of teacher professional development that embody some of the best of what we know about enabling teachers to change their practice in significant and meaningful ways. All the chapters deal with projects focused on creating change in the mathematics and/or science areas, and although the specific changes addressed flow from the systemic reform that has been occurring in these content areas for the last decade (Wise, Spiegel, & Brunning, 1999), the lessons learned and the strategies described have applications beyond these subject areas. Likewise, recognition of the need to change teaching and learning environments, a primary purpose of the three models described here, is part of the broad reform movement currently taking place in education. As an introduction to this division of the yearbook, I briefly review the major themes associated with this movement.

Context and Content

The Context of Educational Reform

The past two decades have witnessed a period of intense pressure to change schools, colleges of education, and teacher education. Many working within the educational domain have put forward ideas and created structures geared toward fostering substantive educational change. Among the most prominent are the Holmes Group, founded in 1985 and reorganized as the Holmes Partnership in 1996, which reported on teachers (1986), schools (1990), and schools of education (1995); the National Network for Educational Renewal (Goodlad, 1994) and the Coalition of Essential Schools (Sizer, 1984), both based on a set of guiding principles; the National Commission on Teaching and America's Future (1996), which focused on issues of standards and quality assurance; and the Association of Teacher Educators report on restructuring teacher education (Association of Teacher Educators Commission on Restructuring Teacher Education, 1991), which called for changes in the way teachers are educated. Although each of these initiatives has its own unique features and foci, all appear to have some common elements that are also present in most other educational reform initiatives. Among the most obvious are these:

- Establishing high-quality standards for all
- Focusing on teaching for understanding
- Providing a quality learning environment that facilitates success for all children
- Stressing active, applied learning that focuses on processes, higher level thinking, and the integration of subject matter
- Developing collaborative governance structures
- Forming connections among and between content areas, people, and institutions
- Enhancing the professional status of teachers, teaching, and teacher education

A Sketch of the Chapters

Although many questions remain unresolved, much has been learned as a result of such educational reform efforts. Among the most important findings has been the recognition that teachers are a crucial element in making change successful (Elmore, 1996). Teachers have great discretion in implementing policy and practice in their classrooms, becoming, in essence, the decision makers regarding what will and will not be incorporated into the teaching/learning environment (Galuzzi, 1998). They are thus an essential force in creating schools in which all children can attain higher standards through active learning processes (Andrew, 1997; National Commission on Teaching and America's Future, 1996). The chapters in Division I stress the need to foster the development of teachers. The authors recognize that the role of teacher educators must encompass not only preparing teachers but also actively working with them to enhance teaching and thus improve schooling. This brief sketch of each of the chapters is meant to provide a sense of their content and unique characteristics.

In Chapter 1, Thomas, Cooper, and Ponticell describe a program aimed at integrating mathematics and science in upper elementary school, which focused on changing teaching approaches. An interesting transformation occurred in the second year of implementation as teachers assumed a greater responsibility for their own learning and for that of their colleagues. Issues related to the teaching of context and the need to allow and foster risk taking in teaching are also addressed in this chapter.

In Chapter 2, Goodell, Parker, and Kahle report on a project that addressed the sustainability of a professional development experience for middle school mathematics teachers. Their conclusions highlight the need for creating and continuing teacher support networks to assist teachers in implementing change over time.

In Chapter 3, Bainer and Wright describe a project aimed at enhancing elementary teachers' capacities to teach science by using a constructivist approach. A major feature of this project was to allow each teacher to develop his or her own plan for professional development. The project was built around a theoretical framework based on research on effective professional development approaches. Involvement in this process helped teachers change their beliefs and practice, serving as an avenue for personal growth and development.

Providing a Framework

Although each chapter in Division I is unique, all three chapters encompass three important concepts:

1. Teaching/learning environments must become more facilitative.
2. The teacher role in these environments and in learning how to create and maintain them must change.
3. Effective professional development is an important aspect of helping to change the teaching role and to create these facilitative environments.

A brief overview of these concepts will help establish a framework for reading the chapters in Division I.

Creating Facilitative Teaching and Learning Environments

Constructivism is one of the primary concepts driving educational change in the teaching/learning contexts of schools and colleges of education (Ishler, 1996; Kaufman, 1996). Constructivism is focused on the notion that individuals are at different levels of understanding and learn in unique ways at differing rates. Teaching strategies in constructivist learning settings include active student and teacher engagement in learning and meaning making, inclusion of problem solving and inquiry as a part of the learning process, and use of assessment procedures that focus on application. The strategies used are meant to create teaching/learning environments that facilitate, rather than direct, learning. Making connections across domains is strongly encouraged and is a significant feature of the Thomas, Cooper, and Ponticell (Chapter 1) model in which mathematics and science are interwoven and integrated.

The concept of constructivism in these models is stressed not only as something K-12 teachers should incorporate into their teaching but also as the preferred method of teaching for university faculty, who modeled constructivist practices for and with K-12 teachers as they engaged in professional development activities. This modeling reflected the notion that those people learning new skills within a profession must have the opportunity to construct their own knowledge as a part of the learning process (Guyton, Rainer, & Wright, 1997).

Reconceptualizing Teacher Roles

Creating classrooms in which a constructivist approach is used necessitates a change in the role of the teacher. In the models described in Division I, this change not only relates to the use of teaching strategies and the relationship of the teacher to the student but also involves the way in which the teacher functions as a professional. These models of teacher education seek to move teachers from conceiving of themselves as working on solving problems related to the teaching of their subjects to viewing themselves as problem solvers who continually inquire about their teaching and their students' learning. An important element in such continuous inquiry is the ability to engage in reflective practice (Brubacher, Case, & Reagan, 1994). Reflective practice is considered by some to be an essential quality in enabling individuals to improve their practice and enhance their own professional development (Schön, 1983, 1987). All the models described here stress this capacity and incorporate both training and opportunities to practice reflection within the role of the teacher.

An interesting commonality in these chapters is that the university faculty involved appeared to view themselves as learners as well as teachers, seeking information about the impact of their work and striving to understand the experience of the teachers with whom they were working. Thus, the faculty members became co-learners rather than experts, and the dividing line between teachers and professors blurred as the two groups became more interdependent. Such relationships are important building blocks in bringing wholeness to the profession (Kochan, 1999).

Another aspect of the changes in the teacher's role highlighted in these chapters deals with teachers' control over their own professional development. Although the professional development experiences in which these teachers engaged were directed toward facilitating teacher adoption of new teaching strategies, all had some degree of choice about how to construct their learning experiences. Thus, the teachers were treated as professionals and placed in positions of power when determining how they would learn. Such empowerment is an important element in teachers' willingness to change their practice (Tunks, 1997).

Implementing Effective Professional Development Strategies

In addition to giving teachers power over their professional growth, our concepts of how to bring about changes in individuals and the ways in which they teach have undergone dramatic revisions in recent years (Abdal-Haqq, 1996). Although the 1-day "shotgun" approach to professional development is apparently still used in many areas, the most effective method for facilitating changes in teacher knowledge and behavior is based on long-term sustained experiences in which teachers can practice and apply new strategies. Collaborative networks and systems of support are often used to assist them in their development efforts (Breck, 1995; Mevarech, 1995; Sparks, 1994).

All three models described in Division I were designed to change the way teachers think about teaching and learning and to give them the knowledge and skills to implement constructivist teaching strategies. Teachers were immersed in the topic over a short period of time and then had the opportunity to apply the ideas and concepts to practice. They also received additional support and engaged in further professional development experiences for at least 1 year after the initial training session. The authors of these chapters also emphasize that teachers participated in these activities because the tasks, knowledge, and skills they were learning and applying were closely related to their practice. Thus, they perceived the professional development activities as relevant to them, an important element in adult learning (Brookfield, 1986).

Another important aspect of the professional development activities described in Division I was that teachers were part of a network of support through which ideas could be shared and questions could be answered. These networks provided a vital link in building teachers' confidence and in sustaining their growth. They were powerful avenues for overcoming the isolation of teaching that so often hinders the professional growth of teachers (Cochran-Smith, 1991; Dana, 1994; Little, 1981) and for dealing with the stress and anxiety of adulthood (Brookfield, 1986).

Concluding Statements

The school-university relationships reported in these chapters provide us with excellent models in which theory and practice were united, each reinforcing the other, as teachers and university faculty worked and learned together to narrow the theory/practice gap that so often exists (Kochan, 1997). The findings from these studies add to our understanding while at the same time raise some important issues that I address in the Division I Summary.

References

Abdal-Haqq, I. (1996). *Making time for teacher professional development.* Washington, DC: Office of Educational Research and Improvement. (ERIC Document Reproduction Service No. ED 400 259)

Andrew, M. D. (1997). What matters most for teacher educators? *Journal of Teacher Education, 48*(3), 167-176.

Association of Teacher Educators National Commission on Restructuring Teacher Education. (1991). *Restructuring the education of teachers: Report of the commission on the education of teachers into the 21st century.* Reston, VA: Author.

Breck, S. (1995, April). *Implementing professional development schools: Seeking a shared vision.* Paper presented at the annual meeting of the American Educational Research Association, San Francisco.

Brookfield, S. (1986). *Understanding and facilitating adult learning.* San Francisco: Jossey-Bass.

Brubacher, J. W., Case, C. W., & Reagan, T. G. (1994). *Becoming a reflective educator: How to build a culture of inquiry in the schools.* Thousand Oaks, CA: Corwin.

Cochran-Smith, M. (1991). Reinventing student teaching. *Journal of Teacher Education, 42*(2), 104-118.

Dana, N. F. (1994). Building partnerships to effect educational change: Schools, culture, and the finding of teacher voice. In M. J. O'Hair & S. J. Odell (Eds.), *Partnerships in education: Teacher education yearbook II* (pp. 11-26). New York: Harcourt Brace.

Elmore, R. F. (1996). *Restructuring schools: The next generation of educational reform.* San Francisco: Jossey-Bass.

Galuzzi, C. (1998, October). *Policy and professional growth: Teachers reconstructing practice in a climate of state reform.* Paper presented at the annual conference of the University Council for Educational Administration, St. Louis.

Goodlad, J. I. (1994). *Educational renewal: Better teachers, better schools.* San Francisco: Jossey-Bass.

Guyton, E., Rainer, J., & Wright, T. (1997). Developing a constructivist teacher education program. In D. J. McIntyre & D. M. Byrd (Eds.), *Research on the education of our nation's teachers* (pp. 149-171). Thousand Oaks, CA: Corwin.

Holmes Group. (1986). *Tomorrow's teachers: A report of the Holmes Group.* East Lansing, MI: Author.

Holmes Group. (1990). *Tomorrow's schools: Principles for the design of professional development schools.* East Lansing, MI: Author.

Holmes Group. (1995). *Tomorrow's schools of education: A report of the Holmes Group.* East Lansing, MI: Author.

Ishler, P. (1996). President's message. *Action in Teacher Education, XVIII*(2), v.

Kaufman, D. (1996). Constructivist-based experiential learning in teacher education. *Action in Teacher Education, XVIII*(2), 40-50.

Kochan, F. K. (1997, November). *Educational improvement: Understanding the theory and the practice.* Symposium presentation at the annual meeting of the Mid-South Educational Research Association, Memphis, TN.

Kochan, F. K. (1999). Professional development schools: A comprehensive view. In D. Byrd & D. J. McIntyre (Eds.), *Research on professional development schools: Teacher education yearbook VII* (pp. 173-190). Thousand Oaks, CA: Corwin.

Little, J. W. (1981). *School success and staff development: The role of staff development in urban desegregated schools.* Boulder, CO: Center for Action Research.

Mevarech, Z. R. (1995). Teachers' paths on the way to and from the professional development forum. In T. R. Guskey & M. Huberman (Eds.), *Professional education.* New York: Teachers College Press.

National Commission on Teaching and America's Future. (1996). *What matters most: Teaching for America's future.* New York: Author.

Schön, D. A. (1983). *The reflective practitioner.* New York: Basic Books.

Schön, D. A. (1987). *Educating the reflective practitioner.* San Francisco: Jossey-Bass.

Sizer, T. R. (1984). *Horace's compromise: The dilemma of the American high school: The first report from a study of American high schools, cosponsored by the National Association of Secondary School Principals and the Commission on Educational Issues of the National Association of Independent Schools.* Boston: Houghton Mifflin.

Sparks, D. (1994). A paradigm shift in staff development. *Journal of Staff Development, 15*(4), 20-23.

Tunks, J. L. (1997, June). *From isolation to integration: The change process in an elementary school: The teachers' perspective.* Paper presented at the annual meeting of the American Educational Research Association, Chicago. (ERIC Document Reproduction Service No. ED 408 251)

Wise, V. L., Spiegel, A. N., & Brunning, R. H. (1999). Using teacher reflective practice to evaluate professional development in mathematics and science. *Journal of Teacher Education, 50*(1), 42-49.

1 Doing Math the Science Way

Staff Development for Integrated Teaching and Learning

Julie A. Thomas

Sandra B. Cooper

Judith A. Ponticell

Julie A. Thomas is Assistant Professor of Curriculum and Instruction at Texas Tech University, Lubbock. Her funded projects and publications, including *Guidelines for the Science Preparation of Prospective Elementary Teachers* (1996), focus on teaching elementary science education and maximizing learning in science teacher preparation and professional development.

Sandra B. Cooper is Assistant Professor of Curriculum and Instruction at Texas Tech University, Lubbock. Her funded projects and publications focus on the preparation of elementary mathematics teachers, the integration of mathematics and science, professional development, and technology integration. Her work has been included in the *Technology and Teacher Education Annual.*

Judith A. Ponticell is Associate Professor of Educational Leadership at Texas Tech University, Lubbock. Her writing and consulting focus on personal, interpersonal, and organizational influences on learning and change. She has authored more than 27 articles, chapters, and books, including *Enhancing Learning in Training and Adult Education* (1998).

ABSTRACT

Doing Math the Science Way, an integrated science and mathematics staff development project, was funded by Eisenhower Professional Development Grants for 2 consecutive years. The project used integrated content and teaching methodology with a focus on earth science in the first year and geometry in the second year. Funding supported a total of 6 hours of graduate credit for an intensive 3-week summer workshop and a 9-month implementation component for the ensuing school year. This study reports what was learned in Year 1 about teachers' transfer of integrated science and mathematics content and activities learned in the project into their classrooms and influences on that transfer. The chapter also reports on changes initiated in the Year 2 project design resulting from what was learned about staff development.

Introduction

Reports such as *Science for All Americans* (American Association for the Advancement of Science [AAAS], 1989) and *Everybody Counts* (National Research Council [NRC], 1989) stress the interrelatedness of science and mathematics and the natural implications for curriculum development and instruction. Teachers are encouraged to cover less content in more depth and to find more connections across the disciplines to facilitate students' cognitive development. The National Council of Teachers of Mathematics (NCTM, 1989) and the National Research Council (NRC, 1996) both call for science, mathematics, and technology integration to enable students to solve real-world problems.

Some proponents, however, are also concerned that elementary teachers have limited content knowledge in the sciences and therefore may be ill-equipped to plan, develop, or teach integrated science and mathematics (Greenwood, 1996). With limited preservice course work in science and mathematics, elementary teachers may lack content depth, the ability to see connections between science and math, and an understanding of science and mathematics as ways of thinking (Raizen & Michelsohn, 1993).

Perspectives

Doing Math the Science Way embraced several perspectives. First, research on staff development is extensive. In a summary of research on successful staff development, Glickman, Gordon, and Ross-Gordon (1998, p. 351) indicate 14 crucial components. Six of these may be described as relating to the content and process of teachers' learning experiences in staff development: (a) small-group learning activities; (b) concrete and specific content; (c) demonstration, trial, and feedback during training; (d) classroom coaching following training; (e) encouragement of risk taking and experimentation; and (f) regular discussion and problem solving.

Second, change is an individual process. Staff development, often designed for groups of teachers, must be relevant to each teacher (Sparks & Loucks-Horsley, 1989). New ideas and innovations have different meanings for different teachers (Hall & Hord, 1987). For this reason, programs based on assumptions of uniformity, or one best practice, repeatedly fail, whereas programs based on the uniqueness of the teachers and school system involved generally succeed (Elmore & McLaughlin, 1988).

Third, new practice is more likely when teachers perceive that they are empowered to increase their own effectiveness. According to Susan Loucks-Horsley, helping teachers increase their content knowledge is complex, and some well-honed principles of effective staff development need to come into play. We need to help people make informed decisions about what they need to learn (in Sparks, 1997, p. 22). Such informed decisions are facilitated by providing teachers with opportunities to work together, to discuss education issues, and to study student work. Such opportunities make it less likely that teachers will revert back to old ways.

Finally, new learning requires a change in perspective. Mezirow (1981) points out that transformative learning often occurs after some kind of disorienting experience. Reflective and critical thinking linked to real-life problems must be part of teacher learning. Through combined reflection and action, called *praxis* by Friere (1970), one increases awareness of the assumptions one makes and then acts on new knowledge.

Background of the Study

The 17 upper elementary school teachers who volunteered for the project came from seven schools. The researchers selected the schools because they had strong administrative leadership, a positive response to professional development opportunities in mathematics curriculum development, and school populations that included a large percentage of historically underserved students. The schools were in an urban district in west Texas; 79% of the students they served were Hispanic, African American, Asian, or Native American, and 86% were economically disadvantaged.

Four objectives drove the development and evaluation of the project:

1. To increase teachers' content knowledge in earth science and mathematics
2. To increase teachers' confidence in their content knowledge and teaching and thus positively influence their self-efficacy
3. To increase teachers' awareness and understanding of hands-on, inquiry-oriented teaching methods
4. To help teachers develop authentic assessments to measure students' understanding of integrated science and mathematics

The teachers earned three graduate credit hours for a 3-week summer workshop and three credit hours for 18 class meetings scheduled on evenings and weekends throughout the ensuing school year. In the 3-week summer workshop, curriculum included study of earthquakes, atmosphere, and weathering and erosion, together with embedded mathematics processes (see Table 1.1). As teachers learned earth science content, they concurrently used mathematics processes. They also engaged in field investigations and developed elementary classroom applications.

The integrated earth science and mathematics curriculum was developed by project staff and a doctoral student who was an experienced earth science teacher and oil field geologist. Geology faculty in atmospheric science, paleontology, astronomy, and cave exploration and their graduate students served as additional teaching resources.

TABLE 1.1 Summer Workshop in Earth Science

Week 1   Earthquakes
Earthquakes rapidly change the surface of the earth.
Objective: Teachers will identify what an earthquake is, why and how earthquakes occur, the physical results of an earthquake, how earthquakes are measured, and how this information shapes our knowledge of the earth's interior.

Science topic	*Mathematics Process*
Types of forces	Measurement
Measuring earthquakes	Using powers of 10, measurement, rounding, converting measurements within the same system
Locating earthquakes	Coordinates, charts and graphs
Earth's interior	Temperature, measurement, charts and graphs
Earthquakes and plate tectonics	Prediction, probability

Week 2   Air
The atmosphere has different properties at different elevations.
Objective: Teachers will demonstrate an understanding of the structure of the atmosphere and its composition. They will collect data related to the ways in which the sun's energy affects atmospheric conditions.

Science topic	*Mathematics Process*
Structure of the atmosphere	Measurement, graphing, temperature, prediction
Energy from the sun	Scales/ratios, rounding, estimation, converting measurements
Heat transfer	Measuring, temperature, volume, charts and graphs, estimating and solving problems using ratios and proportions

TABLE 1.1 Continued

Science Topic	Mathematics Process
Major air circulation	Charts and graphs, measuring, plotting coordinates
Wind systems	Charts and graphs, measuring, plotting coordinates

Week 3   Weathering and Erosion
The surface of the earth is slowly changing.
Objective: Teachers will collect data on the changing surface of the earth and analyze the processes related to these changes.

Science Topic	Mathematics Process
Weathering	Measuring, estimating
Products of weathering	Collect, organize, and interpret data
	Sampling, perimeter and area, mass, volume
Minerals	Mass, volume, changing measurement with same system, prediction, classifying
Erosion	Communicate an understanding of a problem
	List outcomes in a given situation
	Measurement, volume, mass
Agents of erosion	Prediction, measurement, sampling, perimeter and area

During the school year, teachers attended classes twice a month. New concepts were presented through hands-on experiences. Teachers reflected on the application of these new concepts in their classrooms, constructed curriculum materials, and developed lessons, units, and student assessments in collaboration with project staff and participants.

Resource development was important in Doing Math the Science Way. Project staff selected trade books and field guides for teachers on the basis of accuracy of earth science content and general suitability for upper elementary classroom use. Teachers also received activity books with both class lessons and other types of lessons. Teachers explored earth science resources on the Internet and developed lesson and unit "kits" to share with each other.

Data Collection and Analysis

What did we want to learn? We wanted to learn what influenced teachers' transfer and/or extension of integrated science and mathematics content and activities learned in the project into their own classrooms. In the 3-week summer workshop, teachers completed pre- and posttests on earth science content. We developed the content test to include items reflecting the major concepts in the summer workshop. We made anecdotal notes during workshop sessions. Teachers wrote in their reflective journals after each session.

During the school year, teachers completed pre- and postinventories of self-efficacy. Teachers were asked to rate each item on a 5-point scale from 1, *strongly agree,* to 5, *strongly disagree.* We created items on this 27-item Likert-type inventory from identification of common themes in Bandura's (1977, 1982, 1986, 1993) work on self-efficacy. For example, a common theme across Bandura's work is persistence in the face of difficulty. This theme was reflected in the items "I persist in science-related tasks that are difficult" and "When students have difficulty with science concepts, I persist in working with the students."

Over the school year, we also made anecdotal notes during class sessions, and teachers wrote in reflective journals after each session. We informally observed teachers' lessons and made anecdotal notes. Teachers compiled portfolios illustrating the use of new content and methods in their classrooms. At the end of the year, we interviewed the teachers to gather their perceptions of the influence of the project on their content knowledge, their ability to design and deliver integrated science and mathematics curricula, their willingness to take curricular and instructional risks, and their perceptions of the impact of changes they made on student learning. Interviews were audiotaped and transcribed.

Descriptive statistics were run on the pre- and posttests on earth science content and on the pre- and postinventories of teaching self-efficacy.

Participants' reflective journals, researchers' anecdotal notes of class sessions and teachers' classroom lessons, project portfolios, and interview transcripts were analyzed by using the constant comparative method advocated by Glaser and Strauss (1967) and Strauss (1987). This allowed for ongoing data collection and analysis and the generation and revision of emergent themes. Themes were verified and clarified (see Guba, 1981) through analysis of data by researchers separately and together, discussion of discrepancies between researchers' analyses, and reanalysis of data when any unresolved discrepancies arose.

Findings

Teachers' Science Content Knowledge

Pre-/posttest scores indicated that teachers' content knowledge increased at the end of the 3-week summer workshop. Prior to the workshop, none of the teachers had completed the content test at a 70% mastery level. After the workshop, 7 of 13 teachers (or 54%) completed the posttest at the 90% mastery level, 10 (or 77%) at the 80% mastery level, and 12 (or 92%) at the 70% mastery level. Four teachers did not take the posttest.

Teachers' Confidence in Their Content Knowledge and Ability

Pre-/postproject responses on the self-efficacy inventory indicated that teachers' confidence in their content knowledge and teaching ability increased from the beginning of the school year to the end of the school year. Table 1.2 shows an increase in teachers' confidence in their earth science knowledge, ability to organize and plan for earth science teaching, and ability to help students learn earth science concepts. Table 1.2 also shows an increase in teachers' persistence in working with students who had difficulty with earth science concepts and in participating themselves in earth science-related tasks that were difficult for them. The table further indicates a decrease in teachers' tendency to avoid planning earth science activities, as well as in their tendency to avoid earth science-related tasks when they thought they would not be successful. Finally, the table shows a decrease in teachers' tendency to give up on earth science problems, as

TABLE 1.2 Percentage of Teachers Believing in Their Content Knowledge and Ability to Teach Earth Science

	Pre-School Year	Post-School Year
Earth science ability		
High ability in earth science	27	80
Gain knowledge of earth science	27	94
Gain skill in teaching earth science	27	87
Teach earth science as well as other subjects	40	94
Organizing and planning for teaching earth science		
Organize and implement resources and activities	40	93
Regularly plan challenging earth science activities	27	60
Helping students		
Find different ways to explain concepts to students	53	74
Easily answer students' questions	27	80
Turn students on to earth science	20	67
Help students learn earth science	53	93
Persistence/Avoidance		
Persist in working with students who are having difficulty	60	93
Persist in earth science-related tasks that are difficult	20	60
Tend to avoid planning earth science activities	33	14
Avoid science-related tasks if I will not be successful	40	6
Discouragement		
Discourage easily when students don't show progress	33	20
Give up on earth science problems I cannot solve	40	0

well as in their tendency to discourage easily when students did not show progress in learning earth science concepts.

Teachers' Understanding and Use of Hands-On, Inquiry-Oriented Teaching

Analysis of teachers' reflective journals, researchers' anecdotal notes of class sessions and teachers' classroom lessons, project portfolios, and interview transcripts revealed that teachers were transferring some project content and activities into their own classrooms. The degree of transfer varied widely: 9 teachers used earthquake lessons; 7, soil erosion; 6, fossils and dinosaurs; 6, rocks; 5, planets and solar system; 5, bats and caves; 3, plate tectonics; and 2, pollution. We learned that several factors seemed to influence transfer. These are presented below and include some illustrative teacher comments.

Teachers experienced lesson content and activities as students. Thus, they anticipated students' reactions. For example, lesson content/concepts were made concrete for the teachers through the activities. They were able to connect lesson content/concepts to the activities selected, so activities were viewed as important to learning, not merely cute or clever ways to get students' attention. The hands-on and exploratory nature of the activities made the lessons more motivating for the teachers. Teachers experienced fun in learning and found that fun did not necessarily get in the way of content/objectives. Teachers' verbalizations and questioning of what they were learning were encouraged by project staff. This was perceived as useful in teachers coming to understand new information and problems. All these things teachers anticipated would be true for students as well. Furthermore, by using the content and activities in project classes, teachers could get a sense of timing required to plan, set up, and teach the lesson from start to finish.

Teachers learned new content. They perceived themselves to be learning an "elevated" and "scientific" vocabulary, and they genuinely viewed their posttest results as a mark of their own learning. Teachers were also surprised by how much they did not know about earth science. In the project design, content and activities were intended to provide teachers with extensions and elaborations on existing curricula in their schools. We found that teachers were, in essence, learning or relearning the content. They recognized weaknesses in their own content area knowledge. They experienced challenges. For example, using Venn diagrams and learning science through data gathering, graphing, and drawing conclusions were really difficult.

Teachers were surprised at the number of connections that could be made between science and math. They found that skills they usually taught in math (e.g., graphing, fractions, base 10 numbers, the use of calculators) were equally teachable in the context of science content. They began to question when they taught particular concepts. They primarily followed the sequence of the math or science textbook, but the sequence did not necessarily fit what they were doing in other content areas. Teachers deviated from their set sequences in favor of more "sensible" concept links.

Teachers transferred lesson content and activities to their own classrooms. They observed that materials for the lessons were easily gathered from classroom or household items, and they also received actual classroom materials (e.g., books, Web site locations, completed materials and activity packets from lessons, shoe box kits developed by peers). They saw local area sites as resources. A few teachers indicated that they had lived in this area for 20+ years but had never thought to use natural resources in the community in science teaching. Teachers found that lesson content and activities could be adjusted to fit students' specific needs. This recognition enhanced teachers' willingness to risk teaching new lessons. Brainstorming, planning, and sharing with project peers helped teachers gather ideas about the teaching of the same lessons or about possible extensions into other content areas (e.g., whole language or literature-based approaches to reading and writing or social studies) and see some links to skills on the Texas Assessment of Academic Skills (TAAS test). Teachers thought they had built a network of peers to contact as we continued to use project content and activities. Finally, Internet applications encouraged teachers' exploration of technology integration as well—a primary objective of the school district. Opportunities to "surf the Net" in project classes were, for some teachers, their first exposure to Web sites and their use in the classroom.

Teachers' Understanding and Use of Authentic Assessment

We defined *authentic assessment* as assessment embedded within instructional content. In this type of assessment, the teacher has the purposeful intention to collect information about students' understanding throughout a lesson activity. For example, in one lesson activity, students engage in a simulation of the aftermath of an earthquake. They call a radio station in the role of community residents. Each student identifies an address and specific damage done there. Information gathered across students regarding location and extent of damage enables the identification of the intensity of the earthquake on the Richter scale. From this information, students estimate on a geologic map the epicenter of the quake. Through this simulation, a teacher can learn whether students follow directions, understand written information, represent written information in a logical format, interpret information collected, recognize degrees in a base 10 system, round to tenths, sequence decimal numbers, and estimate. From this information, teachers can draw conclusions about students' factual understanding of concepts, ability to apply concepts, and ability to think, reason, and make decisions.

Analysis of project portfolios and interview transcripts indicated that teachers' knowledge and understanding of authentic assessment were less affected by the project than we had hoped. Most teachers had difficulty seeing how the assessment in the activities linked to actual student grades and TAAS objectives. Only one third of participants actually used authentic assessments in their classrooms. Examination of these teachers' portfolios, classroom observation anecdotal notes, and interview transcripts revealed a kind of continuum from high to low use. This is illustrated in the selected teachers' comments that follow:

Teacher develops a new assessment (1 teacher):

[Student's] final project was to do the ABC's of the earthquake. This came about as we were on-line one day and ran into the child whose parents died, and she had posted the ABC's of a Child and Parent. So, if they were on-line, they could explain the ABC's that would be necessary for them to survive an earthquake. . . . So, as we were looking through the ABC's, our kids kind of spontaneously combusted, erupted into their own ABC books. They went nuts! So, they each have to do two letters of the alphabet . . . a parent's guide to teaching kindergarten [or] maybe first graders about earthquakes and survival.

Teachers use some of the same assessments used in the course (2 teachers):

We did a lot of graphing, and it [helped me understand] where my kids were in math as far as metric system or customary system of measuring concepts. . . . Even sitting down with them and saying, "What do you suppose might happen if this drifts away further, or what might happen if there is a crack in the earth?" and we just go into a brainstorm. I sit with them and discuss things.

Teachers tinker with observation/anecdotal records or student construction of meaning (2 teachers):

Some things that I do in my science lab require a test, a test of knowledge questions, but others require an assessment of how much they've learned, maybe the different steps that they used as they put the experiment together. . . . Instead of using paper and pencil, [I assess] how much they observed or absorbed from the experiment that we did and then have them explain to me [in a conference as the teacher does anecdotal observations] all the steps that they took to put the experiment together.

Teachers retain traditional assessment with minor adjustments (3 teachers):

I like them to have pencil-and-paper practice, and that's an easy place to get grades. . . . I do get a lot of my assessment in watching them work. . . . We've done a lot of group things this year, where I gave assignments and I walked around [while] I was making my assessments as I watched them complete the assignment in groups or in pairs. . . . [Then] we would have a discussion.

Teacher finds no use for authentic assessments (1 teacher):

I haven't used any new assessment ideas. I haven't gotten any assessment ideas out of the class, to be honest with you.

Changes in Year 2 Project Design

As we entered Year 2, our expectations for teacher involvement changed. In Year 1, we planned the order and sequence of the project curriculum and the schedule and pacing of each project class session. We developed all materials for project activities and located and provided all materials. We think we taught teachers to depend on us to be in charge of what was learned and used. Although teachers appreciated the structure provided, we think this same structure may have had a negative influence on teachers deviating from or extending project lessons in their own classrooms. Also, even though we encouraged teachers to experiment, they were not accountable to us or each other for whether or not they did. In essence, we did not empower teachers to take charge of their own learning and change.

In the summer workshop in Year 2, we required teachers to write one integrated mathematics and science teaching lesson each week. The lesson could be an extension of a lesson completed in the workshop or a new, creative integration of geometry and science. During the school year, we required teachers to take the instructional lead for 9 of the 18 class meetings. Over the course of these teacher-led classes, each teacher would share three integrated teaching lessons he or she used in the classroom during the school year. In their presentations, teachers would present evidence of students' responses, peer reactions, possible modifications, assessments, and administrative response.

During the school year, we would develop more structured portfolio requirements with the teachers. In Year 1, teachers were pretty much left on their own. In Year 2, teachers would develop a checklist of portfolio requirements and a portfolio evaluation rubric. Also, we would use reflective writing opportunities to encourage teachers' expression of their understandings, questions, concerns, and ideas for transfer into their own classrooms.

Finally, we rethought how authentic assessment was presented to teachers. We discussed steps whereby teachers could convert authentic measures of student understandings into grades and connections to TAAS objectives. Although this may conflict with theoretical perspectives underlying authentic assessment, it may be important for grounding project content and activities in the reality of teachers' existing school contexts. Ponticell (1995) observed that teachers learn new knowledge and skills within a specific school context that greatly influences what gets transferred into classroom practice. If teachers cannot see and practice how new ideas "fit" within existing school contexts, they may easily give up what they learn and revert to more traditional thinking. In this case, we realized that if we did not specifically help teachers see the fit between authentic assessment of student understanding and traditional grades and standardized test objectives, teachers may not risk using authentic measures.

Implications for Staff Development

Susan Loucks-Horsley observed,

> Professional development has become more integral and central
> in the reform movement. In the science and mathematics reform
> efforts, professional development is on everyone's lips. That rep-
> resents an enormous opportunity and challenge for us. When we
> think about science or mathematics learning for kids, it is very
> much like the learning we desire for adults. (as quoted in Sparks,
> 1997, p. 23)

We learned much in Year 1 of Doing Math the Science Way. It
informed our thinking about the design of Year 2 and about staff development to support teachers' learning to integrate science and mathematics.

Teacher learning is influenced by school and district context. Teachers
filtered new ideas and activities through the screen of other demands
made on them by school, district, or state policies and practices. They
transferred only what "fit." We needed to uncover the filters through
which teachers made sense of new ideas and new practices and to provide
transitional strategies.

Learning is risky. When teachers learned new ideas and practices,
they had to unlearn previous information, perceptions, or misconceptions.
This was risky business; teachers' self-efficacy was vulnerable. Teachers
had to be open to cognitive dissonance (Festinger, 1957); they thought
about themselves in one way, but new information often made them
confront their weaknesses. We needed to attend to teacher self-efficacy;
increased feelings of confidence and competence are crucial to adult
motivation.

Learning is personal. Teachers were in varying personal stages of
understanding, transfer, and adaptation. The network that professors and
teachers formed was a valued resource for individualized support. We
needed the year-long time frame to provide sustained contact and support.

Reflecting is beginning. Not all understanding came from learning
new content and participating in activities. Change also came from delib-
erating and considering new information, skills, and perspectives in relation to old information, skills, and perspectives. We needed praxis (Friere,
1970), opportunities to help teachers wrestle with the fit between the new
and the old.

Sharing is empowering. Teachers became professional friends; we don't get to visit like this at school. We needed the long-term interactions among professors and teachers to build a sense of trust and to enable a confident exchange of triumphs and tragedies.

Change comes with personal experimentation. Teachers actively participated in workshop activities but only replicated those same activities in their classrooms. We needed to empower teachers to take charge of their own learning and change; teachers, not we, needed to be making decisions. Continuous, accessible support enhances continued learning. Highly motivated peers and professors were regularly available and easily accessible.

Reality counts. All of us learned to be sensitive to the realities of these teachers' individual elementary classrooms. If we were to be valued as colleagues and collaborators as teachers worked to improve learning for their students, we all needed to ground our problem solving in their worlds, not in our own or generic generalizations.

Although we know a lot about effective staff development, too many teachers still experience one-shot, 1-day, quick-fix approaches to adult learning. In Doing Math the Science Way, we tried to break that pattern. In doing so, we learned to work together in different ways and to develop learning experiences that built teachers' professional ability and self-efficacy and professors' understanding of teachers as learners.

References

American Association for the Advancement of Science (AAAS). (1989). *Science for all Americans: A Project 2061 report on literacy goals in the sciences, mathematics, and technology.* Washington, DC: Author.

Bandura, A. (1977). Self-efficacy: Toward a unifying theory of behavioral change. *Psychological Review, 84,* 191-215.

Bandura, A. (1982). Self-efficacy mechanism in human agency. *American Psychologist, 37,* 122-147.

Bandura, A. (1986). *Social foundations of thought and action: A social cognitive theory.* Upper Saddle River, NJ: Prentice Hall.

Bandura, A. (1993). Perceived self-efficacy in cognitive development and functioning. *Educational Psychologist, 28,* 117-148.

Elmore, R. F., & McLaughlin, M. W. (1988). *Steady work: Policy, practice, and reform in American education* (R-3574-NIE/RC). Santa Monica, CA: RAND.

Festinger, L. (1957). *A theory of cognitive dissonance.* Stanford, CA: Stanford University Press.

Friere, P. (1970). *Pedagogy of the oppressed.* New York: Herder & Herder.

Glaser, B., & Strauss, A. L. (1967). *The discovery of grounded theory: Strategies for qualitative research.* Hawthorne, NY: Aldine.

Glickman, C. D., Gordon, S. P., & Ross-Gordon, J. M. (1998). *Supervision of instruction: A developmental approach* (4th ed.). Boston: Allyn & Bacon.

Greenwood, A. (1996). Science is part of the big picture. *Science and Children, 33*(7), 32-34.

Guba, E. B. (1981). Criteria for assessing the trustworthiness of naturalistic inquiry. *Educational Communications and Technology Journal, 29*(2), 75-91.

Hall, G. H., & Hord, S. M. (1987). *Change in schools: Facilitating the process.* Albany: State University of New York Press.

Mezirow, J. D. (1981). A critical theory of adult learning and education. *Adult Education, 32*(1), 3-24.

National Council of Teachers of Mathematics (NCTM). (1989). *Curriculum and evaluation standards for school mathematics.* Reston, VA: Author.

National Research Council (NRC). (1989). *Everybody counts: A report to the nation on the future of mathematics education.* Washington, DC: National Academy Press.

National Research Council (NRC). (1996). *National science education standards.* Washington, DC: National Academy Press.

Ponticell, J. A. (1995). Promoting teaching professionalism through collegiality. *Journal of Staff Development, 16*(3), 13-18.

Raizen, S. A., & Michelsohn, A. M. (1993). *The future of science in elementary schools: Educating prospective teachers.* San Francisco: Jossey-Bass.

Sparks, D. (1997). Reforming teaching and staff development: An interview with Susan Loucks-Horsley. *Journal of Staff Development, 18*(4), 20-23.

Sparks, D., & Loucks-Horsley, S. (1989). Five models of staff development for teachers. *Journal of Staff Development, 10*(4), 40-57.

Strauss, A. L. (1987). *Qualitative analysis for social scientists.* New York: Cambridge University Press.

◉

2 Assessing the Impact of Sustained Professional Development on Middle School Mathematics Teachers

Joanne E. Goodell

Lesley H. Parker

Jane Butler Kahle

Joanne E. Goodell is Assistant Professor of Mathematics Education at Cleveland State University. Her research interests focus on equity and reform issues for teaching and learning in mathematics and related disciplines in high schools and universities. She has authored more than 20 conference papers and has two chapters in progress from her recent PhD dissertation entitled *Equity and Reform in Mathematics Education*.

AUTHORS' NOTE: An earlier version of this chapter was presented at the annual meeting of the American Educational Research Association, San Diego, April 1998. All names used in this chapter are fictitious. The preparation of this study was sponsored, in part, by the National Science Foundation, Grant #OSR-92500 (J. B. Kahle and K. G. Wilson, coprincipal investigators). The opinions expressed are those of the authors and do not necessarily reflect the position of the NSF. Analysis of the data was carried out with the assistance of an Australian Postgraduate Award at the Science and Mathematics Education Center, Curtin University of Technology, Western Australia.

Lesley H. Parker is Professor of Higher Education and Senior Deputy Vice Chancellor of Curtin University in Perth, Western Australia. She has published widely on equity and social justice issues as they relate to teaching and learning. Her recent publications include "Equitable Assessment Strategies" in the *International Handbook of Science Education*.

Jane Butler Kahle, Condit Professor of Science Education, Miami University, Oxford, Ohio, is an international scholar in gender differences in science education and in the systemic reform of science and mathematics education. She has recently been appointed Director of the Division of Elementary, Secondary, and Informal Education (ESIE) at the National Science Foundation after having served as Principal Investigator of both Ohio's Systemic Initiative, *Discovery*, and a research project to evaluate systemic reform. Her recent publications include a research monograph for the National Institute for Science Education entitled *Reaching Equity in Systemic Reform: How Do We Assess Progress and Problems?*

ABSTRACT

The study reported in this chapter examines the impact of the Ohio Statewide Systemic Initiative (SSI) on participating mathematics teachers. Quantitative data from 90 SSI-trained teachers and 400 teachers without training, along with qualitative data collected from 7 SSI teachers who were visited in their classrooms, are presented. Analysis of the quantitative data showed that SSI and non-SSI teachers reported significantly different frequencies of reformed teaching practices and held significantly different views about the nature and pedagogy of mathematics. Qualitative data from the interviews highlighted that the SSI professional development experience, the ability to find creative ways to overcome lack of resources, and the teacher support networks formed as a result of their participation in the SSI were three major factors that enabled the SSI teachers to make significant changes to their teaching practices and to sustain those changes.

The Statewide Systemic Initiative (SSI) in Ohio, known as Project Discovery, began in 1991 and continued into 1999. It focused on sustained professional development programs for middle school mathematics and science teachers. This chapter presents the results of a study designed to determine the impact of Project Discovery on participating mathematics teachers. Data on which this chapter is based were collected during the large evaluation study known as *The Landscape Study*, which covered all aspects of Project Discovery. Only the teacher questionnaire and teacher interview data for mathematics teachers are explored here. Other findings of the Landscape Study have been reported elsewhere (Kahle & Rogg, 1996, 1997).

Background

Reasons for the failure of many teacher professional development activities to produce long-term change are well documented (Goertz, Floden, & O'Day, 1996). Summarizing these reasons, Miles (1995) strongly criticized traditional one-shot professional development courses, characterizing them as opportunities for active engagement, being able to demonstrate a link between theory and practice, including time for reflection, and modeling exemplary practice. The facilitation theme included ensuring that the materials were high quality and "user friendly" and that networking was facilitated. The application theme included ensuring that the activities were followed up with support from the planners and that teachers were motivated and empowered as a result of the experience.

More recently, Swafford, Jones, Thornton, Stump, and Miller (1999), in their project with middle-grade mathematics teachers in central Illinois, demonstrated that it was possible to influence significantly the teaching practices of those teachers in their project by including elements of content knowledge, reformed teaching practices, and time for reflection and collaboration.

The Ohio SSI had anticipated most of these features. The adopted model of professional development focused on the role of the teacher as change agent and provided sustained professional development and follow-up with opportunities for networking. Six-week summer institutes for middle school mathematics and science teachers were offered. Sessions were content based and taught in an inquiry mode, and instructors modeled inquiry teaching throughout the institute. Six follow-up, 1-day workshops throughout the next academic year focused on the pedagogy of inquiry teaching. Ongoing support was provided through classroom visits by expert teachers known as *teacher leaders,* as well as through an electronic communication network known as DiscoveryNet. All teachers who took part in the SSI were given access to this network, which included an e-mail account and a "discussion room" where they could communicate on-line with other teachers about their experiences implementing inquiry teaching.

In late 1994, the Landscape Study was initiated to evaluate how this model of professional development had affected the teaching of mathematics and science in middle schools in Ohio. (Other aspects had been evaluated throughout the SSI.) The Landscape Study was a mixed qualitative and quantitative multilevel study. Quantitative components included questionnaires for teachers and principals from a random sample of schools in which at least one teacher had participated in the SSI. In a small subset of these schools, students were given achievement tests and questionnaires, and researchers conducted site visits to collect qualitative data.

Purpose of the Study

The purpose of this chapter is to describe the impact, on participating mathematics teachers, of those specific aspects of Project Discovery that concerned their views of mathematics, their pedagogy, and the involvement of their school principals and students' parents with their work as mathematics teachers. In addition, this chapter provides insights into some facilitators and barriers these teachers saw themselves encountering when trying to implement inquiry teaching in their mathematics classrooms. This chapter builds on earlier evaluative research (Supovitz, 1996) suggesting that Project Discovery teachers made considerable changes to their teaching practices after their participation in the SSI and that these changes were sustained over time. It also complements research by Tims Goodell, Kelly, Damnjanovic, and Kahle (1997), who demonstrated that the mathematics performance of students in SSI groups was significantly higher than that of their non-SSI counterparts across all racial and gender groups.

Data Sources and Instruments

Quantitative Data

The quantitative data analyzed in this study were collected in 1995 from 91 mathematics teachers who had participated in the SSI summer institutes (SSI teachers) and 442 mathematics teachers who had not participated (non-SSI teachers). These teachers were from a random sample of 126 schools across Ohio in which one or more teachers had participated in the SSI.

A team of researchers, both internal and external to Ohio, designed and field-tested the instruments used in this study. The Landscape Teacher Questionnaire (LTQ) was developed by the research team to reflect those principles of inquiry and equity that had been the focus of the SSI since its inception. The analysis presented in this study addresses the first five sections of the LTQ: "How I Teach," "What My Students Do," "My School Principal's Involvement," "Parental Involvement," and "My Views About Mathematics."

The first four sections of the LTQ were similar in structure, in that participants were asked to respond twice for each statement—once about the frequency of that event or behavior and once about the importance of that event or behavior occurring in their classroom. The frequency response consisted of five choices: *Almost Never (AN), Seldom (Se), Sometimes (So), Often (O),* and *Very Often (VO)*. The importance response consisted of four choices: *Very Unimportant (VU), Unimportant (U), Important (I),* and *Very Important (VI)*.

The fifth section, "My Views About Mathematics," had two 4-point Likert scales. The first response had choices of *Strongly Disagree (SD), Disagree (D), Agree (A),* and *Strongly Agree (SA)*. The importance response used the same response scale as in the first four sections.

Qualitative Data

After the questionnaires were completed, site visits were made to four schools in 1995 and three more in 1996. Two criteria were used in selecting the sites: The schools had to have at least 30% minority enrollment, and they had to represent as diverse a geographic area as possible. An SSI teacher at each site was chosen as the "focus teacher." During the site visit,

the researcher observed the focus teacher in her classroom and interviewed the focus teacher, the school principal, and some students from
one of the focus teacher's classes. This study presents the results of the
analysis of the data obtained by interviewing the focus teacher at each of
the seven sites visited.

Data Collection

Quantitative Data

The quantitative data collection occurred through a lengthy sequence
of mailed requests and responses, the aim of which was to ensure as high a
return rate as possible. A contact person was established at each site, and
all correspondence was directed through that person. A personalized
cover letter and address label were produced for every teacher. Envelopes
were provided so that teachers could seal their responses if so desired.
Follow-up letters and replacement LTQs were sent to teachers who had
not returned them. The final sample contained 126 schools, and the number of teachers at each school ranged from 1 to 6.

Qualitative Data

Members of the research team observed the focus teachers' classes and
interviewed each focus teacher for up to 3 hours during the 3-day site visits, or for 1 hour on the 1-day site visits. Researchers focused their interviews around the teachers' LTQ responses. The teachers were given a
copy of their completed LTQs and were asked to comment on any item in
the questionnaire that was important to them. Other issues that arose from
these discussions were pursued. Because all researchers were using the
same instrument as a prompt for interview questions, a formal interview
protocol was unnecessary. Researchers were encouraged to ensure that
interviews remained focused on the factors influencing teachers' attempts
to implement the suggested reforms. All interviews were taped and subsequently transcribed.

Data Analysis

Quantitative Data

A principal-components rotated-varimax method of factor analysis was employed twice: once for the frequency responses and once for the importance responses in the questionnaire. Cattell's Scree test was applied to determine the optimum number of factors for each analysis. For the frequency components, the Scree test identified four factors as the best solution. For the importance components, the Scree test identified five factors as the best solution. Following the factor analysis, the internal consistencies of the factors were determined by using coefficient alpha. Effect sizes were used to investigate differences in the reporting of these factors by SSI and non-SSI teachers. The effect size statistic was selected because this statistic is not affected by the size of the sample in the way a *t* test would be. The effect size is a standardized measure of the difference between two means and provides a measure of the magnitude of the differences (Robinson & Levin, 1997). A *t* test, in contrast, estimates the likelihood of an observed difference occurring. With large sample sizes, even a very small difference becomes unlikely and is reported as statistically significant, which may be misleading, especially when the researcher is trying to determine the practical implications of a difference between means.

Qualitative Data

A qualitative data-analysis software package was sought that would make the analysis of the qualitative data as manageable and meaningful as possible. A comparison of all qualitative data-analysis software packages available at the time (Miles & Weitzman, 1994) indicated that NUD*IST by Qualitative Solutions and Research (QSR) was the best package available for the Macintosh computer at the time the study commenced.

All interview transcripts were entered into the software, and "codes" that described specific things teachers talked about were attached to appropriate segments of text. The codes were based on Rossman's conceptual framework for synthesizing case studies located within the practice of systemic reform. The four dimensions of this framework are as follows:

Technical: Professional knowledge and skills and the means by which they are acquired

Political: Matters of authority, power, and influence, including the negotiation and resolution of conflicts

Cultural: Values, beliefs, and school norms—both in terms of a general ethos and competing perspectives that contend with each other

Moral: Matters of justice and fairness

Codes that were relevant to this particular study came from the technical dimension and were about the professional development experience, the provision of resources to support the suggested reforms, and the establishment and maintenance of teacher support networks. (See Goodell, 1998, for a complete description of the remaining three dimensions.)

Results

Quantitative Data

Frequency Scales

The names of the four factors with their means, standard deviations, effect sizes, and reliabilities are given in Table 2.1. The first factor, CLASSTCH, concerned reformed classroom teaching practices and comprised almost all the items from the "How I Teach" and "What My Students Do" sections of the LTQ. The second factor, PRINSUPP, contained all the items from the section "My School Principal's Involvement." The third factor, HOME, included all the items from the section "Parental Involvement." The fourth factor, NATMATH, contained all the items from the section "My Views About Mathematics." To determine any differences in the way SSI and non-SSI teachers responded to these factors, effect sizes were calculated. These data are shown graphically in Figure 2.1.

Given that an effect size of greater than 0.2 is generally accepted as being of educational significance (Keeves, 1992), it is clear from the data

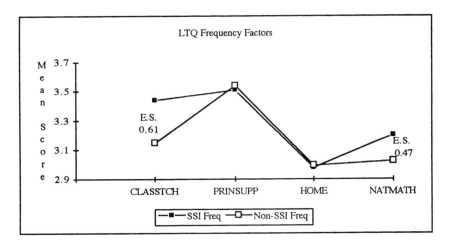

Figure 2.1. Means and Effect Sizes for LTQ Frequency Scale Factors

presented that SSI teachers responded very differently from non-SSI teachers in terms of their classroom teaching practices and their views about the nature of mathematics, although they reported the same levels of principal and home support as their non-SSI counterparts.

Importance Scales

Items from the importance scale did not form the same factors as those from the frequency scale. This result could have occurred because the respondents tended to use the *Important* or *Very Important* response a great deal, and thus a ceiling effect resulted. Items from the "How I Teach" and "What My Students Do" sections were split between the second and third factors, but the other three factors remained as they had for the frequency scales. The names of the five factors identified by the factor analysis with their means, standard deviations, effect sizes, and reliabilities are given in Table 2.2.

The first factor, IMPPRIN, was concerned with the importance of principal support. The second factor, IMPACTVT, was concerned with the importance of students being actively involved in the classroom. The

TABLE 2.1 Reliabilities, Means, and Effect Sizes for LTQ Frequency Scale Factors

Factor	Number of items	Reliability	SSI sample size	SSI mean	Standard deviation	Non-SSI sample size	Non-SSI mean	Standard deviation	Effect size
CLASSTCH	24	.89	81	3.44	0.49	364	3.15	0.47	**0.61**
PRINSUPP	17	.88	74	3.51	0.68	351	3.54	0.61	−0.09
HOME	13	.87	76	2.98	0.55	374	2.99	0.61	−0.08
NATMATH	7	.87	79	3.20	0.44	395	3.02	0.37	**0.47**

NOTE: Significant effect sizes are shown in bold.

TABLE 2.2 Reliabilities, Means, and Effect Sizes for LTQ Importance Scale Factors

Factor	Number of items	Reliability	SSI population	SSI mean	SSI standard deviation	Non-SSI population	Non-SSI mean	Non-SSI standard deviation	Effect size
IMPPRIN	17	.90	76	3.34	0.37	353	3.21	0.39	**0.36**
IMPACTVT	12	.86	86	3.50	0.32	392	3.29	0.33	**0.63**
IMPCOMM	12	.82	69	2.86	0.39	350	2.59	0.49	**0.62**
IMPPAREN	11	.86	78	3.33	0.36	375	3.28	0.40	**0.29**
IMPVIEW	8	.87	71	3.07	0.47	373	2.97	0.44	**0.24**

NOTE: Significant effect sizes are shown in bold.

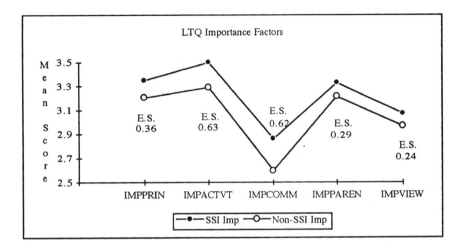

Figure 2.2. Means and Effect Sizes for SSI and Non-SSI Teachers on Importance Factors

third factor, IMPCOMM, was concerned with the importance of teachers and students communicating with each other in the classroom. The fourth factor, IMPPAREN, was concerned with the importance of parental support. The last factor, IMPVIEW, was concerned with the importance of the teachers' views about the nature of mathematics being reflected in their teaching practices. These data from Table 2.2 are presented graphically in Figure 2.2. Again, clear and significant differences were found between SSI and non-SSI teachers in the way they responded about their perceived importance of all factors investigated in this study.

Qualitative Data

Only technical (Rossman, 1993) issues that pertained directly to the implementation of the SSI reforms were included in this analysis. These were the professional development experience itself, the availability of resources to support the new style of teaching advocated by the SSI during the professional development activities, and the importance of teacher support networks in helping teachers make and sustain changes in their teaching.

The Professional Development Experience

All teachers who were interviewed said that the professional development they had participated in through their involvement with the SSI had caused them to change profoundly not only their teaching practices but also the way they thought about teaching. Barb Arnold encapsulated this sentiment as follows:

> I look at everything I teach now—every lesson that I have— wondering how I can do this in an inquiry method. I look at things and think about it each time I have a new lesson that I'm coming up with, thinking about how I could do this inquiry. It kind of sets the seeds going, and all of a sudden it kind of comes together. (Barb Arnold, May 1995)

For another teacher, Kathy, the standards by which she judged her classroom were quite different after her involvement with the SSI:

> I think I was a pretty good teacher pre-Project Discovery, too, according to the standards of pre-Project Discovery. (Kathy Straub, May 1995)

She indicated that although she had always used group work in her classes, she had not previously required her students to demonstrate their understanding in the way they now did:

> They actually have to show an understanding as opposed to just being able to do it. I think that is the difference. Before maybe there wasn't an extreme understanding, just being able to do the problems. (Kathy Straub, May 1995)

For some teachers, the SSI experience was one of several major influences on their teaching practices. Ms. Michaels, previously a special education teacher, was experienced in using cooperative groups. She acknowledged, however, that her SSI experience had helped her make the transition into mainstream teaching and become student centered in her classroom. She indicated that she had not really changed her teaching style a great deal but that she had changed the focus of some of her activities to make them more inquiry oriented. She also expected her students to have a deeper conceptual understanding than before.

Resources to Support Reformed Teaching Practices

All the schools visited in the Landscape Study were struggling financially. The problem of lack of manipulatives, however, was overcome to some extent in this SSI by providing all teachers who participated in the summer institutes with materials for their own classes. But because these materials were not sufficient for every situation, some teachers found creative ways to cater to their students. Ms. Arnold was ingenious in her use of resources, using everyday objects rather than relying on expensive equipment. Ms. Michaels had access to a wide range of equipment but, being department head, was concerned about the lack of equipment for the rest of her staff if she was always using it. She seemed to use the equipment infrequently, relying instead on group work and interactive questioning to involve her students. Ms. Golf felt guilty asking for tightly managed money, particularly when she thought she was virtually the only person requesting money for extra equipment. Ms. Fisher, however, had a roomful of equipment that she never used and, not surprisingly, she did not think she needed any more. Her teaching style and classroom environment were the least reformed of all those visited as part of this study. So, for her, having a roomful of equipment did not mean that she was able or willing to use it.

Some teachers mentioned that their students were unable to supply their own calculators. To overcome this, Ms. Arnold had a box of mathematics equipment, including a ruler, compass, and calculator, available at all times on each group of desks. Items were rarely lost or stolen from these boxes. Students respected the trust she showed them. Ms. Michaels had one class set of calculators that she used quite often, but when another teacher required them for a test, she had to go without them.

In summary, financial resources, or the lack of them, were not always a barrier to implementing reform. Individual teachers came up with creative ways of overcoming many difficulties imposed on the provision of equipment by financial constraints.

One further issue related to resources was important at more than one site. This was the availability of appropriate written curriculum materials to support inquiry-based teaching. It was a particularly important issue for Ms. Arnold. During the first visit in 1995, she stated that she did not use the textbook her school district had adopted, but relied instead on photocopying worksheets from a wide range of curriculum-support books. Because this was time-consuming and expensive, in 1996 she joined a national program known as Mathline, which she describes in the following interview segment:

> Mathline provided us with the videotapes that had three lessons on them and an overview. The activities were similar to types we did with Project Discovery: They're inquiry-type activities. They're actually done in a classroom and were videotaped. They provided the paperwork to support it. It describes the activity and what materials you need and what lesson, what's being taught in it, what's being met in it, whether its probability or whatever and any kind of, if you need a game board or something. It gives you the master to duplicate for that so then you can present it in your class exactly the way it was done there, or you can modify for whatever your needs are. (Barb Arnold, May 1996)

During the second visit, Ms. Arnold used the Mathline resources in several lessons observed and indicated that she had made extensive use of these resources throughout the year because she thought the materials were very appropriate to inquiry methods of teaching. The issue of availability of appropriate inquiry-style teaching resources was also raised at other sites visited, although none of the focus teachers at those sites were using Mathline. Clearly, Ms. Arnold was convinced of the need to continue teaching in an inquiry mode and was motivated to find new resources to support this.

Teacher Support Networks

The model of change followed by the SSI concentrated on the individual teacher as the change agent but recognized the need to provide teachers with continuing support. All participants were given an e-mail address and access to an electronic discussion group and other services. Because some teachers came from schools where no other teachers had been previously involved with the SSI, the electronic network known as DiscoveryNet, established just for SSI teachers, proved to be an important element in facilitating the change process, as shown by the following comments made by Betty Michaels during an interview:

Interviewer: Do you use DiscoveryNet very much?

Betty: Actually, I do. I check the lounge a lot and see what's going on. Right now my system is down, but I check it at home and see what's going on and talk to people.

Interviewer: Is that an important thing to you?

Betty: I think it's good because, especially now, here I have other people in my building who are Discovery. I have Joan, who is math, and I'm math. And then we have Debra with science. And there are two sixth-grade teachers who did Discovery science. We can talk to each other about "What are you doing?" But in a building when you are the only one, I think that's very important to be able to communicate and ask, you know, "Gee, I'm trying this, what ideas do you have?" Or when you are trying to make changes, that at least you have some other people behind you that can say, look, you know, here are all these people out here that are doing this and how can we get involved here? And the instructors that we had were excellent and have been very supportive, and I feel that I can contact them on DiscoveryNet when I've needed something—I need the address to this or how do I find out about that—and they have responded. It's been good. (Betty Michaels, May 1996)

In some cases, the support network was the main reason why some teachers were able to sustain the changes they were making:

Interviewer: What would you say are the most important things that you are taking from Discovery?

Diane: Well, I think some of the things we did in the follow-up, where we shared ideas with other teachers from other parts of the state. You know, "I tried this in my classroom, and it worked, but you might want to try it this way." Or, "This failed." It's like, gee, other people fail at things. This is how you can build on it and go from there. You try, you fail, you have a tendency not to try it again. But you could improve on it and try again.

Interviewer: How would it change things if you didn't have that support network?

Diane: I think that you get back into the same old routine, the same old rut, get discouraged. With that, you're more likely to have a fresh outlook. (Diane Young, May 1995)

Conclusions and Implications

The study described in this chapter demonstrated significant differences between SSI and non-SSI teachers in terms of their views of mathematics and their pedagogy, with SSI teachers reporting practices and perceptions more consistent with the reforms espoused by Project Discovery. The study also showed little difference between the two groups in terms of their perceptions of the involvement of their school principal and students' parents with their work as mathematics teachers, although SSI teachers considered these dimensions to be more important than non-SSI teachers did. In addition, the qualitative data obtained from the site visits provided some insight into those factors that seemed to assist SSI teachers in implementing reforms. These were the professional development experience itself, the willingness to find creative ways to overcome lack of resources, and the establishment and maintenance of teacher networks. Without these three aspects, it is doubtful whether SSI teachers would have been empowered to sustain the changes they made to their teaching beyond 1 or 2 years after their participation in the summer institutes.

The findings presented in this chapter need to be appreciated in the total context of evidence now available in relation to Project Discovery (e.g., Supovitz, 1996; Tims Goodell et al., 1997). Although a causal relationship cannot be established, all the evidence, when taken together, provide a compelling argument for the effectiveness of the model of professional development adopted by Project Discovery. Overall, the findings of this research have significant implications for those trying to effect reform in middle school mathematics classrooms. Although many aspects of this SSI contributed to its long-term success, central to its effectiveness was the use of sustained professional development, with continued involvement and support through follow-up activities and networking opportunities.

References

Goertz, M. E., Floden, R. F., & O'Day, J. (1996). *The bumpy road to education reform* (CPRE Policy Brief No. RB-20). Philadelphia: University of Pennsylvania, Graduate School of Education, Consortium for Policy Research in Education.

Goodell, J. E. (1998). *Equity and reform in mathematics education.* Unpublished doctoral dissertation, Curtin University of Technology, Perth, Australia.

Kahle, J. B., & Rogg, S. R. (1996). *A pocket panorama of the Landscape Study.* Oxford, OH: Miami University.

Kahle, J. B., & Rogg, S. R. (1997). *A pocket panorama of the Landscape Study, 1996.* Oxford, OH: Miami University.

Keeves, J. P. (1992). The design and conduct of the Second Science Study. In J. P. Keeves (Ed.), *The IEA Study of Science III: Changes in science education and achievement: 1970 to 1984* (pp. 42-67). Elmsford, NY: Pergamon.

Miles, M. B. (1995). Foreword. In T. R. Guskent & M. Huberman (Eds.), *Professional development in education: New paradigms and practices* (pp. vii-ix). New York: Teachers College Press.

Miles, M. B., & Weitzman, E. (1994). Choosing computer programs for qualitative data analysis. In M. B. Miles & A. M. Huberman (Eds.), *Qualitative data analysis* (pp. 311-317). Thousand Oaks, CA: Sage.

Robinson, D. L., & Levin, J. R. (1997). Reflections on statistical and substantive significance, with a slice of replication. *Educational Researcher, 26*(5), 21-26.

Rossman, G. (1993). *Building explanations across case studies: A framework for synthesis.* Boulder: Colorado University School of Education. (ERIC Document Reproduction Service No. ED 373 115)

Supovitz, J. (1996). *The impact over time of Project Discovery on teachers' attitudes, preparation, and teaching practice.* Raleigh, NC: Horizon Research.

Swafford, J. O., Jones, G., Thornton, C. A., Stump, S. L., & Miller, D. R. (1999). The impact on instructional practice of a teacher change model. *Journal of Research and Development in Education, 32*(2), 69-82.

Tims Goodell, J. E., Kelly, M. K., Damnjanovic, A., & Kahle, J. B. (1997, March). *Classroom factors associated with systemic reform in science and mathematics education.* Paper presented at the annual meeting of the National Association for Research in Science Teaching, Chicago.

3 Teachers' Choices About Their Own Professional Development in Science Teaching and Learning

Deborah L. Bainer

Dinah Wright

Deborah L. Bainer is Associate Professor of Teaching and Learning at The Ohio State University, Mansfield. Her research examines the impact of school-based partnerships and constructivist professional development. She has coauthored one textbook and more than 30 articles, books, and chapters.

Dinah Wright is a first-grade teacher and Science Coordinator at Scottish Corners Elementary School in Dublin City School District, where she provides leadership in constructivist professional development programs.

ABSTRACT

This chapter describes a program that provides professional development in science teaching and learning following a constructivist philosophy. Teacher choices and thinking are described as the teachers developed and implemented individualized professional development plans. Teachers engaged in a range of learning opportunities to enhance their professional development, chosen on the basis of their self-perceived needs, their learning styles, and the direct applicability of the experience to their professional situation. Most projects they completed were directly applicable to their instruction and in line with district guidelines and policies. Other projects enabled them to develop professional skills or to reflect on the evolution of their teaching approach. The constructivist program resulted in change in the way teachers think about learners and learning science, how they view themselves as professionals, and how they provide instruction. Although teachers deemed the program effective, their recommendations for refining the program are provided.

Introduction

The need for professional development of elementary teachers in science education is well documented. Elementary science teachers are poorly prepared by university teacher education programs to teach science, lack sufficient content knowledge in science to interpret and teach basic concepts, and are unaware of or reluctant to use effective instructional methods (Raizen & Michelsohn, 1994). Professional development programs therefore must target specific weaknesses in order to improve the quality and quantity of science education in elementary schools.

Notions of effective professional development have changed in recent years. Generally, the literature does not support as an effective approach the use of short, one-shot workshops provided on an irregular basis by outsiders. Rather, effective professional development programs are characterized by (a) the development of a coherent plan, (b) in-depth and long-term programs such as intensive courses or institutes, (c) substantial follow-up as teachers return to the classroom, (d) a critical mass of teachers and/or administrators to build internal support structures, and (e) use of teachers in training and support roles (Loucks-Horsley, 1989).

Sparks (1994) identifies three powerful ideas "altering the face of professional development in this decade" (p. 42). The first is the notion of *results-driven professional development.* That is, the effectiveness of professional development efforts must be judged by whether the program alters instruction in ways that benefit students. Honig (1994) points out that reform efforts are not typically organized around improving teachers' content knowledge or enhancing their ability to collaborate to improve instruction.

A second guiding notion is *systems thinking*, which recognizes the complex, interdependent interrelationships among various parts of the educational system. Professional development efforts in the 1980s showed that teacher-by-teacher strategies are not powerful enough to transform a school because 85% of barriers to reform reside in the school's organization and process (Sparks, 1994). Collective efforts that involve a critical mass of staff committed to improving student performance and to making instructional changes are needed to initiate systematic reform in science education.

A third notion is *constructivism*. Constructivism, long applied as a theory for learning in children, holds that individuals learn at different rates and through different modes and that learning is a social experience. For constructivists, a good learning climate includes time for mental processing; other learners with whom to interact, collaborate, and reflect; and a variety of alternatives for reaching the learning outcome.

Constructivist professional development extends this learning theory to working with adults. With this approach, teachers identify their professional strengths and weaknesses and develop a plan to meet their individual professional needs by using multiple forms of job-embedded learning. Staff developers provide consultation, planning, and facilitation services, as well as training (Sparks, 1994). Further, networks are established that focus on instruction and learning and on bringing schools and community resources together to broaden perspectives and offer collegial support. The goal of constructivist professional development is to change the way teachers think about teaching, learning, and learners. This change in thinking, it maintains, is necessary for instructional change.

The purpose of this chapter is to describe the professional development program in science teaching and learning undertaken by one school district that springs from a constructivist theoretical framework. The 3-year program aimed to alter elementary science instruction in ways that benefited students by creating a critical mass of teachers within and across grade levels who were committed to improving student performance and to making changes in their instruction to reform science education in the district. The professional development program was constructivist in that teachers were challenged to identify their strengths and weaknesses in science teaching and to implement a plan to meet these professional needs. The program was teacher-led, supported by multiple levels of administration, and facilitated by university personnel. Periodic meetings among teachers and with stakeholders established support networks within the system and sought to bring grade levels and schools together to broaden perspectives and to offer collegial and instructional support.

Further, this chapter describes the choices made by teachers as they developed individualized professional development plans. How those choices were made and the impact of the choices on science instruction and on the teachers themselves are also explored. Finally, teachers' evaluations of this constructivist professional development approach are presented.

Methodology

The School District

The study involved a middle-class suburban school district near a major urban center in Ohio. In this fast-growing district, the student body of 10,800 is predominantly white (86.9%), and 96% of graduates go on to higher education. The number of teachers employed has doubled since 1986 to 750. Teachers have an average of 11 years of teaching experience, and 48% hold master's degrees or are pursuing doctorates. The pupil:teacher ratio is 19.5:1. The general fund's annual expenditure per pupil is $6,293, slightly above the state average of $6,019. The 10 elementary schools, which were the focus of this professional development effort, provide an integrated, whole language, literature-based curriculum based on constructivist theory. The science and mathematics curricula are process based but have traditionally been secondary to the strong language arts program. Nevertheless, for 1996 and 1997, the fourth-grade proficiency test scores were above the state average for science (state = 59% pass rate; district = 79% for 1996; state = 58%, district = 79% for 1997) and for the five content area tests overall (state = 50%, district = 74% for 1996; state = 36%, district = 57% for 1997; the exam was changed for 1997, which resulted in lower scores overall).

The Participants

When the constructivist professional development program was introduced to all 250 district elementary teachers in August 1995, 66 teachers elected to participate in the year-long project. Of these, 59 taught in self-contained classrooms in grades K-5 throughout the district. Data from only these teachers are presented in this chapter. Most of the teachers (54) were females. More than half (35 teachers, or 59.3%) taught in primary grades (K-3), whereas 21 teachers (35.6%) taught intermediate grades (4 and 5). Three teachers taught in classrooms that were a 3/4 split.

The elementary building most familiar to the researchers was selected for a closer look at the impact of the professional development program 1 year later (in spring 1997). The K-5 building has 25 teachers; 10 were enrolled in the program. Of these, a purposive sample of 8 teachers representing a range of grade levels and recommended by the science coordinator as most articulate agreed to participate. Teachers were observed and interviewed on-site, student-developed artifacts were examined, and an on-site focus group was conducted. Questions explored the long-range impact of the program on science instruction in classrooms and the building, teacher attitudes toward science teaching and learning, and barriers teachers perceived to science education reform at the building and district levels.

The Program

During the 1994-95 school year, a districtwide team of 15 to 18 teachers representing all elementary grades and buildings modified the district science course of study (COS) to comply with the new state framework. Recognizing that teacher development was needed to implement the new COS successfully, during the summer of 1995 a subcommittee developed a plan to enhance teachers' skills and content knowledge. A university faculty member joined the team to facilitate program planning, gaining university credit, and identifying resources. Based on an analysis of the needs expressed by the teachers, a menu of professional development opportunities was identified. The plan, implemented throughout the 1995-96 school year, required participating teachers to document at least 30 contact hours of professional development training and to submit a culminating authentic project reflecting their participation and growth in science teaching and learning.

The menu of professional development opportunities involved a variety of options throughout the school year. These included five after-school, 3-hour sessions presented by academicians. Topics selected on the basis of teacher need were concept development, inquiry-oriented lesson planning, earth systems approaches to science education, integrating children's literature into the science curriculum, and authentic assessment of science learning. An in-service day focused on grade-level science curriculum planning, and a year-end session to debrief and share projects and resources was also scheduled. A tour of the Eisenhower National Clearinghouse (ENC), focused on resources available to teachers, was scheduled. Full-day training sessions in Project Wild, Aquatic Wild, Project WET, and Project Learning Tree were Saturday options. Teachers were encouraged to use learning experiences and resources throughout the community and university to construct a plan that best addressed their professional needs. As a follow-up, two levels of Project AIMS workshops were available to district teachers during the following summer.

Data Sources and Analysis

To improve the validity of the study, data triangulation was used (Denzin, 1970). Multiple data sources were collected, including notes and logs from organizational meetings, university guidelines and syllabi, time sheets showing teacher-selected activities throughout the year, teachers' final projects, evaluation reports, interview and focus group transcriptions, and observational notes. Time and space further triangulated the data (Denzin, 1970); that is, data were collected and examined over a period of 2 years. Further, interviews and focus groups were conducted on-site at the convenience of the participants, were varied as to the day and time of day, and were conducted over a period of weeks. These efforts provided a means of validating and reinforcing findings.

The research questions driving the analysis of the data were as follows: When teachers make choices about their own professional development,

1. What will they choose to do, and how do they make those decisions?
2. What is the quality of their work?

3. How do the decisions affect them and their teaching?

4. What is their evaluation of this constructivist approach?

Data were transcribed, collected, and organized to allow for an ongoing analysis throughout the collection process. Categories derived from the data were chosen during and after the data were scrutinized (Altrichter, Posch, & Somekh, 1993). Inductive analysis was performed (Patton, 1990), which allowed patterns and themes to emerge from the data. As the researchers became more immersed in the program and the data, certain concepts and ideas were repeated across participants and were reiterated by the same participant. Descriptive statistics were also used in summarizing and drawing meaningful conclusions from the data.

Trustworthiness in this study was developed in several ways (Guba & Lincoln, 1981). To avoid distortions resulting from the researchers' presence, data were collected over a period of 2 years. To avoid distortions from the researchers' involvement with the participants and to maintain objectivity, transcriptions of data were provided for them to review, correct, and expand or react to. Transcriptions were also checked by a disinterested peer for consistency and accuracy.

Results

The findings of the study are presented with respect to the four guiding research questions:

1. *When teachers make choices about their own professional development, what will they choose to do, and how do they make those decisions?* At least half of the participating teachers chose to attend the after-school sessions throughout the year (lectures, planning days, ENC tour). The Saturday workshops were attended by 11 or 17 teachers each. However, 36 other activities were located and attended by participating teachers. Among the other activities chosen by teachers were educational tours of the zoo and science museum, field trips, and science fairs. Table 3.1 shows activities that teachers chose for their professional development.

TABLE 3.1 Professional Development Experiences Chosen by Teachers

	Experience Participants (N = 59)	*% Total Participants*	*Total Time (in hours)*
Structured Meetings:			
Concept development	31	52.5	92
Lesson planning	34	57.6	102
Earth systems	42	71.2	125
Literature and science	34	57.6	102
Assessment	25	42.3	75
Curriculum planning session	59	100.0	354
Debriefing/Sharing session	46	78.0	137
ENC tour	36	61.0	108
Workshops:			
Project Learning Tree	11	18.6	67
Project WET	17	28.8	102
Project WILD	11	18.6	80
Aquatic WILD	17	28.8	134
Other	36	61.0	161
Other experiences:			
Zoo	6	10.2	21
COSI	8	13.6	29
Field trips	18	30.5	43
Science fair	11	18.6	121
Other	27	45.8	149

Requirements for the culminating project were loosely structured. Projects were to be job-embedded to enable researchers to determine what teachers considered to be meaningful ways to demonstrate their professional growth. Of the 59 projects collected, most were resource books or lists for personal, team, or district use (26 projects, or 44.1%); 19 teachers (32.2%) developed unit plans; and others wrote in-depth reflection papers of their teaching and learning in science instruction, initiated a buildingwide constructivist science fair, conducted action research, implemented and evaluated new teaching methodologies, or provided buildingwide leadership in science education reform to demonstrate their growth. Of the 59 projects, 49 (83.1%) were directly and consciously related to the district curriculum, 9 were indirectly related, and 1 was for personal/professional growth but not related directly to the school curriculum or context. Table 3.2 presents a summary of the types of projects that teachers completed.

When teachers were interviewed about how they chose experiences for their individualized professional development plans, the foremost criterion mentioned was the *nature of the experience.* That is, they selected experiences that met a professional need they identified about themselves (e.g., provided science content on a specific topic, provided networking experiences with other professionals, provided experience in leading hands-on science lessons), that were an area of interest for them professionally (e.g., literature useful in teaching science), or that reflected their learning style (e.g., level of structure, involvement, pace, and background required). The second criterion cited was *applicability of the topic to the teacher and to the COS.* Teachers chose experiences that "fit" with what they were doing already but that enabled them to do those things better. The third criterion, mentioned by two of the eight teachers, was *time.* One teacher shared that, at the beginning of the school year, she chose experiences on the basis of professional benefits but that, near the end of the school year, she needed to log 30 hours of contact time so she resorted to "crunching" experiences in whenever time was available. Another teacher reportedly "paced" her professional development program so that she participated in one activity each month.

2. *When teachers make choices about their own professional development, what is the quality of their work?* All but two of the participating teachers documented at least 30 contact hours of professional training. Contact time ranged from 24.0 to 51.5 hours, with a mean of 33.8 hours. Whereas 41 teachers (69.5%) documented exactly 30 hours of participation, 16 teachers (27.1%) reportedly engaged in more than 30 hours of professional development.

When compared with the level of work submitted by master's-level students in a traditional teacher-directed graduate-level university sci-

TABLE 3.2 Professional Development Projects Chosen by Teachers to Demonstrate Learning

Type of project	Number of projects	Percent of projects
Resource book or list	26	44.1
Curriculum unit	19	32.2
Reflection paper	6	10.2
Science fair	3	5.1
Action research	2	3.4
New methodology	2	3.4
Instructional leadership	1	.1

ence methods course, 36 projects were rated at the same level of performance (equivalent to a B+ grade), 14 were above the standards for that course (equivalent to an A), 8 were slightly below the standard level of performance (B or B–), and 1 was unacceptable (below C).

3. *When teachers make choices about their own professional development, how do the decisions affect them and their teaching?*

Changes in Teachers. Five themes emerged from the interviews and other data regarding the impact of the professional development program on the teachers themselves. Half of the teachers shared that *their thinking about good teaching and good science had not changed as a result of the program but that now they were equipped with the knowledge, skills, and strategies to implement their philosophies.* One teacher expressed that the program "crystallized the importance of hands-on learning" in her mind. Others noted that not only did they now know how to "do it" but they also had become comfortable teaching learner-centered science "even when you don't know what will happen."

A second prominent theme was that *teachers gained a new understanding of, and relationship to, their students as learners.* Teachers now viewed themselves as co-learners with the students, especially when learning new content. This was accomplished by "watching it happen and the students making sense out of it" and by "having fun with science and kids and learning." The teachers' new role as facilitator of hands-on science was possible because of a new understanding of how students learn actively. One teacher stressed that she benefited greatly from assuming the role of a learner in science activities during the professional development program. She experienced a range of emotions: anxiety with pacing that was too fast or too slow; frustration from time limits; a casual attitude toward an apparently superficial activity until friendly competition developed among the teams. Taking this student perspective during activities enabled her to understand the emotions her students would face when she led them in activities, and it enabled her to adjust her instruction to reduce frustration and heighten motivation. As teachers watched their students engage in activity-based science, many gained respect for the young learners. "They are incredible thinkers," one teacher shared. "I had not given them enough credit before."

A third emergent theme was that *the teachers viewed themselves as growing professionals, as professionals "in process."* For some, the growth in science teaching skills was a relatively easy transfer of many strategies they already used in inductive language instruction. For others, the growth was more of a struggle, often conveyed through emotional verbiage such as "dread, scary, reflective, then finally fun because I could see that students were excited and empowered." About half of the teachers expressed that they "need to keep growing" or, more optimistically, that although they are more confident with inquiry teaching, they "will be more so in 5 more years!" As one teacher shared, "I'm growing, but I'm not a new person . . . yet!"

A fourth theme of teacher change was that *teachers found a new sense of empowerment or freedom.* They began to see the need to change their curriculum and felt empowered to do so. Although some became "100% sold" on the new curriculum, which they "didn't buy into at first," all the teachers did not yet fully understand the new course of study. One teacher confessed that initially she dreaded the new curriculum but that, through the professional development program, she felt empowered by what the new curriculum approach could do for her and her students. "I realized that I was tired of frogs and toads and the other topics; I was renewed by the concepts in the new curriculum and how I could branch off of those topics into areas that were the kids' interests." Teachers also seemed to feel a new freedom in their ability to teach by using a process approach despite their perceived weakness in science content. Two teachers discussed their feelings of inferiority because of their weak content background and then shared their realization that their lack of content was not a barrier when using a process approach. "I'm probably a better teacher without the science content," one confessed. "That way, I have to focus the kids on figuring it out for themselves!"

Although these four themes suggest that the professional development program had a positive impact on the professional growth and attitudes of the teachers interviewed, a fifth, somewhat disturbing theme also emerged from the data. That was an almost universal theme that *they wanted to collaborate and communicate more with other teachers, especially about the new course of study.* Although some spoke of mentors or a science coordinator from whom they gathered ideas, most still felt isolated in their building, rather than a part of a grade-level team. Many said it was because of a lack of time; others thought it was because they were "waiting for someone to take the initiative to get us talking with each other." Even though the professional development program provided such a forum for communication during 1 year, it seems that this did not carry over into the following year, at least not at this building site or to the degree that some teachers had hoped. "Of course, whose fault is that?" one teacher summarized. "We are the only ones who can change that by making time to talk and work with each other. We have to take the initiative if it is important to us."

Changes in Instruction. The data suggested three main aspects in the way the teachers' instruction had changed as a result of the professional development program. The first was in the way instruction was carried out. Teachers noted that they were talking less and that students were talking more during science lessons. Also, student talk had changed from simply responding to analysis and questioning—questioning themselves, each other, and the teacher. Science lessons were also more student centered. Teachers moved beyond "this is what we're going to learn" to selecting topics of student interest that fulfilled COS objectives, finding out what the students already know, what they want to know, and what questions they would like to have answered. Students gave input into what they were studying and the depth with which they wanted to explore each topic. Thus, instruction was more meaningful to the students. Students had less textbook and printed material to simply recall;

more emphasis was put on making connections rather than on covering fragmented material. One teacher replaced a traditional dinosaur unit that she was "totally sick of yet that used to be in the integrated course of study" with a student-centered study of endangered species to "make it more real to the kids." She observed that "basically it was the same concepts and ideas but it was under their control.... [I]t took more time ... but I felt it was more meaningful to them because they can do something about this." Another teacher noted an interesting example of empowerment attributable to more student involvement in the curriculum: "It used to be that the fifth grade book buddies came to our class to read to the children. Now, my second graders are teaching the fifth graders what they learned in science class."

The second aspect was that instruction became more process oriented. Observing, labeling, questioning, open wondering, and investigation increased. An emphasis on problem solving permeated the science lessons, focusing on how to find information to answer questions. This process emphasis was evolving for all teachers, although they were at different levels in their proficiency with the approach. Whereas some teachers shared that they had just begun to replace their "same old same old" approach with a more facilitative teaching style, others were clearly farther along the instructional continuum and were moving away from guided discovery toward true inquiry teaching.

A third aspect of instructional change was in student assessment. Although many teachers used the same assessment tools as they had prior to the professional development program, they now used them differently. As one teacher shared, "I still use the same science logs. Before, students recorded their observations in the logs; now, they record the why and how. Their writing needs to be much more in-depth." Many adopted new assessment methods that were more "hands-on." Students were asked to write, explain, develop clay models, draw, or demonstrate what they had learned in a variety of other ways. One teacher assessed students with rubrics that they helped develop. Most teachers, though, talked of a different focus during assessment. Whereas before they had looked at a product, now they were observing students as a way of assessing learning. They watched to see whether students were making connections across concepts and ideas, and they watched for changes in each individual child. One teacher summarized her new assessment as

". . . you have to watch the big picture. You have to see what they do [the product] but also observe and see what seems to be clicking."

4. *When teachers make choices about their own professional development, what is their evaluation of this constructivist approach?* When queried about strengths and weaknesses of a year-long, constructivist professional development program, teachers were overwhelmingly positive. One strength they especially liked was the menu of options. They liked to be able to "pick and choose things I needed." As one teacher explained, "If I could make the choice myself of whether or not I want to give up a Saturday [to attend a workshop], I don't mind doing it, but it's when you are dictated to that I mind." Several teachers appreciated the variety of speakers and facilitators, not "the same voice throughout." More important, the optional experiences were at a variety of levels so that teachers could make choices based on their expertise with hands-on science. Those who needed structure built it into their professional development plans by attending the lectures because they were not yet ready for the loosely structured, inquiry-oriented options. Teachers also appreciated that most experiences were provided on-site rather than at the university. One teacher shared that on-site sessions enabled her to relax and learn more. "Bringing the course out to where the teachers are is the best gift you can give us" because teachers didn't have to rush from the school, to class, and back to their families.

A second strength that teachers identified about this professional development approach was the time frame and flexibility. When commenting about how the program spread across the academic year, one teacher said,

> I love that . . . because I could reflect on everything that I was doing in my old units. I rethought it. Is this a valuable thing to do? Does this really tie in? Am I more skill oriented? What's the content there? . . . I was questioning some things, and I was jotting some things down in a journal. I wanted and I needed time to let it all soak in.

This notion was reiterated across teachers: The year-long approach allowed teachers to work through new concepts and teaching methods more slowly and completely and to assimilate the changes into their teaching approach as they went along. Thus, the changes in teaching and teacher growth were truly developmental. Teachers overwhelmingly voiced favor for the flexible time schedule because "it motivates me."

A third strength of the districtwide program was the networking opportunities. Although many of the experiences provided opportunities for networking with professionals outside the district, more valued by the teachers was the opportunity to talk and process with others located in the next classroom or the next building.

Finally, teachers appreciated the active nature of the professional development program; that is, they learned from the program instructors. More important than learning content was the fact that they experienced hands-on science as students and that they saw leaders model the facilitator role. These experiences changed their thinking about how to conduct and facilitate activities in their own classrooms.

Of course, all was not rosy with the professional development program. Several teachers wanted even more options. Some wanted more time built in to work with their specific district curriculum to "come to grips with how we are really going to plan this out." A few were still overwhelmed by what they heard and experienced. One teacher shared in frustration, "I felt that a lot of it went over my head and I just couldn't catch a hold of it."

Conclusion and Discussion

Researchers concluded that when teachers were involved in a constructivist professional development program, they made responsible choices to develop a personalized professional development plan. Their choices were based on their perceived needs as teaching professionals and on experiences that, because of their learning styles and circumstances, they would be able to maximize. Further, they chose experiences that were directly applicable to their professional situations and that would enable them to better fulfill their responsibilities. Although time was a factor in selecting activities, developing professionally was a greater factor.

Further, the choices teachers made about projects to demonstrate their learning suggest that they selected meaningful, directly applicable projects that they undertook seriously in an attempt to enhance their instruction in line with district guidelines and policies. When given the choice, however, some appreciated the opportunity to develop professional skills (especially in the area of technology use) or to wrestle with and reflect on their notions of science teaching and learning and to chart the evolution of their ideas across the span of an academic year through journals or action research. That is, teachers thusly empowered about their own growth make serious, responsible choices and complete rigorous, meaningful projects to demonstrate their growth.

The result of individualized professional development, the data seem to suggest, is change. Teachers' thinking about and ability to teach science in an inquiry-oriented fashion were strengthened as teachers either transferred existing skills from their language arts curriculum or learned new strategies. Teachers changed their thinking about their learners by joining them in the process of science and by being more in tune with the frustrations that learners often experience when doing inquiry. This made the teachers better facilitators. Teachers saw themselves as growing professionals, in process themselves. They were able to look at the newly adopted curriculum more positively and even with enthusiasm and felt less encumbered by their lack of science content knowledge because of the process approach that curriculum requires. This resulted in instructional change, with science lessons that were more student-centered, student-directed, and meaningful to students. Teachers also assessed learning differently, changing the focus of assessment from judging products to watching for signs of growth and learning in individual students.

For most teachers, the constructivist approach to professional development was effective. The reasons they cited for its effectiveness support the idea that a constructivist theory of learning applies to adult learners as well as to children. Teachers valued the opportunity to choose experiences they needed and wanted to participate in. They valued a longer time frame in which to reflect on and implement what they had learned. They valued the districtwide scope of the program because it provided networking and conversation about the science curriculum. These comments suggest that the program was effective in providing a climate for learning as described by constructivist theory. Sadly, teacher laments that more communication and networking were still needed suggest that social learning, an essential element for a learning climate, was not sustained beyond the initial year of professional development, at least not at the level needed by some of the teachers.

This study provides suggestions for school districts engaging in professional development programs. Instructional change and education reform are possible only when teachers change the way they conceive of and think about teaching, learning, and learners. This study suggests that those changes in teacher thinking result when a constructivist approach is applied to professional development of adult learners. This requires districts to establish a climate for learning. Essential elements for this climate include implementing professional development across a period of time—at least across 1 year. This element provides teachers with time for reflecting and assimilating and accommodates different learning or developmental rates among teachers. Establishing this climate also requires that the professional development effort be at the building or, preferably, district level. This ensures that a critical mass of teachers will be involved in each building, thus providing opportunities for interaction, collaboration, and mutuality, which make learning a social experience. Further, the climate requires that teachers be provided with a variety of options to reach and demonstrate the learning objectives or professional development. By thoughtfully developing individual plans based on a personal assessment of their professional needs, developmental level, and cognitive approach, teachers are able to maximize professional development.

This study suggests that, when given the freedom to make choices about their own professional development, teachers construct programs that lead to changes in their thinking about teaching and learning. Instructional change in the direction of "good science" is the result. How long these changes endure if the conditions for constructivist learning are not sustained, however, is open to question.

References

Altrichter, H., Posch, P., & Somekh, B. (1993). *Teachers investigate their work.* New York: Routledge.

Denzin, N. K. (1970). *The research act.* Hawthorne, NY: Aldine.

Guba, E. G., & Lincoln, Y. S. (1981). *Effective evaluation.* San Francisco: Jossey-Bass.

Honig, B. (1994). How can Horace best be helped? *Phi Delta Kappan, 75,* 790-796.

Loucks-Horsley, S. (1989). *Developing and supporting teachers for elementary school science education.* Washington, DC: The Network.

Patton, M. Q. (1990). *Qualitative evaluation and research methods.* Newbury Park, CA: Sage.

Raizen, S., & Michelsohn, A. (1994). *The future of science in elementary schools.* San Francisco: Jossey-Bass.

Sparks, D. (1994). A paradigm shift in staff development. *Journal of Staff Development, 15*(4), 26-29.

TEACHER PROFESSIONAL DEVELOPMENT AS A SOURCE OF EDUCATIONAL REFORM: IMPLICATIONS AND REFLECTIONS

Frances K. Kochan

The chapters in Division I offer us hope, challenges for the future, and questions for reflection. In this summary, I present a brief analysis of each of the chapters individually, followed by a more general discussion based on the themes of hope, challenge, and reflection.

Analysis of the Chapters

Doing Math the Science Way: Staff Development for Integrated Teaching and Learning

Thomas, Cooper, and Ponticell (Chapter 1) describe an exciting project that depicts not only a teacher educational model but their own openness to learning. The authors' decision to give more control of the program to teachers during the second year and the changes they made in their approach to authentic assessment are indicators of their own constructivist approach to teaching. Their ability to provide open, trusting environments in which teachers could learn and fail and to work with these teachers in a collaborative manner is an excellent example for us to emulate.

The authors' ability to help teachers identify avenues for finding resources in practical, inexpensive ways was a particularly important dimension to their work. Although this might seem insignificant, it appeared to have a powerful impact on the teachers and their ability to implement active, applied, process-driven curricula.

The findings that teachers became more persistent about teaching and learning science, more able to make connections between disciplines and content, and more able to deviate from texts as they taught provide causes for optimism regarding the potential for changing teacher behavior through effective professional development.

Authors and teachers must learn how to uncover the context in which people must operate and how to connect that with their desire to change, even when the system does not understand, honor, or support such change. This learning is a challenging process of monumental significance. The authors focus on a crucial point when they suggest that we must "uncover" the context and determine how to help teachers cope with the reality of what is as they seek to create a new reality.

Here are some issues for reflection that flow from their work:

- How can university educators become more sensitized to the context of the K-12 teaching/learning environment in which teachers function?
- How can teachers become more aware of the barriers they face in trying to change and more adept at overcoming them?

Assessing the Impact of Sustained Professional Development on Middle School Mathematics Teachers

Goodell, Parker, and Kahle (Chapter 2) provide a context and content slightly different from those of the other authors in Division I. Their work is broader in scope, examining a statewide effort, and the outcome gives us a glimpse of the potential for long-term growth, development, and change in teacher beliefs and practice that effective professional development activities can stimulate. The use of an electronic network and periodic conferences to sustain the new relationships formed between the teachers involved in the effort were important factors in enhancing their ability to continue to inquire about and change their classroom practices. The use of such networks offers others a viable means for nurturing similar professional development activities. Likewise, the concepts of "teacher as expert" and "teacher as change agent" place teachers in pivotal roles as leaders. Research on organizational change suggests that a leader or leaders are needed to make change successful (Schaffer, Nesselrodt, & Stringfield, 1997), and placing teachers in leadership roles to facilitate changes in teaching practice promises to be an excellent way of developing school-based leaders.

The importance of resources and of assisting teachers in acquiring and creating them was highlighted in this chapter. The authors stressed that we must not forget the hectic world of the classroom and do all we can to support teachers as they strive to balance all the demands made on them. This is an essential factor in implementing changes in classroom practices and must not be overlooked. A crucial finding in this study was that students in classrooms taught by teachers who had been part of the professional development project achieved at higher levels than those taught by nonparticipating teachers. This finding challenges us not to ignore the value of such information. Too many reform efforts stop short of examining their impact on student performance, leading to criticism about their purpose and value.

A distinctive feature of this project was the concern about school leadership, a discussion often missing in individual teacher change initiatives. Teachers who participated in the professional development activities indicated that principal support was an important factor in their ability to implement the new teaching strategies and approaches they had learned.

Not all teachers who were eligible volunteered to participate in this initiative. This, along with the use of teacher leaders in a variety of ways and the issues related to school administrative leadership, suggests some questions for further research:

- How can we stimulate those who chose not to participate in professional development activities to do so?
- How important is principal support in facilitating and sustaining teacher change?
- How can we facilitate teacher leadership in initiating and sustaining educational change?

Teachers' Choices About Their Own Professional Development in Science Teaching and Learning

Bainer and Wright (Chapter 3) offer us a hopeful vision of how to affect practice by focusing on how professional development activities affect teachers' beliefs about teaching and learning. It appears that the experiences teachers engaged in either changed or reinforced their beliefs in powerful ways that led them to change their practice. Teachers also changed their concepts of themselves and reported feeling empowered and more knowledgeable about their subject area and how to facilitate student learning. It is worthwhile to note that university faculty members also revised their approach to teaching, making the experience more relevant and convenient for teachers by conducting on-site classes and by establishing a structural system that would permit teachers to design their own learning activities.

The fact that teachers continued to think of themselves as learners who needed to continue to grow, even after the professional development activities were completed, may be an indication that changes within their thinking and ways of operating will continue. Thus, effects of the professional development model appear to have the potential to affect teachers, children, and learning, and possibly schools, for years to come. These findings suggest that achieving a critical mass of practitioners within a school, coupled with effective professional development, could be an avenue for overcoming the inertia, bureaucracy, or leadership vacuum that sometimes prevents schools from changing.

Chapter 3 also leads us to some thoughts for reflection. Although a communication system had been created for these teachers while they were active participants in the program, the communication between and among them did not appear to continue over time. This finding led the authors to express concern about the sustainability of the changes reported, even in cases where a critical mass of teachers was present within the school and evidence was clear that the teachers continued to change their practice. The findings raise three important questions:

1. Will the internal changes in beliefs or reinforcement of beliefs of teachers, the sense of empowerment that teachers derived from their involvement, and the perceptions they gained about themselves as professionals be strong enough forces to sustain them as they seek to change their practice?

2. What will be the long-term impact of the lack of a consistent communication and support system among and between these teachers?

3. What types of strategies can be built into support networks to sustain them over time to enhance teacher change and development and take advantage of the presence of a critical mass of teachers with a common belief system within a school?

Discussion and Implications

The authors in Division I offer us exemplary models for professional development focused on teaching and learning that have changed teachers' beliefs and practices. This focus is extremely important, as, rather surprisingly, improving teacher knowledge is often not the principal notion around which educational reform movements are developed (Honig, 1994). It is interesting to note that the student populations served by the participants in these studies were diverse in nature (upper middle class, historically underserved, and those who were part of a statewide effort), lending credibility to the capacity of the strategies used to bring about effective change.

Others may wish to consider some common strengths across all three programs when developing their own programs aimed at enabling teachers to change or enhancing teaching practice. Such programs should consider the following:

- Focusing professional development on issues of teaching and learning
- Modeling the practices that are being recommended
- Providing opportunities for teachers to apply their newly learned skills and knowledge to their practice
- Ensuring that the learning environment for teachers is safe, allowing for failure as well as success
- Using adult learning principles in creating professional development activities by recognizing that adults

  - have many roles and responsibilities and pressures on them
  - are motivated to learn when the learning serves a purpose they view as important
  - bring many diverse experiences to the learning task
  - want to have control over their own learning (Brookfield, 1986)

- Establishing and using networking and support systems both during and after professional development activities are being conducted

Signs of Hope and Challenges for the Future

At a time when education appears to be under a continuous barrage of criticism, these authors offer us much to be hopeful for. Evidence is strong that teacher beliefs, behavior, and practice were changed as a result of their involvement in the programs described. This performance-based outcome of professional development that judges changed teaching practice, not teacher satisfaction, as a primary outcome is exemplary in nature (Sparks, 1994). Teachers in these studies became more reflective, thought of themselves as learners, and changed their relationships with their students. In the often dire reports of failed educational change (Myers & Goldstein, 1997), such reports are uplifting.

The authors also noted some difficulties, however, which direct us to challenges we must heed as we proceed in our work. The most substantial of these challenges deals with the sustainability of teacher change over time. Goodell, Parker, and Kahle (Chapter 2) make a strong case for the absolute necessity of maintaining contact by using both technology and personal contact. The authors of the other two chapters also support the need for some type of networked support system. Liberman and Grolnick (1997) reinforce the value of such networks, suggesting they can have "powerful effects on their members" (p. 212). They further state that successful networks must be built around a common purpose, make decisions on whose knowledge will be included, and include some type of formal structure and membership criteria.

Funds, time, and support are always issues when considering how to build and maintain systems of support for teachers. Here are some possible methods that may be feasible, in addition to those offered by the chapter authors:

- Build peer/buddy mentoring programs into the training in which partners agree to continue to work together within a school or across schools
- Let teachers develop their own long-term plans for maintaining contact
- Seek business partners to conduct annual on-line or personal conferences and let teachers present their work
- Establish videotape networks in which teachers can videotape lessons, share them with each other, or use them for self-analysis
- Create newsletters and alternative teacher responsibility for submitting ideas and questions

A second challenge touched on slightly by Goodell, Parker, and Kahle (Chapter 2) deals with the role of the school and system leader in supporting teacher changes. The data indicated that many teachers who participated in the training thought that principal support was important. Research tells us that the role of the principal in bringing about successful change in a school is critical (American Association of School Administrators, 1991; Duttweiler, 1987). Participating teachers did not, however, appear to have any greater support than their nonparticipating counterparts. One must ask, What is the meaning and importance of these responses? Teacher educators must become more active in dealing with the issue of school administrative and district support for teachers and teacher change. The issue of the role of teacher leaders should also be more thoroughly addressed. Murphy (1999) suggests that it is time for teacher education and educational administration to become more closely united. These chapters lead us to reflect on that suggestion and to consider how we should respond.

A third challenge that must be addressed is teacher resources. The authors were adept at helping teachers create and find resources more easily. The data indicate that this is an important factor in whether teachers actually implement active learning and apply their beliefs into their practice. These findings challenge us to keep the realities of the classroom in mind when framing professional development activities. Building in opportunities for teachers to create or access materials, continually feeding them information about what is available, and incorporating this issue into networks of support are all possibilities that should be considered.

Reflections

In addition to challenges for action, the authors lead us to some questions for reflection that are an outgrowth of what we have learned from their efforts and an attempt to connect their findings with the context in which teacher education and educational reform are functioning. Among these questions are the following:

- Although the voices of the teachers in this study speak eloquently of their desire to change, grow, and relate to students in different ways, many voices are missing. This leads us to ask, How can we, as a profession, stimulate those teachers who choose not to volunteer or participate in these educational experiences to do so? What is the impact of nonparticipating teachers on teachers who are trying to change? What is our role and responsibility toward them?
- In this age of accountability, with its focus on a technical approach to education measured primarily through standardized test data (Olson, 1999), how can we support teachers who want to create open, active classrooms? How can we help them connect their constructivist learning with the measurement standards being used so that they can be successful in meeting external demands while still operating as inquiring, facilitative teachers?

- What kind(s) of data can we collect, facilitate the collection of, and educate others about that will demonstrate that students are benefiting from teacher professional development? Furthermore, how can we deal with and change the belief systems of our constituents regarding what should be measured and how?

As always, research and inquiry guide us toward more research and inquiry, and so it seems that our authors have provided us with both ideas to strengthen our own work and questions to pursue as we strive to improve our educational environment, ourselves, and our profession. The role of teachers in educating our youth is crucial to their welfare and the welfare of our nation and our world. As one of our past teachers, Christa McAuliffe, reminded us, "I touch the future. I teach."

A note of gratitude, then, goes to all those teachers who engaged in the activities reported in Division I and to those who worked with them. Their work and its outcomes are inspirational. Their efforts give us concepts and knowledge that will enable many in the field to design, implement, and explore ideas, activities, methods of teacher education, and practice that can make a difference in teachers' beliefs and practice and their concepts about their role and stimulate their use of strategies that can foster deeper levels of understanding and meaning making for both teachers and students.

References

American Association of School Administrators. (1991). *America 2000: Where school leaders stand* (Report No. ISBN-0-87652-172-3). Arlington, VA: Author. (ERIC Document Reproduction Service No. ED 344 325)

Brookfield, S. (1986). *Understanding and facilitating adult learning*. San Francisco: Jossey-Bass.

Duttweiler, P. C. (1987). *Dimensions of effective leadership*. Austin, TX: Southwest Educational Development Laboratory.

Honig, B. (1994). How can Horace best be helped? *Phi Delta Kappan, 75*(10), 790-796.

Liberman, A., & Grolnick, M. (1997). Networks, reform, and the professional development of teachers. In A. Hargreaves (Ed.), *Rethinking educational change with heart and mind* (pp. 192-215). Alexandria, VA: Association for Supervision and Curriculum Development.

Myers, K., & Goldstein, H. (1997). Failing schools or failing systems? In A. Hargreaves (Ed.), *Rethinking educational change with heart and mind* (pp. 111-127). Alexandria, VA: Association for Supervision and Curriculum Development.

Murphy, J. (1999, April). Reconnecting teaching and school administration: A call for a unified profession. *University Council for Educational Administration Review, XL*(2), 1-3.

Olson, L. (1999, January 11). Report cards for schools. *Education Week, 18*(17), 27-29.

Schaffer, E. C., Nesselrodt, P. S., & Stringfield, S. C. (1997). *Impediments to reform: An analysis of destabilizing issues in 10 promising programs.* Washington, DC: Office of Educational Research and Improvement. (ERIC Document Reproduction Service No. ED 408 676)

Sparks, D. (1994, April). A paradigm shift in staff development. *Education Week*, p. 42.

DIVISION II

Inquiry and Reflection

TWIN NEEDS FOR IMPROVED
TEACHER EDUCATION

W. Robert Houston

Allen R. Warner

W. Robert Houston is Professor, Moores University Scholar, and Executive Director of the Institute for Urban Education, College of Education, University of Houston. He is Editor of the first edition of the *Handbook of Research on Teacher Education*, Past President of the Association of Teacher Educators (ATE), and Chair of the Commission on Teacher Educator Standards. In 1997 he was honored as ATE's first Distinguished Teacher Educator.

Allen R. Warner is Professor and Dean, College of Education, University of Houston and President-Elect of the Association of Teacher Educators (ATE). He is Past Chair of ATE's Leadership Foundation for Teacher Education, represents the association to the National Council for Accreditation of Teacher Education (NCATE), was elected as a Distinguished Member of ATE, and is the recipient of five Presidential Service Awards from five different ATE presidents.

Reflection and Inquiry:
Twin Opportunities in
Teacher Education Research

For nearly a century, the hallmarks of both professionals and professional education have been *inquiry* and *reflection*. At whatever level of expertise, educators are prepared to avoid the *ritual of formal pedagogy* and engage instead in *thinking*. The purpose of reflection and inquiry is to bring disparate data, ambiguous situations, and conflicting perceptions into focus.

Reflection was defined by John Dewey (1916) as a disciplined way of thinking that involves the "reconstruction and reorganization of experience which adds to the meaning of experience, and which increases ability to direct the course of subsequent experience" (p. 76). He wrote that "without initiation into the scientific spirit one is not in possession of the best tools which humanity has so far devised for effectively directed reflection" (p. 189).

A major responsibility of teacher education is to facilitate professional self-reflection. In an insightful analysis, Eleanor Duckworth concluded that teachers must be able to reflect on themselves as *learners* before they can reflect on themselves as *teachers* (Meek, 1991). From the beginning, teacher education programs should help prospective teachers understand themselves and their values and drives prior to helping them understand their students' needs and aspirations and the effectiveness of their own instructional strategies. Such inquiry and reflection should be made with tentativeness in conclusions as new data provide new insights.

Borrowing from the scientific community and mirroring Dewey's admonition, educators too often have adopted algorithms or prescriptions for inquiring about educational issues, misunderstanding the tentativeness of scientific conclusions:

Scientific knowledge is fallible; scientists seek the truth and often think they have found it, but when pushed they usually concede that one day they may be shown to be wrong—the tide of opinion, and of evidence, may turn against them. Thus, Newtonian physics prevailed for several centuries, but eventually it succumbed to Einstein. (Phillips, 1985, p. 49)

Conclusions about self, students, and self as teacher should be considered tentative and changing. The same principle applies to educational theories and movements. Tools of inquiry change and become more precise and valid, modes of analysis are strengthened, and knowledge of learning is increased through new research. All such changes should, but too often do not, restructure educational practice. Educators continue to draw on antiquated instructional methods, modes of inquiry, and limited access to reflection because they either do not know about the new evidence or choose to continue the less challenging and more familiar modes of education. Far too often, conventional wisdom (what *everybody* knows) and professional folklore learned in the teachers' lounge (e.g., don't smile until Christmas; be fair, firm, and friendly) tend to interfere with the absolute need for teachers to be introspective and to engage in a healthy, ongoing process of self-critique.

Approaching reflection from a somewhat different perspective from Dewey or the so-called scientific method, Schön (1983, 1987) proposed "reflection-in-action" as an alternative to more formal sequences of conscious steps in a decision-making process. According to Schön, knowledge is inherent in the action, based partially on the past experiences of the practitioner and the attributes of a particular situation. This interaction brings forth and expands on an individual's tacit knowledge that is not consciously articulated at the time. "This way of thinking . . . is neither linear nor conscious" (Clift, Houston, & Pugach, 1990, p. 11).

More recently, the theoretical foundations of *constructivism* are holding sway in many areas of education—the notion that each of us constructs our own reality, our own knowledge, attitudes, and beliefs from our interactions with the world around us. Constructivism appears to be a useful position from which to view the personal/professional growth of educators because it is indeed in the relationships between self and others that teaching lives.

A major responsibility of teacher education is to facilitate the self-monitoring necessary to function as active, critical, and progressive thinkers. Reflection and inquiry are not learned by listening to a lecture or by reading a book. They become professional habits through use and further reflection *on* such use.

Portfolios, Case Studies, and Teacher Research

The three chapters in Division II delineate three approaches to data collection and reflection—teacher research, case studies, and portfolios. Nevárez-La Torre and Rolón-Dow (Chapter 4) conducted a year-long seminar that met once a month with five bilingual teachers. Studying research and research findings, using observation techniques, and relating them to their own classrooms resulted in teachers who felt more effective and became dissatisfied with traditional professional development.

Chapter 5 analyzes the differences in teacher development and perception when case studies are presented in print or in video formats. Rowley and Hart found that preservice teachers rated both formats high in instructional value; however, the video format resulted in greater engagement and was preferred by about three fourths of participants.

In Chapter 6, Wood explores portfolios as tools for reflective teaching. Novice teachers participated in a year-long seminar in which reflection was emphasized. Participants reported that reflection provided a viable approach to professional growth, increased experimentation with different teaching strategies, and increased understanding of student differences.

Three Characteristics in Teacher Education

Vincent Rogers (1985) identified several characteristics of teacher education programs that promote reflection and inquiry. As you read the three chapters in Division II, consider the relevance of three of his opportunities.

1. *The opportunity to practice the art of perception:* To teach well, one must learn to see with all of one's senses. Painters, dancers, poets, musicians, comedians, and other artists have developed this skill far beyond the level of ordinary people. They see the subtleties, the nuances, the absurdities in everyday life that others often overlook. To teach, teachers

must know the people who populate their world inside and outside schools. Such knowing depends on one's ability to see and understand the subtle cues and signals given by children, colleagues, and others with whom one comes in contact.

2. *The opportunity for reflection:* Teacher education, and indeed teaching itself, is often a hurried, time-dominated activity. One learns to deal with daily crises but seldom has time to search for the meaning inherent in events. Thus, there is a need to stand back, to examine events from more than one perspective, and to apply theory to practice, and indeed practice to theory.

3. *The opportunity to engage in genuine inquiry:* Inquiry is, essentially, "finding out." It need not be goal oriented (although it usually is), and one does not necessarily know in advance what one is seeking. Teachers need to inquire about education; to learn how it functions in certain settings; to identify and isolate problems; to see, gather, analyze, and synthesize data; to build theory as well as test it; and to share and discuss these theories with their colleagues in training and in schools (Rogers, 1985, pp. 251-252).

References

Clift, R. T., Houston, W. R., & Pugach, M. C. (Eds.). (1990). *Encouraging reflective practice in education.* New York: Teachers College Press.

Dewey, J. (1904). The relationship of theory to practice in education: Part I. In J. Dewey, S. Brooks, & C. A. McMurray (Eds.), *The third yearbook of the National Society for the Study of Education.* Chicago: University of Chicago Press.

Dewey, J. (1916). *Democracy and education.* New York: Macmillan.

Meek, A. (1991). On thinking about teaching: A conversation with Eleanor Duckworth. *Educational Leadership, 48*(6), 30-34.

Phillips, D. C. (1985). On what scientists know and how they know it. In E. Eisner (Ed.), *Learning and teaching the ways of knowing: Eighty-fourth yearbook of the National Society for the Study of Education.* Chicago: University of Chicago Press.

Rogers, V. (1985). Ways of knowing: Their meaning for teacher education. In E. Eisner (Ed.), *Learning and teaching the ways of knowing: Eighty-fourth yearbook of the National Society for the Study of Education*. Chicago: University of Chicago Press.

Schön, D. (1983). *The reflective practitioner: How professionals think in action*. New York: Basic Books.

Schön, D. (1987). *Educating the reflective practitioner*. San Francisco: Jossey-Bass.

4 Teacher Research as Professional Development

Transforming Teachers' Perspectives and Classrooms

Aida Nevárez-La Torre

Rosalie Rolón-Dow

Aida Nevárez-La Torre is Assistant Professor of Education, Curriculum, Instruction, and Technology in the Education Department of Temple University, Philadelphia. Her publications and research have focused on teacher preparation responsive to a diverse student population, family-school partnerships as a resource to education, and Latino participation in educational reform. Her most recent publication is an edited issue of *Education and Urban Society* titled "Latino Communities: Resources for Educational Change."

Rosalie Rolón-Dow is a doctoral student of Urban Education in the Educational Leadership and Policy Studies Department, Temple University, Philadelphia. Her research interests include teacher research in diverse settings and the influence of gender and ethnicity on the schooling experiences of diverse students.

ABSTRACT

This chapter explores the use of teacher research as a tool for the professional development of in-service bilingual teachers in a Northeast city of the United States. The premise is that teacher research promotes the transformation of bilingual teachers in two basic ways: as professionals and as practitioners. The analysis focuses on how teacher research expands the thought process of bilingual teachers to grow as professionals by assuming a new role—that of researchers in linguistically diverse settings. In addition, the chapter examines how teachers use the acquired insights and skills to affect practice and discusses the changes that occur in the way teaching and learning are facilitated in bilingual classrooms where teacher-guided inquiry happens. The authors suggest that participation of bilingual teachers in this collaborative inquiry group leads them to an understanding that empowers them to be advocates for change and outline implications for in-service professional development and teacher research in other contexts.

Introduction

The [teacher research] Forum has been helpful because it has awakened me to question my effectiveness as a teacher. After so many years of teaching, it is so easy to fall into a boring routine not really dealing with or welcoming challenges. . . This forum helps me hear myself thinking. (Dora)[1]

This quote supports the notion that teacher research is a tool for change and transformation through reflection and action. Within linguistically diverse settings,[2] teacher-guided inquiry offers many opportunities for growth and empowerment. In this chapter, we describe the journey bilingual teachers[3] take as they conduct research in their own classrooms. Ultimately, we illuminate the contributions that the voices of bilingual teacher-researchers may bring to the greater teacher research community.

Rationale and Theoretical Framework

Teacher research is growing in popularity as an effective means of including teachers' voices in the community that produces knowledge about effective classroom practices. Erickson (1986) contends that an essential characteristic of master teachers should be the ability to reflect critically on one's classroom practice and to communicate to others the insights from that reflection process. We concur with Cochran-Smith and Lytle's (1993) assertion that a major objective of teacher education is to encourage teachers to engage in inquiry and that schools ought to be used as research sites that can produce knowledge.

Teacher research as a tool for professional development is a recent development in in-service teacher programs. Its growing importance has emerged, in part, from the fact that this research process values inquiry, collaborative work, and teachers' voices (Harste, 1990; Louis, Marks, & Kruse, 1996). In teacher research, inquiry becomes a vehicle to reflect about and improve the teaching and learning processes. Furthermore, sustained professional contact with colleagues can facilitate intellectual work, improve practice, and strengthen the practitioners' commitment to work (Louis et al., 1996). Finally, through teacher-based research, practitioners reframe their understanding of teaching and learning in meaningful ways, and their voices contribute to the creation of knowledge about schooling in particular contexts (Harste, 1990; Ulichny & Schoener, 1996).

Despite the benefits of conducting teacher research, there is a scarcity of teacher research carried out by practitioners working with linguistically diverse populations. Lack of professional validation may be one factor hindering participation of bilingual teachers in research activity. For example, Flor Ada (1986) uncovers this limited validation when she explains that bilingual teachers often lack support and face a great deal of criticism:

> Bilingual teachers, caught between the accepted practices they are required to follow and the sound theories and research that contradict those practices, are especially vulnerable to attack. Most bilingual teachers were not educated in bilingual programs, nor did they have the experience of teaching in bilingual schools that receive full societal support. In many instances they themselves have been victims of language oppression and racism; thus,

in order to empower their students to overcome conditions of domination and oppression, they must first be empowered themselves. (p. 386)

Recent movements like English Only and California's Proposition 227 suggest that bilingual teachers today experience a similar adverse professional atmosphere. Other possible reasons for lack of participation in research suggested by this study include job insecurity and lack of awareness of teacher research. *Job insecurity* refers to the vulnerability of bilingual programs to attacks from sectors that want to reduce funding substantially or to eliminate these programs completely. The constant threats against bilingual education programs burden bilingual teachers with the added responsibilities of support and advocacy. Bilingual teachers may have to serve as advocates in the schools and community, representatives of bilingual programs in multiple committees and functions, and defenders of this educational approach in public forums. In addition, job insecurity refers to the fact that many bilingual teachers lack teaching certification. Because of a nationwide shortage of bilingual teachers, school districts need to hire bilingual individuals who will work as full-time teachers while they are also enrolled in certification programs (Garcia, 1990; Griego-Jones, 1995; U.S. Bureau of the Census, 1993). These multiple responsibilities thus limit the time and capacity that bilingual practitioners have to pursue different forms of professional growth.

Finally, the lack of awareness that bilingual teachers have about teacher research might be attributable to the limited amount of teacher research conducted in bilingual settings that is discussed at professional meetings and published in scholarly journals. The need for teacher research with linguistically diverse students is especially poignant, given the changing population trends in urban centers, such as the growing number of diverse students (Archer, 1996; Weiser Ramirez & Linde, 1994). These trends demand comprehensive and innovative educational approaches that will promote success for all students. The involvement in practitioner research of teachers who work with linguistically diverse students is one way to respond to the demands brought forth by the changing trends.

Our research in bilingual settings supports the contention that, through teacher research, practitioners engage in the process of examining their practice to develop a course of action that is appropriate for the specific context in which they work. The course of action should then bring about liberating and empowering practices that improve teaching and learning within linguistically diverse settings. Furthermore, the inclusion of teacher research as a strategy in professional development programs can expand the potential of in-service teachers as agents of change in their diverse classrooms.

Context

The Bilingual Teachers' Research Forum is a collaborative research project for practitioners working in linguistically diverse settings. The forum is an inquiry group consisting of five bilingual teachers and two university facilitators in a Northeast urban center. The group meets regularly to explore their classroom practice and the collaborative process of research through reflection. The forum teachers' experience working with linguistically diverse students ranges from 5 to 20 years. The teachers possess expertise in teaching elementary and middle school students, English as a second language (ESL), special education, and reading. The group members have varied levels of experience with teacher research, from teachers who have carried out and presented teacher research projects to teachers who are new to the process. The facilitators are one faculty member and a doctoral student from an urban university who have experience as bilingual classroom teachers, as well as professional knowledge and experience conducting research and working with teacher researchers. The group meets once a month to learn about research methodology, critique articles about teacher research and about teaching in linguistically diverse settings, discuss videotapes from the teachers' classrooms, and share progress and receive feedback on individual teacher research projects. In addition, meetings between the facilitators and individual teachers are scheduled at least once a month at each teacher's school site.

Research Methodology

The two forum facilitators conducted this research. As facilitators, we coordinated meetings and participated in group discussions. Our main role as researchers was that of participant-observer. In this role, we responded to teachers' inquiries by providing feedback after classroom visits and collaborated in the analysis of their videotaped lessons. We constructed our research role as that of supportive colleagues seeking to part-ner with the teachers as they embarked on their inquiry journey.

Qualitative methods of data collection were used for this study. These methods allowed us to capture the complexity of the teacher research pro-cess within bilingual settings. This form of research is best suited to our inquiry process because it is deliberately open ended, takes a develop-mental view, and allows for the use of multiple sources of data (Hitchcock & Hughes, 1989). Data were gathered from teachers' monthly journal entries, from conversations at monthly forum meetings, and from semi-structured interviews done twice with the teachers. The journals docu-mented how teachers reflected on their own classroom practice and brainstormed about changes they wanted to see in teaching and learning in their classrooms. In addition, journal data showed the process through which teachers developed and refined their particular research ques-tions and the use of specific data collection strategies (e.g., observations, interviews). Data from monthly forum meetings described teachers' learning about the research process and highlighted the journeys and challenges as the teachers developed their individual research projects. Data from these discussions also identified the contextual factors influenc-ing the teachers' inquiry in bilingual settings. The open-ended interview questions generated data on teachers' perceptions about their roles as teachers and teacher researchers and the effects of their research involve-ment on their practice. The meetings and interviews were recorded and transcribed, and all data were coded and analyzed to extract outstand-ing themes relevant to the research questions (Bogdan & Biklen, 1992; Burgess, 1984). Analysis of data from journal entries, meetings, and inter-views focused on the influence of the research process on teachers' con-ceptualization of themselves as professionals and on teachers' knowledge about their classroom practice in bilingual settings. Findings discussed here represent data gathered during the first year of the forum's work (July 1997 to May 1998).

Findings and Discussion

Transformation as Professionals

According to Avery (1990), teachers' growth as professionals involves the development of self-assurance in their own teaching, the ability to manage ambiguity in the learning process, and the skill to problematize teaching and learning in classrooms. Three themes emerge from the data that suggest professional growth: (a) their perceptions about their role as researchers, (b) their questioning of traditional ways of professional development, and (c) the development of a critical view about empowering themselves to grow.

The first area of professional growth is teachers' perception of their new role as researchers. Teachers are at different places in an awareness continuum, from seeing themselves solely as teachers to seeing themselves as teacher researchers. In the beginning months of the forum, two participants—Dora and Minerva—mostly thought of themselves as teachers, not as researchers who work with linguistically diverse students. This meant that, as teachers, they believed that their role was to instruct children with the information specified in the prescribed curriculum. They were solely responsible for the learning of their students, whom they saw as passive learners. This reflects the "banking concept of education" (Freire, 1970). Similarly, research, to these teachers, could be conducted only by using traditional approaches (e.g., quantitative, positivistic, and done by university experts). Through the forum meetings, however, the teachers are gradually expanding their understanding of research and their role in this activity.

> Learning about teacher research has been more of a change in thinking for me. Now I am more focused and interested in why something is working or why something is not working rather than I have to get through Chapter 5 and I have to hurry up. . . . But you have to stop and think, But why? You have to make connections . . . and just be more reflective. (Dora)

This teacher has gradually discovered the importance of questioning her own practice to create an atmosphere conducive to growth and improvement in her classroom. She also recognizes and is assuming an active role in developing as a teacher through posing her own questions and learning from them. Both Dora and Minerva are still discovering the benefits of research and are exploring how they can best integrate research into their practice.

Initial meetings of the forum also revealed that two other teachers— Nereida and Trina—were already sensitized to the importance of research and to different research paradigms. Research activity, however, was for university people. These teachers did not know how to develop their own inquiry-based practice. Through forum activities, these bilingual teachers have begun to use inquiry in their particular classrooms, thus gradually making a transition to conducting research. Some aspects of conducting research that these two teachers have begun to use and benefit from are the value and importance of learning as part of a community of teacher researchers through critical dialogue, observation, and ongoing inquiry. The classroom investigations these teachers are conducting have gradually revealed to them the importance of a systematic and theory-grounded reflective process. The teachers' awareness of their role as researchers is still partial, however, as revealed by the fact that these teachers are ambivalent about calling themselves researchers, investigators, or experts. Two teachers' comments illustrate this view:

> And just the idea that what we have is valuable. Lots of time I think, other than for my own self, we don't think that what we have to say or what we have to share is so important or so valuable. (Nereida)

> The fact that we are teacher researchers. . . . Not that we are experts but just our experience in the classroom. (Trina)

One teacher—Mercedes—speaks in ways that suggest she is actively assuming a teacher researcher role in her classroom, as well as in the school. She is starting to integrate an investigative approach to how she looks at students' behaviors, interactions, and her own teaching. She interprets teaching and learning through questioning, rather than through descriptions of what she sees and experiences. In addition, she is discovering the potential of teacher research to transform school policies. In this regard, she is actively using research as a tool for advocacy on behalf of bilingual education in her school.

> The question of bilingual education is a highly political question for which I feel passionately about. . . . When we are arguing [defending bilingual education], we need to take hold of the data. We need to argue with the research in our hands. . . . We need to say, "Because research demonstrates, because it has been found. . . ."

> To me, teacher research means the necessary constraints to all this passion.... Because it means I have to have discipline in the analysis.... It is no longer enough to say, "This is the way because I feel it is." [Instead] this is the way to help this child because I have research to back this up.... I have data on which I can fall back and say, "It is not because I say so or because I feel so strongly for our children but because I have this data." (Mercedes)

Mercedes is integrating the role of researcher into her classroom practice, as well as into the political dynamics of her school. She is uncovering the significance of the researcher as an agent of change within a linguistically diverse setting.

We expect that the evolution of these practitioners' roles from teacher to teacher researcher will continue as they conduct further research and reflection. As discussed by Avery (1990), becoming a teacher researcher is a process that influences the thinking and behavior of teachers and thus needs to be gradual, systematic, and continuous.

The second area of professional growth is the questioning of traditional ways of professional development. This is particularly significant for bilingual teachers because most states do not have mandates for bilingual certification. Many universities do not offer courses that expose bilingual teachers to theory about bilingualism and pedagogy effective for bilingual classrooms, including dynamic and interactive ways of learning. Therefore, school districts rely heavily on in-service workshops to present bilingual theory and practice.

The forum teachers see research activity as an effective professional development tool that differs from the traditional professional development provided by school districts. They identify differences between the two forms of professional development in what is expected from their participation and in how their participation time is used. In terms of teacher participation, these bilingual teachers value the reflective and dynamic nature of conducting research as part of a community of practitioners while they question the benefits of passive listening and prescriptive approaches to change that are prevalent in traditional staff development. They also value learning through critical dialogue with other practitioners and the opportunity for a collective inquiry effort even though they work at different schools. (This approximates descriptions of the process of collective inquiry in other teacher research groups included in the literature;

see, e.g., Louis et al., 1996, and Ulichny & Schoener, 1996.) One teacher explains,

> I think the difference with the forum is [that] we continue to talk about it. With the workshops and the presentations, I'm the audience. I'm sitting there, and somebody is telling me what to do and how to do it and so on. And showing me their children's work. With the forum, it's the opposite. I'm showing my students' work, I'm talking about what they are doing and I am doing, and getting feedback . . . like I'm part of the team. (Nereida)

Participation in the forum has prompted the teachers to question the way their time in professional development activities is used. According to these teachers, teacher research requires time to be developed, to be expanded, and to be meaningful to their work in bilingual settings. In contrast, the teachers perceive traditional staff development activities as limiting the time that is needed to learn and grow. Meyer (1995, 1997) and Wells (1994) make similar critiques based on their work with other teacher researchers. Nereida commented,

> Because many professional developments are kind of one shot, 1-day dog and pony shows, and sometimes not even a day. Sometimes it's half a day. And then the presenters always say, you know, we have 2 days' worth of things we want to teach you, but we have to cram it in 2 hours. But already it's rushed. You don't have time to process. You don't have time to ask questions. With the forum, I think, as things come up, you can jot them down, and you can bring them back to the group. And again, the growth happens over time. It's on a continuum.

Data indicate that the third area of professional growth of teachers is the development of a critical view about empowering themselves to grow. Teachers have begun to look critically at school conditions that support or impede their growth as bilingual professionals and at how they can facilitate their own growth through research. Although they describe their schools as not actively promoting growth through reflection and inquiry, they see the forum as providing these learning opportunities. They say that forum participation gives them some control over their own growth process and connects them with a larger educational audience.

> I guess knowing that there is a bigger audience out there. That it is not just my classroom. The fact that I went out and presented in a state conference to a bigger group of people. . . . It is sharing what we are doing in the [forum] group to an outside audience. I think it has opened up my eyes to what I am doing in the classroom that not only affects the children but other bilingual programs elsewhere. (Trina)

The development of a critical stance toward traditional teacher roles and professional development activities is both a foundation for, and a sign of, growth (Meyer, 1997). The experience of conducting research in their classrooms has empowered these five bilingual practitioners to identify ways to promote their own learning. The teachers have now established a dialogue within a community of bilingual practitioners and are engaged in ongoing reflection that moves them to action. All these experiences have promoted the teachers' growth as professionals. The inquiry-based teaching process has also promoted their growth as practitioners. In the next section, we discuss how they are experiencing this growth.

Transformation as Practitioners

The research forum has served as a vehicle for promoting reflection about changing classroom practice. Transformation involves being open to reexamine classroom practice and to explore alternative ways for improving teaching and learning (Noffke, 1995). Data suggest that forum teachers are transforming their classroom practice in several different yet interconnected ways. First, they are observing both their practice and their students with a renewed critical view. Second, they are using the knowledge they gain from observations to reflect on their current practice and to seek possible explanations for what is happening in their classrooms. Finally, they are actually making changes in the way they conceive of their practice as teachers and in the way they structure teaching and learning for their students.

The role of observer is often new for teachers. Teachers seldom have time to observe carefully what is happening in their classrooms because their time is spent carrying out plans. (For an expanded discussion of teachers' use of time, see Cochran-Smith & Lytle, 1993.) The forum helps teachers find ways to create spaces in their school day for observation. These observation exercises lead to opportunities for reflection. In the following quote, a forum participant shares how reflection allows her to look at situations from new angles and to challenge her own taken-for-granted assumptions about what works in her ESL classroom:

> I know that it [the forum] is a vehicle for potential growth. I think growth for, you know, time for you to reflect on your teaching practices, helping you to try to think through the situation. Like my problem with Janitza, just helping me to look at it from all different angles that maybe I never would have thought about in that way. (Dora)

Reflection through observation is a key component of the research process because it encourages teachers to revisit their classroom practice and to explore the reasons why certain practices are effective whereas others are limited in promoting classroom learning. Thus, reflection that is prompted by observations can provide motivation for teachers to consider new possibilities for their practice. One teacher shares:

> Another thing too, I was thinking about; if teachers are going to change, if anybody's going to change, before you change, you have to see a reason to want to change. And things like the research forum have me think, oh, I shouldn't be doing this. There's a better way to do things. 'Cause it's a lot easier to sit there and just do something the way you've done it for years. (Nereida)

Facilitating opportunities for teachers to reflect about their classroom practice during and after their observations is important also because it is one of the first steps necessary to involve teachers in investigating, modifying, and generating theories about classroom practice. Thus, observation and reflection are part of a cyclical process that produces grounded theory. Clarke (1994) asserts that the traditional theory/practice dichotomy and discourse are dysfunctional because teachers are placed in a position to accept theoretical proclamations without being involved in the process of examining them and deciding what to reject and what to modify, given their unique experiences and needs. Thus, involvement in teacher research can encourage a new paradigm in which theory and practice are interdependent and closely linked to the everyday realities of teachers. The forum teachers explain how the ongoing and interconnected processes of observation and reflection help them examine theory in the light of their particular teaching context:

> Doing research as part of the forum has helped me to stand back from the students and record what I saw happening, to question what I saw happening, and to assess my classroom practice in terms of theories I know. And lastly, to make changes as a result. (Nereida)

Observation, reflection, and theorizing are worthwhile goals and necessary to teacher research. They become particularly meaningful, however, when change or action in the teachers' classrooms follows them. Teachers engaged in classroom inquiry are usually interested in improving their practice. They become part of a community of teacher researchers because they see the need for altering some facet of their work. The continuum of observation, reflection, and production of theoretical insights is therefore crucial to the teacher researcher as it becomes the catalyst for changing classroom practice. Trina explains how change and improvement are inevitable outcomes of conducting classroom research:

> Just having to keep a journal to reflect on what's going on in the classroom, to be able to sit back and write it and look at it and go back and think about it and go back again and read it, to have your classroom videotaped and be able to observe what goes on in your classroom, you have to grow. I mean there is no other way to go about it. When you look at what you are doing, you want to do something either better or change something or just to look back and say I like what is happening in my classroom. (Trina)

We have identified several ways in which teachers in the forum have begun to make changes that affect their practice. In the first way, as the teachers reflect about their classrooms, they begin to reconsider how they should construct their practice as teachers in their bilingual or ESL settings. One teacher explains how her experiences as a teacher researcher have helped her assume a more facilitative role in her classroom:

> But I see myself more as a coach with my students—more as a coach, more as an observer. And that has really been a change for me because when I started in first grade I wanted to wipe noses, I wanted to tie shoes, I wanted to button. . . . I wanted to do everything. And I've just seen myself mentally changing and the need for the kids to be active, interactive, learning, and having them do it for themselves in order to discover things for themselves. I don't want them to be dependent on me as the sole source of information. (Dora)

In the second way in which teachers are transforming their classroom practice, as the teachers change their classroom practice, they also begin to look at their students differently. New information about students is helpful in that it challenges teachers to rethink their assumptions and can lead to new plans for how to work with particular students. Observation of students influences instruction and allows teachers to focus on how teaching can be altered to meet the needs of students. This change is illustrated in the following excerpt in which Nereida reflects about what stood out for her from a video of one of her lessons:

> Every time I look at it (the video) I see more and more detail. And also, every time I look at it, I try to zero in on one child and just see who's doing what, just focusing maybe on one child, and watch all their behaviors. . . . And I think it just shows me, even things with body language, what they're doing with their fingers, how they're behaving. Like what I noticed was Crystal, I could tell that she's getting bored because it's too easy for her. She may get bored and say, "Oh, the heck with this. I already know this." So, I need to have things to challenge her. I could also use her as a tutor to help Edwin. Those are some of the things I've thought about. (Nereida)

The previous examples illustrate how teacher research encourages teachers to take control of their practice and make actual changes. Clarke (1994) asserts that there is "no objective truth out there waiting to be discovered, written up and delivered to teachers by researchers and theoreticians" (p. 20). Instead, he proposes that the new understandings that teachers gain as they scrutinize their own experiences should be used as the basis for action. The forum activities serve as a tool for teachers to examine and change their practices. As the forum teachers move through the research process, they begin to gain more assurance concerning what area of their practice they want to examine and often begin trying out new strategies as a way of addressing their research questions. One teacher explains how the discussions that are part of the research forum help her gain a clear perspective of the facet of her practice that she wants to investigate in her ESL classroom:

> All I know is, I guess the more I talk about it [her research] the more I look at it, the clearer it's become what I want to do. Yeah, I see it now . . . now I see the connection as to Janitza's situation, Juan's situation, and my practice and what I do. Basically it's focusing on the type of instruction for children who are older kids that have not had the opportunity to academically be where they should be. (Dora)

This teacher moves from a description of her topic of inquiry to specific strategies she wants to try in her practice to help her answer her research question. She elaborates:

> All of these questions came to mind when I started working with Janitza. I believe through writing she will learn how to read [in English]. Also, I want to begin using emergent literacy books to track progress and using a tape recorder to record success. I want her to see herself as a reader and writer and see if this works for her. (Dora)

For some teachers, actual changes in classroom practice come slowly. These teachers spend more time on careful observation and reflection before attempting to make any concrete changes. For another teacher, the reflective process has always been intertwined with concrete action strategies. From the beginning of her participation in the forum, Nereida has been actively involved in learning more about what happens when she implements strategies for promoting English literacy among her first-grade ESL students. Nereida explains how her instruction has changed since she has become involved in her inquiry project:

What I used to do is when they did writing I used to tell them to write about . . . to use words they already know. So what I found was that a lot of them were just copying from their literature book. So there wasn't that creativity. And now instead of spending time . . . I don't even use the workbook. So, what I find that's different this year is I spend more time on the writing. So, I've spent more time on the writing because I've seen the value. And then I've also seen how it helped with the reading. (Nereida)

The process of examining their classroom practices has helped the forum teachers question their own taken-for-granted assumptions about how to educate their linguistically diverse students. In addition, it has given the teachers confidence to try new ideas that are based on their own knowledge of what they want their practice to be and of what their students need as learners. The data provide evidence that teachers' practices are changing as a result of the forum. It is still too early in the process to know what the long-term effects of forum participation will be on the teachers' classroom practice or on the students the teachers work with. We do notice, however, that the teachers are invested in the changes they make because these changes come from their own initiative and from their desire to alter classroom practice in ways that will benefit their bilingual students.

Conclusions, Limitations, and Implications

The discussion in this chapter exposes the growth process of bilingual teachers who inquire about their own practice as part of a teacher research group. These teachers have added the dimension of researcher to their role as teachers, and through this new dimension they are transforming their role as professionals and their practice in bilingual settings. We contend that teacher research in linguistically diverse settings facilitates awareness of what it means to be a teacher researcher, leads teachers to critique traditional professional development tools, and guides them to assume more control over their growth as professionals. We also assert that, through observation, reflection, and theorizing, teacher research leads practitioners to make meaningful changes that are responsive to the demands of their practice in linguistically diverse settings. We suggest that participation of bilingual teachers in a collaborative inquiry group leads them to an understanding that empowers them to be advocates for change. As mentioned earlier, teachers have different levels of awareness of themselves as teacher researchers; thus, the degree, type, and intensity of change initiated by these teachers vary according to their particular growth and transformation patterns as teacher researchers.

The work described in this chapter is important because of the scarcity of research documenting teacher research in linguistically diverse settings. Our seminal work has limitations that need to be addressed in further research with bilingual teachers. As with other qualitative work, our research is limited in its potential for generalization. Educators wishing to learn from our work need to consider that this study was conducted with a small group of teachers whose experiences are shaped by their unique growth trajectories and prior experiences as teachers and by their specific classroom and school district settings. This is especially important to consider as bilingual programs differ dramatically both within and between school districts. Another important limitation is that the work reported here documents only the first year in the journey of these teachers as they engage in teacher research. Longitudinal analysis is needed to document the long-term impact of conducting teacher research in bilingual settings. Multiyear studies will help researchers capture the intricacies and details that arise from contextual factors in bilingual settings. The ways in which these factors shape the research process and the experiences of teacher researchers will best be determined through extended analysis.

Our work with bilingual teacher researchers offers possibilities to redefine the way in which in-service teachers can grow as professionals. Administrators who develop school district models of professional development for bilingual teachers need to be cognizant of the unique contextual factors that influence the growth process of bilingual teachers. To facilitate this growth, in-service designs for the professional development of bilingual teachers should incorporate components of the teacher research process. These components include ongoing opportunities for critical dialogue, observation, and reflection that can empower bilingual teachers to take positive action over teaching and learning in linguistically diverse settings.

Our work also has implications for reconsidering the role of teacher researchers in other settings. The critical stance of conducting research is one that has, at times, been neglected in the discourse about teacher-guided inquiry (Shannon, 1990). Bilingual teacher researchers conduct their research in a context surrounded by contradictions and ambiguity where their work is constantly contested. As Mercedes' experiences suggest, teacher research in this environment demands that teachers assume positions of advocacy and activism. Thus, teacher research conducted by bilingual teachers can illustrate the importance of looking critically at the context where any teacher research is carried out. In this way, the critical dimension of research may be placed at the center of the teacher research discourse.

Notes

1. To respect the anonymity of participants, their names have been changed.
2. *Linguistically diverse settings* refers to classrooms, schools, and neighborhoods where other languages in addition to English are used to communicate and learn.
3. *Bilingual teachers* refers to practitioners who promote teaching and facilitate learning in two or more languages.

References

Archer, J. (1996, March). Search in Hispanic enrollment predicted. *Education Week*, p. 3.

Avery, C. S. (1990). Learning to research/Researching to learn. In M. W. Olson (Ed.), *Opening the door to classroom research*. Newark, DE: International Reading Association.

Bogdan, R., & Biklen, S. K. (1992). *Qualitative research for education: An introduction to theory and methods*. Boston: Allyn & Bacon.

Burgess, R. G. (Ed.). (1984). *Field methods in the study of education*. London: Falmer.

Clarke, M. (1994). The dysfunctions of the theory/practice discourse. *TESOL Quarterly, 28*(1), 9-26.

Cochran-Smith, M., & Lytle, S. (1993). *Inside/outside: Teacher research and knowledge*. New York: Teachers College Press.

Erickson, F. (1986). Qualitative methods in research on teaching. In M. Wittrock (Ed.), *Handbook of research on teaching* (3rd ed., pp. 119-161). New York: Macmillan.

Flor Ada, A. (1986). Creative education for bilingual education teachers. *Harvard Educational Review, 56*(4), 386-394.

Freire, P. (1970). *Pedagogy of the oppressed.* New York: Seabury.

Garcia, E. (1990). Educating teachers for language minority students. In W. R. Houston (Ed.), *Handbook of research in teacher education.* New York: Macmillan.

Griego-Jones, T. (1995). *Implementing bilingual programs is everybody's business.* Washington, DC: NCBE.

Harste, J. C. (1990). Foreword. In M. Olson (Ed.), *Opening the door to classroom research.* Newark, DE: International Reading Association.

Hitchcock, G., & Hughes, D. (1989). *Research and the teacher: A qualitative introduction to school-based research.* London: Routledge.

Louis, K. S., Marks, H. M., & Kruse, S. (1996). Teachers' professional community in restructuring schools. *American Educational Research Journal, 33*(4), 757-798.

Meyer, R. (1995). Servicing-in: An approach to teacher and staff development. *Teacher Research, 2*(1), 1-16.

Meyer, R. (1997). Staff development rooted in composing, disrupting, and inquiring. *Teacher Research: The Journal of Classroom Inquiry, 4*(2), 59-72.

Noffke, S. E. (1995). Action research and democratic schooling: Problematics and potentials. In S. E. Noffke & R. B. Stevenson, *Educational action research: Becoming practically critical.* New York: Teachers College Press.

Shannon, P. (1990). Commentary: Teachers as researchers. In M. W. Olson (Ed.), *Opening the door to classroom research.* Newark, DE: International Reading Association.

Ulichny, P., & Schoener, W. (1996). Teacher-researcher collaboration from two perspectives. *Harvard Educational Review, 66*(3), 496-524.

U.S. Bureau of the Census. (1993). *U.S. summary: Population and housing summary.* Washington, DC: Author.

Weiser Ramirez, E., & Linde, K. (1994). *The state of Hispanic education, 1994.* Washington, DC: Aspira Institute for Policy Research.

Wells, G. (1994). *Changing schools from within: Creating communities of inquiry.* Toronto: Ontario Institute for the Study of Education.

5 Print and Video Case Studies

A Comparative Analysis

James Rowley

Patricia Hart

James Rowley is Associate Professor of Education at the University of Dayton. His research and writing agenda has focused on applying Donald Schön's notion of the reflective practicum to the preservice and in-service education of classroom teachers. He has coproduced two video case series (for the Association for Supervision and Curriculum Development, 1994, 1995) and written articles and book chapters on the topic of case methods in teacher education.

Patricia Hart is Associate Professor of Education at the University of Dayton. Her writing and research agenda has focused on the design, development, and study of video-based case studies. She has coproduced two video case series (for the Association for Supervision and Curriculum Development, 1994, 1995) and written articles and book chapters on the topic of case methods in teacher education.

ABSTRACT

The purpose of this study was to compare the use of print format and video format cases in a preservice teacher education setting. Employing written and videotaped versions of a case of an eighth-grade social studies teacher's efforts to engage a challenging student, the authors sought to understand better the comparative value of the two media as perceived by preservice teachers. Two similar groups of prospective teachers were systematically exposed to both case formats. The dependent variables of interest were students' engagement in the case-based lessons and students' postintervention assessments of the overall quality of the alternative professional development experiences. Although the subjects gave high marks to both case formats, 72% preferred the video version. In addition, a statistically significant difference was discovered with regard to student engagement favoring the video format of the case. The chapter concludes with recommendations regarding the development of multimedia cases that can capture the respective advantages of print and video cases.

Introduction

In the past decade, the case method of teaching has been increasingly employed by teacher educators to promote preservice teacher reflection. To date, the vast majority of cases produced in the field of teacher education have been print format cases. Despite the dominance of the written, narrative case, calls have been made for the development of cases that employ different media. Sykes and Bird (1992), Brooks and Kopp (1990), and Shulman (1993), for example, have all written about or made references to video-based and computer-based cases as vehicles for delivering case-based instruction. In addition, other writers have described their efforts to develop and study the use of electronic media teaching cases (Richardson & Kile, 1992; Rowley & Hart, 1993; Saunders, 1992). Guided by Schön's (1987) definition of the *reflective practicum,* we have been developing video cases designed to serve as virtual worlds of practice in which novice and veteran teachers can practice professional decision making (Rowley & Hart, 1994, 1995).

The purpose of the study was to explore and describe the differences between print format and video format case studies as used in the professional development of preservice teachers. More specifically, the study focused on how the two forms of case studies might differ with regard to student perceptions of instructional quality and the relative power of the two media to engage students' minds.

The subjects in this study were two groups of preservice elementary education students attending a private midwestern university. The subjects were participating in a BLOCK program consisting of 17 hours of professional development courses integrated with a 6-week field experience. The 53 students were arranged into two instructional sections, one with 26 students and the other with 27. The subjects self-selected into the study by enrolling for the BLOCK program. A coin toss determined which section would be designated as the video format group (video group). The other group became the print format group (print group). The two groups were virtually identical in terms of age, gender distribution, and prior experience with case studies in teacher education.

Research Design

In an effort to understand better how print and video cases might differ with regard to student perceptions of instructional quality and intellectual engagement power, the following design was employed. First, a video case study titled *What to Do About Raymond* (Rowley & Hart, 1995) was selected as the video case for the study. The video case was designed to engage preservice and in-service teachers in reflecting on the challenges of trying to motivate a reluctant middle school learner named Raymond. As the case unfolds, teachers gain new perspectives on Raymond's school history and family background and are challenged to develop strategic responses to Raymond's off-task and disruptive classroom behaviors. Using the transcript from the video case, the researchers created a print version of the case designed to be similar to the video case in content. In many instances, the dialogue between the characters was drawn verbatim from the video case. At the conclusion of the study, the subjects were asked to rate the *content similarity* of the two versions of the case, with *content* operationally defined as the main story line and characters of the case. Fully 62% of subjects found the two cases *highly similar*, and the remaining 38% found them *similar* in content.

The researchers engaged the services of a part-time university instructor who was not known by the subjects. The researchers trained the instructor to present both the video and the print cases, controlling for a variety of instructional factors including enthusiasm and questioning technique. More specifically, the instructor was asked to promote discussion of the case by probing students' thoughts, feelings, and possible actions and was instructed not to share her personal opinions relative to the case or to draw conclusions about the case. At the conclusion of the study, subjects were asked, on a scale of 1 to 10, with 1 being *poor* and 10 being *excellent,* to rate the performance of the professor according to the above criteria. The mean score for the 53 subjects was 9.45.

The research design was executed in two phases over a 1-week time period. In Phase I, the instructor presented the video version of *What to Do About Raymond* to the video group and the print version of the same case to the print group. Instructional time, physical setting, and instructor performance were controlled. Identical data collection methods relative to instructional quality and engagement were employed for both groups.

In Phase II, the same instructor met with each group and introduced each to the opposite form of the case they were exposed to in Phase I. In other words, the video group *read* and discussed the print version of the case, and the print group *viewed* and discussed the video version of the case. Again, instructional time, setting, and instructor behavior were controlled. The purposes of Phase II were to expose the subjects to the alternate case study format, to provide an opportunity for subjects to express possible preferences for one form of the case, and to allow participants to articulate the reasons for any preference. Toward that end, a 3-item questionnaire was administered to each group after they were exposed to the alternate case study format.

Data Collection

Student Engagement

For the purposes of this study, *student engagement* was defined as the power of the medium (video or print) to capture and hold learner interest across a period of instructional time. Engagement was measured with a 60-point semantic differential scale developed by the researchers and referred to throughout this chapter as the Student Engagement Scale (SES). The subjects self-reported their level of intellectual engagement by checking the SES during the case-based lessons. Participants were instructed to inventory and record their level of engagement when signaled by the sounding of a bell, which the researchers rang on 10 occasions at 7-minute intervals.

TABLE 5.1 Bipolar Pairs for Instructional Quality Index (IQI)

A Pair	B Pair
1. relevant/irrelevant	6. meaningless/meaningful
2. disengaging/engaging	5. fast/slow
3. realistic/unrealistic	8. artificial/authentic
4. worthless/valuable	9. significant/insignificant
7. interesting/boring	10. stimulating/not stimulating

Instructional Quality

The second dependent variable in this study, *instructional quality*, was defined as a composite of five factors: relevance, engagement, realism, stimulation, and significance. Instructional quality was measured with a 10-item semantic differential developed by the researchers and referred to throughout this chapter as the Instructional Quality Index (IQI). Analysis of the IQI for internal consistency using Cronbach's alpha resulted in a reliability coefficient of .82. The five factors mentioned above were measured by two items each (see Table 5.1). For example, the relevance of the lesson was measured on one item with the polar adjectives *relevant* and *irrelevant* and on a second item with the polar adjectives *meaningful* and *meaningless*. Finally, at the end of the Phase II sessions, identical questionnaires were administered to the video and print groups, asking them three questions designed to uncover their relative views of the two forms of the case.

Results

Student Engagement

The mean SES score for the video group was 50 on the 60-point SES, compared with 37 for the print group. As is discussed later, these results were highly consistent with the statistically significant differences in student engagement discovered in the IQI.

TABLE 5.2 Total Mean Scores and *t*-Test Results for Video Group
           ($n = 27$) and Print Group ($n = 26$) on the Instructional
           Quality Index (IQI)

	Mean IQI	SD	Independent t	p
Print group	41.9	6.56		
Video group	45.7	7.86		
			– 1.87	> .05

NOTE: $t(51) = -1.87$, $p > .05$, no significant difference.

Instructional Quality

The mean score for the video group on the IQI, with 60 being the highest possible total score, was 45.7 (see Table 5.2). The mean score for the print group was 41.9. A *t* test for independent samples with alpha set at .05 revealed no significant difference between the mean total scores for the two groups.

When IQI subtest scores for the two groups were analyzed, however, some interesting results were observed (see Table 5.3). First, no statistically different results were found on Subtest 1, which measured the degree to which subjects found the case-based instruction to be *relevant* and *meaningful* in their professional development. Both the print and video groups gave their respective case-based lessons relatively high scores. Not surprisingly, nearly identical results were achieved on Subtest 4, which asked students to rate the instructional experience as being *significant* and *valuable.* Here again, results were very similar, with both groups giving their respective lessons relatively high marks.

The remaining three IQI subtests did produce statistically significant differences between the print and video groups. Of particular interest to the researchers was the significant difference on Subtest 3, which requested subjects to rate their respective case for realism and authenticity. The significant difference between the print group's score of 10.57 and the video group's score of 8.25 may well have resulted from the subjects in the video group having discerned that several video scenes from *What to Do About Raymond* must have been staged because they captured teachers,

TABLE 5.3 Mean Instructional Quality Index (IQI) Subscores, Standard Deviations (*SD*), and *t*-Test Results for the Print and Video Groups

IQI items	Print Group		Video Group			
	Mean	SD	Mean	SD	t	p
Relevant/ Meaningful (Q1,Q6)	9.76	1.77	9.96	1.45	−0.43	>.05
Engaging/Fast (Q2,Q5)	6.03	2.40	8.18	1.81	−3.67	<.05*
Realistic/ Authentic (Q3,Q8)	10.57	1.62	8.25	2.44	4.07	<.05*
Significant/ Valuable (Q4,Q9)	9.26	1.95	9.96	1.72	−1.37	>.05
Interesting/ Stimulating (Q7,Q10)	6.30	1.19	9.53	1.83	−7.13	<.05*

NOTE: * denotes statistical significance.

students, parents, and school administrators in settings not typically viewed by the public and certainly not filmed.

The statistically significant results obtained on the remaining two IQI subtests were especially interesting because they were highly consistent with the results obtained on the SES. Analysis of data from Subtest 2, which measured student perceptions of how engaged they were in the lesson and how quickly time passed (Csikszentmihalyi, 1978) indicates that the video group subjects were more engaged in the lesson than were their print group cohorts. Statistically significant results were similarly obtained on Subtest 5, which asked students to rate their respective case-based lessons as being interesting versus boring and stimulating versus not stimulating.

Phase I Questionnaire

At the end of the Phase I sessions, the video and print groups were given identical questionnaires consisting of five items. The first item,

TABLE 5.4 Video Group and Print Group Analyses of Their Case-Based Lessons With Respect to Other Cases

	Video Group (%)	Print Group (%)
Similar	31	76
Different	66	21
No answer	3	3

which consisted of two parts, was designed to collect data on the extent to which subjects had prior experience with case-based instruction in their teacher preparation programs. Predictably, the vast majority of the 53 subjects (94%) indicated that they had prior experience with case studies. Only three students (6%) reported that they had no prior exposure to case-based instruction.

The second part of the item asked subjects whether the case-based lesson they had just experienced was similar to, or different from, other cases they had analyzed (see Table 5.4). In the print group, 20 subjects (76%) reported that they found the case to be similar to other cases they had analyzed in their teacher education classes. Comparatively, only 8 video group subjects (31%) indicated that they found the case to be similar to others they had experienced. Asked to describe briefly why they thought the video case lesson they experienced was different from other case studies, video group subjects identified several reasons. Four subjects stated they were used to written cases; in all four instances, the students expressed in slightly different words that they liked the video better. The remaining explanations were more specific and included such observations as "This was more visual. We could take into account the verbal and nonverbal cues," "This was much more interesting to me," and "I like the way we stopped the tape and discussed it at critical points. I enjoyed hearing the views of my classmates."

The second question asked subjects to compare the lesson in which they had just participated with other teacher education lessons by assessing its relative instructional quality (see Table 5.5). As indicated in Table 5.5, 52% of the video group rated their video case lesson as one of the best or above average. Comparatively, 41% of the print group rated

TABLE 5.5 Video Group and Print Group Ratings of the Instructional Quality of Their Respective Case-Based Lesson

	Video Group (%)	*Print Group (%)*
One of the best	14	3
Above average	38	38
Average	41	45
Below average	7	14
One of the worst	0	0

their print-based lesson as one of the best or above average. Results of this item were consistent with results of the *t*-test analysis of the video and print groups' total mean scores on the IQI, with the video group rating their lesson modestly higher than the print group.

The researchers were intrigued, however, by the different explanations rendered by the two groups in support of their ratings. In briefly explaining their choices, the print group subjects were universally to the point. For example, 17 subjects (65%) stated that the class was "too long," "too boring," or "poorly organized." The remaining 9 subjects (35%) simply indicated that the lesson was "useful" or "interesting." Comparatively, the video group explanations were more varied in nature as indicated by the following representative responses:

I liked hearing the opinions of my classmates throughout the case. It caused me to reflect on my own thoughts and feelings about what I would do in the various situations.

This lesson really opened my eyes about what not to do in certain situations.

I think it is important to put us through simulations like this. It forced me to think like a teacher.

It forced us to reflect on how teachers interact with students and with parents.

TABLE 5.6 Video Group and Print Group Assessments of the Realism
of Their Respective Cases

	Video Group (%)	Print Group (%)
Highly realistic	17	55
Realistic	59	41
Undecided	10	0
Unrealistic	14	3

The class discussion was too long and drawn out. I often wished
the instructor would start the tape instead of allowing us to discuss each scene so long.

The third item on the Phase I questionnaire asked subjects to assess
how realistically they thought the case represented school life. Once again,
questionnaire results were consistent with results obtained from the IQI.
As indicated in Table 5.6, 55% of the print group rated their written case to
be highly realistic, compared with only 17% of the video group rating their
video case to be highly realistic. Although 59% of the video group rated
their case as realistic, overall results favored the print version of the case as
being more realistic.

Analysis of the written explanations from the two groups once again
resulted in some interesting observations. First, the 26 print group responses were highly consistent, following a pattern of response that
expressed "There are children like Raymond in almost all classrooms,"
"There is a student in my BLOCK class that reminds me of Ray," and "This
was very realistic. In my class now there are three students like Raymond."

Comparatively, the video group responses were considerably more
varied and tended to deal with the issues of the case with greater specific-
ity. Interestingly, no video group subjects responded by saying that the
case was realistic because they had a student like Raymond in their
BLOCK class. Here are some representative responses:

I can see this situation happening, and I can see teachers acting in
this way as well. I think a lot of teachers become frustrated and do
not handle situations in the best manner.

TABLE 5.7 Video Group and Print Group Preferences for Print and
Video Case Formats

	Video Group (%)	*Print Group (%)*
Prefer the print format	41	15
Prefer the video format	59	85

There are always going to be students who aren't interested in what you are teaching, and it is important to know how to handle them.

I think it is realistic because more and more students come from homes where parents do not have a big impact on their school careers. I think it is also realistic that teachers can fail to communicate and that students can slip through the cracks.

Unrealistic. I would like to think that out of all those teachers, someone would have found a way to interest Raymond in school and get him on the right track.

This was unrealistic because no one in the school had a clue about what was going on. They did not handle the situation properly.

Phase II Questionnaire

At the conclusion of Phase II, a second questionnaire was administered to both groups. The first item stated, "You have just been exposed to another version of the case study *What to Do About Raymond.* If you had a choice of participating in a case study lesson using the printed or video version of the case, which version would you prefer?" (see Table 5.7). Next, the subjects were asked to describe the chief advantages of the version of the case they selected.

After being exposed to the video version of *What to Do About Raymond,* only four print group subjects (15%) expressed a preference for the print version of the case. These four students cited several reasons for their preference. For example, one student stated that he (or she) liked "to look back and check information." Comparatively, another expressed that she (or he) liked "to read the case all the way through without interruption." Still another explained that she preferred to "form her own pictures in her head." Finally, another pointed out that the video case tended to evoke "more emotional decisions."

The 22 print group students (85%) who expressed preference for the video version of the case described various reasons in support of their preference. Half of this group cited seeing "body language" and "facial expressions" as the reasons for their preference. Four students argued that the video version was preferable because it was helpful to see how the characters "interacted," "communicated," or "responded" to one another. Three other students explained that the video case helped them get a better sense of the character's "feelings," "emotions," or "attitudes." Many students expressed more than one reason for their preference, including the following: "It was more entertaining" and "Many details picked up in the video cannot be captured in print."

After being exposed to the print version of *What to Do About Raymond,* 11 video group subjects (41%) expressed a preference for the print version of the case. Interestingly, all 11 explained that the print version provided more background information. Eight subjects explained that they liked to "reread" or "make notes" and that the print version was preferable for those reasons. Three students observed, using slightly different words, that it was "beneficial to know the thoughts behind the character's actions." The variety of other responses included "I react better to print material" and "The print gives you more time to think and reflect."

In the video group, 16 subjects (59%) stated that they would prefer the video version of the case and articulated several reasons for their preference. For example, 12 students described how they felt more "involved," "engaged," "part of," or "caught up in" the video version of the case. Many responses included a reference to the way the video was viewed, stopped, and discussed and how that contributed to their engagement. Nine subjects explained that the video allowed them to "get a better feel for" or "better understand" the reactions of people. Three students simply stated that they were "visual learners" and that the video case was more appropriate to their learning style.

Conclusions

Interpretation of the results of this study yielded the following four conclusions regarding the relative merits of written and video case studies for teacher education. First, with regard to how preservice teachers might rate the educational merit of the two case formats, the preservice teachers in this study gave high marks to both formats as having instructional value; 52% of the video group and 41% of the print group rated their respective format above average or one of the best lessons they have experienced in their professional preparation.

Second, with regard to the question of student engagement, subjects in this study were more engaged by the video format of the case. Administration of the IQI yielded statistically significant differences with regard to how interesting, stimulating, and engaging the subjects rated the comparative formats. This evidence favoring the video format was reinforced by written responses on the first questionnaire, which indicated that 65% of the print group found the print case lesson to be "too long" or "too boring."

Third, after being exposed to both forms of the case *What to Do About Raymond,* subjects in this study expressed a strong preference (72%) for the video version of the case. As the basis for their preference, students cited a variety of reasons dealing with the video version's ability to provide insight into human interactions, communications, feelings, and attitudes.

Finally, although the majority of students preferred the video case, many of the remaining students (28%) expressed a preference for the print version. Common among the reasons given for their preference was a need to be able to "review, rethink, or reread" the case to clarify their thinking. Consequently, the results of this study suggest that teacher educators may best meet the needs of their students by using both video and print case studies. Video cases, as used in this study, place preservice students in a virtual world of practice in which many professional decisions must be made quickly and in what Schön (1987) has called the "indeterminate zone" of practice. Conversely, print cases offer students the opportunity to take more time to reflect on issues of professional decision making, whereas practitioners may have the luxury of more time to consider alternate actions and their possible consequences. A second alternative, which has special appeal to us, is the development of multimedia cases that employ video representations of professional practice supplemented and enhanced by written artifacts.

References

Brooks, D., & Kopp, T. (1990). Technology and teacher education. In W. Houston (Ed.), *Handbook of research on teacher education* (pp. 498-513). New York: Macmillan.

Csikszentmihalyi, M. (1978). *Beyond boredom and anxiety.* San Francisco: Jossey-Bass.

Richardson, V., & Kile, S. (1992). *The use of video cases in teacher education.* Paper presented at the American Educational Research annual meeting, San Francisco.

Rowley, J., & Hart, P. (1993). Catching and releasing expert teacher thought. In M. J. O'Hair & S. A. Odell (Ed.), *Diversity and teaching: Teacher education yearbook* (Vol. 1, pp. 122-137). Orlando, FL: Harcourt Brace.

Rowley, J., & Hart, P. (1994). *Mentoring the new teacher* [Videocassette series]. Alexandria, VA: Association for Supervision and Curriculum Development.

Rowley, J., & Hart, P. (1995). *Becoming a star urban teacher* [Videocassette series]. Alexandria, VA: Association for Supervision and Curriculum Development.

Saunders, S. (1992). *The nature of preservice teachers' comments in discussing a videotaped teaching case.* Paper presented at the American Educational Research Association annual meeting, San Francisco.

Schön, D. (1987). *Educating the reflective practitioner.* San Francisco: Jossey-Bass.

Shulman, L. S. (1993). Toward a pedagogy of cases. In J. H. Shulman (Ed.), *Case methods in teacher education.* New York: Teachers College Press.

Sykes, G., & Bird, T. (1992). Teacher education and the case idea. In G. Grant (Ed.), *Review of research in education* (Vol. 18, pp. 457-521). Washington, DC: American Educational Research Association.

6 Teaching Portfolios

*Tools for Reflective Teaching in
Inner-City Teacher Induction*

Ann L. Wood

Ann L. Wood is on the faculty at California State University, Long
Beach. She is a Trainer for the California Formative Assessment Support System for Teachers. Her research interests are teacher induction
and educational reform; she has authored an educational monograph
and other articles.

ABSTRACT

Reflection helps teachers understand how teaching practices influence student learning. This study describes how 17
novice teachers learned and used reflective teaching practices
in their first and second years of teaching. Using a phenomenological approach, the study explores the meaning of teachers' experiences through an analysis of qualitative (observations, interviews, content analysis of written reflections and
studies) and descriptive statistical (pre- and postprogram
questionnaires, a program evaluation, and a second-year
follow-up survey) data. Three central findings emerged from
data triangulation. Using teaching portfolios as tools for reflective teaching results in novice teachers' (a) recognition and use
of reflection for professional growth, (b) increased experimen-

tation with different teaching strategies, and (c) enhanced awareness and valuing of student difference.

Introduction

The reflective portfolio process has become a significant part of school reform (Tierney, 1992). Successful teachers are viewed as engaged in ongoing reflection about their practices and in examining evidence of their students' learning. Research demonstrates that portfolios are effective means for teachers' reflections on their professional growth experiences (Stone, 1998). The practice of writing reflections about one's teaching in portfolio entries is considered to be useful in becoming a reflective teacher (Grant & Huebner, 1998). This practice creates habits of the mind that foster continuing professional development. Lyons (1998) states, "The power of these habits of mind should be examined in longitudinal studies of portfolio makers" (p. 126). This is a longitudinal study of how inner-city, novice teachers learn to reflect in a collaborative, standards-based, teacher induction program and how they continue their reflective practices in their second year of teaching.

Theoretical Framework

The perspective of reflection on which this study is based is that of Schön's "reflection-on-action" (1987). Reflection-on-action occurs as a retrospective analysis of a teaching experience that is usually completed through writing. Teachers analyze, synthesize, and evaluate their teaching experiences to make informed changes in practice to meet students' needs (WestEd, 1997). Reflection enables teachers to frame and reframe teaching situations and then to formulate new student-based plans of action (Schön, 1991).

Teaching portfolios are generally defined as selective collections of information about a teacher's practice or structured collections of evidence of a teacher's accomplishments over time (Wolf, 1991, 1996). The purpose of teaching portfolios is to provide teachers with opportunities to explore, extend, and reflect on their own and students' learning (Dietz, 1995). The type of teaching portfolio chosen as the basis of this study is a growth portfolio (WestEd, 1997) or learning portfolio (Bartell, Kay, & Morin, 1998). As Wolf and Dietz (1998) state, "The learning portfolio is the best choice when the goal is to stimulate and strengthen teachers' reflection and practice" (p. 19).

Portfolio questions are constructed to guide teachers' reflections on practice through an evidence-gathering process. Writing reflections for portfolio entries pushes teachers to examine their teaching. Teachers become researchers of their own practice. Novice teachers explore portfolio questions that continue to evolve as a part of their ongoing professional development (Grant & Huebner, 1998).

Context of the Study

Beginning Educator Seminars on Teaching (B.E.S.T.) is a collaborative program between one of the nation's largest school districts and a western university's teacher education program. It is a series of professional development Saturday seminars for inner-city novice (first-year) teachers that is grounded in the *California Standards for the Teaching Profession (CSTP)* and the California Teaching Portfolio model (WestEd, 1997). Unlike California's formative assessment and support program Beginning Teacher Support and Assessment (BTSA), B.E.S.T. is conducted on 16 Saturdays (9 a.m.-1 p.m.) to avoid the overextension of time that new teachers experience in mandated after-school Monday through Thursday commitments.

B.E.S.T. seminars are grounded in the six standards of the CSTP (California Department of Education & the California Commission on Teacher Credentialing, 1997). On the basis of best practices research, the CSTP represents a developmental and holistic view of teaching (Bartell et al., 1998). The CSTP functions as the lens through which novice teachers analyze their instructional and classroom management strategies and on which they base their future teaching practices.

The portfolio process is built on a plan, teach, reflect, and act cycle (WestEd, 1997). Novice teachers plan teaching strategies, practice them, reflect on them, and revise them on the basis of students' learning outcomes. The process includes reflective conversations, written reflections, and a focused portfolio collection of evidence of CSTP-based teacher and student work. Teachers' written reflections are completed at each B.E.S.T.

seminar and include interactive journal entries between the novice teachers and the seminar instructor.

Novice teachers' portfolios center on two standards: (a) creating and maintaining effective learning environments for student learning and (b) engaging and supporting all students in learning. Based on research from the California New Teacher Project, these two standards are considered to be central to issues in first-year teaching (California Commission on Teacher Credentialing & the California Department of Education, 1992). Each B.E.S.T. teacher formulates a classroom-based research question grounded in one of these standards and collects evidence on it. Portfolio evidence is always accompanied by written reflections. Reflections may include comparisons of what transpired with what was planned, connections between teachers' actions and student learning, suggestions for improvements in teaching, and/or identification of next steps for professional development (WestEd, 1997).

B.E.S.T. novice teachers are assigned a district mentor teacher as a critical friend/coach. Mentors are matched to beginning teachers on the basis of grade level, subject matter, and similarity of school sites. They observe the novice teachers monthly and help them gather CSTP-based evidence for their classroom-based research questions. After each observation, novice teachers are asked to complete a Reflective Observation Form. They answer questions such as, "What have I learned about my students?" and "What have I learned about my teaching?" Some of these responses are incorporated in the case study data.

The overall goal of this study is to describe a teacher induction model that promotes reflective teaching through the use of a teaching (growth) portfolio process based on professional teaching standards. The study's objectives are to assess whether novice teachers (a) learn how to reflect on their teaching, (b) value reflection as a teaching practice, and (c) continue to value and use reflective teaching practice in their second year of teaching. To answer the objectives of this study, the following research questions were generated:

How can teaching (growth) portfolios be used to teach novice teachers how to reflect on their teaching practices?

How does a standards-based, reflective portfolio process influence novice teachers' practices in their first years of teaching?

Will novice teachers practice these reflective strategies in their second year of teaching?

Method

Because of this study's purpose and research questions, it uses qualitative methodology (Strauss, 1987). Qualitative methods enabled us to understand how these teachers perceived and interpreted their lived experiences as first-year teachers in an induction program (Patton, 1990). Phenomenology is the approach that grounded the research and guided the data collection, analysis, and interpretation (van Manen, 1990).

Participants in this study were selected for the diversity of their educational, linguistic, and cultural backgrounds, as well as of their teaching assignments. The 17 participants included 14 females and 3 males and 16 first-year elementary and 1 middle school teacher. Informants' cultural backgrounds were 6% African American, 6% Asian American, 41% Latino American, and 47% European American. They ranged in age from 24 to 48. Former occupational backgrounds of these first-year teachers included one ex-attorney, one ex-military professional, one former union representative, and three former teacher's aides.

Denzin and Lincoln (1998) recommend "triangulation" for data collection involving more than one source of information. All study participants completed pre- and postprogram questionnaires on reflective teaching and the teaching portfolio process. Mentor teachers conducted monthly, formal observations of B.E.S.T. teachers. Observations were recorded on an adapted version of the BTSA Observation Form. Participants' classroom-based research questions were collected. Participants conducted peer reviews of each other's portfolios, and field notes were taken on these reviews. A second-year follow-up survey was administered, and an external program evaluation was conducted.

Five participants were selected as case studies on the basis of their educational and cultural diversity, as well as of their teaching assignments. Two semistructured, in-depth interviews were conducted with them in their first and second years of teaching. Questions asked included "What impact did reflection have on your teaching practices?" and "Did constructing a teaching portfolio help you become a reflective teacher?" Second-year, postprogram interviews were conducted after follow-up surveys were collected. Participants were asked such questions as "With regard to reflective teaching practices, how do you compare your first and second years of teaching?" and "How did the process of constructing a teaching portfolio influence your teaching this year and last year?"

Qualitative data were analyzed by using the constant comparative method (Strauss, 1987). The experiences of five participants were documented in case studies. Cross-case analysis (Patton, 1990) was used to look across the case studies to identify patterns as well as variance that occurred in the teachers' responses. Each case, however, was treated as a holistic entity (van Manen, 1990) that could stand alone because of the unique perspective of each teacher. Quantitative data analysis and interpretation, including the application of descriptive statistics, were conducted for the pre- and postprogram questionnaires, the second-year follow-up survey, and the external program evaluation. Descriptive statistics, teacher responses, and all documents were examined to identify common underlying themes (see "Results").

To illustrate the diversity of novice teacher experiences, excerpts from four of the case studies are presented below. Pseudonyms are used for anonymity, and all identifying information about study participants has been changed to protect study informants' confidentiality.

Kim

Kim is a 25-year-old second-grade teacher who was born in Thailand and speaks Spanish, Thai, Chinese, and English. Prior to entering B.E.S.T., she completed a university internship program. Under California law, graduates of intern programs are eligible for 1 year of a teacher induction program. As an intern, Kim had received an award for her outstanding teaching practices and entered her first official year of teaching filled with enthusiasm.

Kim's first classroom was in a school in a culturally mixed neighborhood with Chinese, Latino, Thai, and Hmong residents. Kim's research question was "How can I use my multicultural classroom to connect students' life experiences with second-grade curriculum objectives?" Throughout the year, she instituted classroom activities that captured the essence of her students' cultural backgrounds. Colors, sights, and sounds abounded in her print-rich classroom. Kim remarked that formulating her portfolio inquiry question had been "a motivation to get things done." She commented, "It forced me to reflect on my teaching."

Kim was methodical about taking photographs of classroom activities. Her portfolio bulged with class snapshots. Perhaps because of the prolific number of class projects that Kim instituted, writing reflections about her practices was more difficult for her. She would forget to write reflections about lessons and then not remember critical thoughts about them or revisions for them.

She commented, "B.E.S.T. became my model of how to reflect on my teaching." The required reflection on each portfolio entry forced Kim to write her thoughts about each CSTP-based piece of evidence. Kim became more cognizant of the importance of consistently writing portfolio reflections on teaching evidence. She began to write more regularly after experiencing "the frustration of forgetting what happened during a lesson."

Putting her analysis of each teaching strategy into written form demanded a discipline of practice for Kim. The writing contained an element of commitment for or against a teaching practice. Negative evaluations of a particular strategy called for further exploration of other teaching strategies or learning activities. Looking back at the B.E.S.T. program as a second-year teacher, Kim stated, "Reflections helped me explore using different strategies to teach diverse students."

Thomas

Thomas is a 34-year-old European American man of Irish heritage who left the legal profession and entered teaching because he married a teacher and decided that "teachers were nicer than lawyers." Raised on the East Coast and transplanted to the West Coast via Japan, Thomas entered teaching as a trilingual professional. His own cultural exposure and language proficiency made him particularly empathic to the wide cultural and linguistic diversity of his first-grade class.

Thomas's first teaching assignment was a first- and second-grade combination class in which he team-taught science, social studies, and art. Of his students, 25% spoke Tagalog, 15% spoke Spanish, and 10% spoke Vietnamese; 10% were African American, and 40% were European American. During the school year, he was observed teaching his first graders to say *good-bye* in six languages.

Because of class-size reduction, Thomas's class contained 18 students, including several children designated as gifted. His classroom-based portfolio question was "How do I use different instructional strategies to meet the needs of students at a variety of literacy levels?" During the year, Thomas researched and implemented a variety of literacy strategies and described the impact of his portfolio question as making him "focus on language arts acquisition in the classroom." He made the students book bags and had them take home special books each night. He discovered that he enjoyed "the process of helping slow developing readers become strong readers." He had regular read-alouds and helped students make their own books. Thomas commented on how he "tried many, new literacy strategies as a result of being in B.E.S.T."

During his first year of teaching, Thomas's wife was expecting their first child. This first year was preparation for a career that would balance his own child's care with his time as a classroom teacher. This may have put subtle pressure on him to learn more and faster than other beginning teachers. Reflective writing became very important to him in keeping track of details about his students, as well as his ideas about teaching. "Reflection helped me become more aware of who my students are and what they bring to the classroom." During his second year of teaching, Thomas returned to his same school site in a shared teaching arrangement. Both teachers, he and his wife now shared child care and teaching responsibilities. He also began to keep a journal to reflect on his teaching and to note changes he wished to make in his practices. "Keeping a journal since that time (in B.E.S.T.) has proved to be an invaluable tool."

Jose

Friendly and with twinkling eyes, 38-year-old Jose continuously tried different teaching strategies with his kindergarten children throughout his first year of teaching. Fluent in Spanish, Jose commented that he liked "working with urban, bilingual students and other students who live in poverty. They respond to my attempts to teach them in a positive way." Jose participated in B.E.S.T. as an emergency credential teacher (emergency credential teachers in California make up over one third of the state's teaching force).

Jose taught in a large, year-round elementary school in which he received much support from a team teacher. The school was 90% Latino, 8% African American, 1% Asian, and 1% European American. His class of 19 was an even split of boys and girls, one gifted child, and three special needs children. All children were identified as English language learners, and 100% were eligible for free meals.

Jose's portfolio question was "How do I employ literacy strategies that teach to the many different developmental levels of my students?"

Jose found it helpful to think about and collect evidence on this question. He stated, "I kept the question in my head all the time, the whole year, and was able to work on an answer over time."

Although he loved reflective thinking, Jose was less enthusiastic about reflective writing. He sometimes struggled to put his thoughts on paper. Like other novice teachers, sometimes he thought that writing took more time than it was worth. It was a difficult journey to incorporate written as well as oral reflections in his repertoire of teaching skills. One issue that changed this was how his colleagues perceived Jose's sense of professionalism.

Jose had volunteered to tutor his students in English on Saturdays. Some of his colleagues resented his willingness to put in extra, unpaid time. It was around this issue that Jose started to feel the value of reflection with his seminar peers. He was visibly relieved and buoyed by his B.E.S.T. peers' support of his extra work. He had written several reflections around this issue, and the reflective conversations that centered on these writings strengthened his own resolve to continue practicing teaching in his own manner.

These reflective conversations bolstered Jose's confidence in himself as a competent teacher and helped him resist peer pressure to do less work. Writing reflections about these experiences helped him be more open to writing as a vehicle for reflective processes. In the second-year interview, Jose stated that he "incorporates reflective teaching practices into his present teaching. Reflection helps me to assess my teaching and make adjustments in an organized, ongoing way."

Katarina

A 33-year-old soccer player, Katarina is a special education teacher and a first-generation Italian American mother of one small child. Organized and brightly decorated, her room invited students to learn. Her 11 students ranged in age from 7 to 11 years and included one student with hearing impairment, one student with speech disability, and nine students with learning disability. One student was an English language learner.

A graduate of a traditional student teaching program, Katarina often expressed her sense of preparedness for teaching a learning handicapped special education class with grades 2 through 5. Although she worried aloud and worked long hours, Katarina managed her classroom with fairness and resoluteness. She frequently shared advice on classroom discipline with her peers:

> I don't mind working with learning disabilities or behavior problems. The children are what I enjoy, not the learning problems or management problems. Behaviors like students shouting, getting out of their seat, or other off-task actions are just problems to work around.

The student behavioral management system and role responsibilities that Katarina implemented helped her focus on students' academic learning. Her classroom-based research question was "How can I use student portfolios to promote self-direction and reflective learning in emergent readers and writers?" This research question helped Katarina fulfill a school mandate to use student portfolios while she learned about teaching portfolios. She stated, "I learned a lot about myself, my teaching, and my school from doing the teaching portfolio and this question. I had to focus, and I tried things that I probably wouldn't have done otherwise."

During her second-year interview, Katarina talked more about the value she sees in reflective teaching practices:

> The main thing that I got out of B.E.S.T. was the concept of reflection. I never really thought about reflecting on how I teach, but now I am constantly doing that. I continually question how my teaching is going and why I do things a certain way. Then I decide how I can better my teaching.

Results

Analysis of the triangulation of data yielded the following three central findings.

Recognition and Use of Reflection for Professional Growth

Findings of this study underscore the importance of reflection as a valued and regularly used teaching strategy for first-year teachers. At the initiation of B.E.S.T., 25% of these first-year teachers reported that they did not know what reflective teaching was. By the completion of the B.E.S.T. seminars and their first year of teaching, 100% of participants demonstrated their knowledge and use of reflective teaching practices. "Reflection has been a wonderful tool to slow down and think, to make decisions based on observations and classroom needs, rather than moving blindly on," stated one teacher. Program evaluation results show that, of all the skills gained from B.E.S.T., participants rated reflective teaching the most valued. "Teaching practices are based on research, so why not have the classroom as my research lab where I can practice my teaching, succeed, fail, rethink, redo, reflect, and move on?"

Reflective teaching practices became ingrained in these novice teachers' repertoires of teaching strategies. "It helped me assess my teaching and make adjustments in an organized, ongoing way." Teachers noted that learning about reflection, especially constructing their own teaching portfolio based on an identified classroom-based question, had influenced them to review their teaching practices continuously. "The documentation of what worked and what didn't work enabled me to remember and reflect some more." Findings from the second-year follow-up survey showed that 100% of teachers stated they continued to value and use reflection as a tool for quality teaching.

Increased Experimentation With Different Teaching Strategies

Barth (1990) suggests that creating opportunities for professional discourse leads to greater experimentation among teachers. One teacher commented, "I tried many new things as a result of B.E.S.T. and reflecting on my teaching." Case study and other participants reported an increase in experimentation informed by their reflective conversations with their B.E.S.T. mentors and peers. "Sharing reflective writings with others' ideas of what is important and what materials they use, helped me prioritize and try different things."

As she began her second year of teaching, one participant reminisced, "I'm using the lessons that were successful and trying new techniques shared by the B.E.S.T. speakers last year." Of the second-year follow-up survey respondents, 75% reported that participation in B.E.S.T. still influences them to experiment with different teaching strategies in their classrooms. "Now I realize the importance of probing more deeply into why students are not learning and changing my teaching when they aren't getting it."

Enhanced Awareness and Valuing of Student Difference

In their portfolio inquiry questions, participants identified areas of professional growth that shared one common theme: The majority of their portfolio inquiries centered on the issue of student difference. Examples of these questions are "How can I develop math learning centers that address the needs of students' different ability levels?" and "How can I use kinesthetic and tactile strategies to match students' individual learning styles?" One teacher stated,

> I seek out help from references, resources, other teachers, and other classrooms to meet the needs of the individual students, not just the majority.

> Teachers' classroom-based portfolio questions focused on the individual child within the group. Individual students became the focus of teachers' increased awareness. I need to be aware of the culture of my clientele, and this is no easy task. I need to know my students individually. Many times, we as teachers speak a foreign language to our students and are not aware of it. I think the challenge lies in making the connection from each student's culture to their learning.

Of the second-year survey respondents, 63% reported that participating in the B.E.S.T. program had influenced how they teach culturally diverse students. They found that writing portfolio reflections increased their sensitivity to individual student needs. A second-year teacher participant commented, "I reached an awareness level that I probably might not have and an understanding of diverse students."

Discussion

It is believed that the findings of this study underscore the importance of including reflective portfolio processes in teacher induction pro-

grams. Portfolios have become regular features of many teacher education programs (Wolf, 1996) and are used at every phase of teacher
development (Bartell et al., 1998). Numerous educators across the United
States who use portfolios acknowledge their potential for promoting
learning and reflection (Anderson & DeMeulle, 1998).

This study contributes to the understanding of standards-based
reflection in teacher education and specifically in teacher induction programs. Results suggest that reflection offers a promising means to
promote novice teachers' professional development. Findings also suggest that reflection may foster novice teachers' professional growth
through subsequent years of teaching. Most research on teaching portfolios occurs at the preservice level (Schram, 1995; Wade & Yarbrough,
1996). More longitudinal studies are needed that examine reflective teaching practices from preservice through induction and teachers' ongoing
professional development. Further research is needed to compare the
results of teaching reflective teaching strategies through teaching portfolios versus other strategies. More longitudinal research needs to be conducted on the long-term effects of the use of reflection in portfolio-based,
teacher induction programs on teachers' ongoing reflective teaching
practices.

What implications can be drawn from this study? First, reflection can
be taught successfully to first-year teachers. Standards-based, reflective
teaching strategies do not add to novice teachers' overloaded professional
duties; they help new teachers sort out teaching tasks. "Reflecting on my
teaching helped me prioritize what I wanted to do in the classroom."
Reflection helps novice teachers take on the professional role of teacher
and adopt a perception of themselves as competent teachers (Clark, 1992).
For this study's novice teachers, learning how to reflect created a continuum of positive influences on the teachers' skills. For teachers who began
their first-year by putting pressure on themselves and being unduly harsh
in their self-assessments, reflection offered reassurance and increased
self-acceptance. For new teachers who did not know or did not use best
practices, standards-based reflection caused them to make improvements
in their teaching.

Second, using reflective teaching practices may help foster novice
teachers' increased awareness of, and sensitivity to, students' cultural
diversity. Reflection calls on teachers to think about whom they are teaching and how they are teaching. As the diversity of the K-12 student popu-

lation grows more complex in the 21st century, it may be useful to conduct further research on the influence of specific reflective teaching practices on teachers' responsiveness to student difference.

Third, a significant number of first-year teachers in this study were switched into different combination grade-level classrooms for their second year of teaching. This move, in essence, asks them to begin their careers again and has significant implications for the type of appropriate, continuing support that novice teachers need beyond their first year of teaching.

Fourth, the external evaluation demonstrated that Saturday seminars were well liked by most participants. Originally viewed as the most risky aspect of B.E.S.T., Saturday mornings turned out to be the preferred format. Each Saturday became the beginning teachers' quiet time to think slowly and deeply about their teaching practices and professional growth. A Saturday seminar format should be considered for other teacher induction programs.

B.E.S.T. is not a prescriptive model for all teacher induction programs. Findings of the study clearly indicate the power of standards-based reflection to foster novice teachers' professional development. It is hoped that this chapter will encourage designers of teacher induction programs to incorporate reflective teaching practices into their programs and to work toward establishing teaching standards as the groundwork for reflective processes.

Research suggests that teachers' professional development occurs as a result of teachers' daily involvement in defining and shaping the problems of practice (Lieberman, 1995). That is the essence of standards-based, reflective teaching practices. The teaching portfolio process inspires and supports teacher reflection—alone and with others, in writing and in conversation, and in planning and documenting one's teaching. There can be no more powerful tool for the lifelong development of educators than teaching novice teachers to incorporate reflection that is grounded in teaching standards into their daily, ongoing teaching practices.

References

Anderson, R. S., & DeMeulle, L. (1998, Winter). Portfolio use in 24 teacher education programs. *Teacher Education Quarterly,* 23-31.

Bartell, C. A., Kay, C., & Morin, J. A. (1998, Winter). Portfolio conversation: A mentored journey. *Teacher Education Quarterly,* 129-139.

Barth, R. (1990). *Improving schools from within.* San Francisco: Jossey-Bass.

California Commission on Teacher Credentialing & the California Department of Education. (1992). *Success for beginning teachers: Final report of the California New Teacher Project.* Sacramento: Authors.

California State Department of Education & the California Commission on Teacher Credentialing. (1997). *California standards for the teaching profession.* Sacramento: Authors.

Clark, C. M. (1992). Teachers as designers in self-directed professional development. In A. Hargreaves & M. G. Fullan (Eds.), *Understanding teacher development* (pp. 75-84). New York: Teachers College Press.

Denzin, N. K., & Lincoln, V. S. (1998). *Collecting and interpreting qualitative materials.* Thousand Oaks, CA: Sage.

Dietz, M. (1995). Using portfolios as a framework for professional development. *Journal of Staff Development, 16,* 40-43.

Grant, G. E., & Huebner, T. A. (1998, Winter). The portfolio question: A powerful synthesis of the personal and professional. *Teacher Education Quarterly,* 33-43.

Lieberman, A. (1995). Practices that support teacher development: Transforming conceptions of professional learning. *Phi Delta Kappan, 76,* 591-596.

Lyons, N. (Ed.). (1998). *With portfolio in hand: Portfolios in teaching and teacher education.* New York: Teachers College Press.

Patton, M. Q. (1990). *Qualitative evaluation and research methods.* Newbury Park, CA: Sage.

Schön, D. A. (1987). *Educating the reflective practitioner.* San Francisco: Jossey-Bass.

Schön, D. A. (1991). *The reflective turn: Case studies in and on educational practice.* New York: Teachers College Press.

Schram, T. (1995). Using portfolios to mediate learning and inquiry among interns and teachers. *Teaching Education, 7*(2), 71-80.

Stone, B. A. (1998, Winter). Problems, pitfalls, and benefits of portfolios. *Teacher Education Quarterly,* 105-114.

Strauss, A. L. (1987). *Qualitative analysis for social scientists.* New York: Cambridge University Press.

Tierney, D. (1992). *Teaching portfolios: 1992 update on research and practice.* San Francisco: Far West Laboratory for Educational Research and Development.

van Manen, M. (1990). *Researching lived experience.* Albany: State University of New York Press.

Wade, R., & Yarbrough, D. (1996). Portfolios: A tool for reflective thinking in teacher education? *Teacher and Teacher Education, 12,* 63-79.

WestEd. (1997). *A guide to preparing beginning teachers and support providers to work with the California teaching portfolio.* San Francisco: Author.

Wolf, K. (1991). The schoolteacher's portfolio: Issues in design, implementation, and evaluation. *Phi Delta Kappan, 73,* 129-136.

Wolf, K. (1996). Developing an effective teaching portfolio. *Educational Leadership, 53,* 34-37.

Wolf, K., & Dietz, M. (1998, Winter). Teaching portfolios: Purposes and possibilities. *Teacher Education Quarterly,* 9-21.

DIVISION II

Summary

REFLECTION ON INQUIRY AND REFLECTION IN TEACHER EDUCATION: IMPLICATIONS AND REFLECTIONS

W. Robert Houston

Allen R. Warner

The three chapters in Division II represent three approaches to reflection and inquiry. Each is designed to help teachers make explicit for themselves the intentions and underlying assumptions, knowledge, values, and sensitivities that guide their practice.

Implications of the Three Studies

In Chapter 4, Nevárez-La Torre and Rolón-Dow approached reflection and inquiry through teacher research. Their sample was composed of five bilingual teachers who met with two university faculty for a year. Their goal was to expand the vision of bilingual teachers to include research in linguistically diverse settings. Even with a small *n*, the teachers ranged widely in their initial understanding and ultimate use of teacher research. Noting this wide variance among teachers is an important finding for those striving to develop teachers as inquirers.

With a small number of participants and extensive time together, the teachers made progress during their year of study. Observing others and observing their own videotaped lessons became an important change agent. Changing teaching practices, particularly fundamental shifts such as using inquiry, takes considerable time—both concentrated time and length of the change process. Following intensive change processes, teachers, like all *Homo sapiens*, tend to return to practices not too dissimilar from those that preceded the change process. Apparently, this did not occur with these five teachers. Their reflections varied and their teaching styles changed, but each made progress. Why? Because they were treated as individuals in the same way they were expected to treat their students as individuals. Throughout their year of in-service study, the teachers and university faculty had opportunities to practice perception, opportunities for reflection, and opportunities to engage in inquiry, providing all three of Rogers' opportunities for all participants, university and school faculty.

In Chapter 5, Rowley and Hart compared and contrasted two approaches to case studies for prospective teachers: print and video. The authors drew on five factors to assess the two approaches that could be organizers for other research on instruction: *relevance, engagement, realism, stimulation,* and *significance.* Although reflection was enhanced by both approaches, students preferred the video format. The two approaches complemented each other, however; video induced greater cognitive involvement and provided cues to the behaviors of participants, whereas print permitted prospective teachers to reread and compare sections of the case study.

The authors drew on Rogers' three opportunities but in different ways than in Chapter 6. The study's structure (one group completed the print case study and then the video case study while the other group completed the video case study first and then the print case study) permitted the authors to reflect on the attributes of each presentation type. Participants in the study were able to engage in the first two of Rogers' opportunities—perception and reflection—but not the third—engaging in genuine inquiry. As the authors analyzed the data from the study, they alone inquired into the meaning of findings.

In Chapter 6, Wood drew on all three of Rogers' teacher education opportunities that promote reflection: (a) opportunity to practice the art of perception, (b) opportunity for reflection, and (c) opportunity to engage in genuine inquiry. The participants, first- and second-year teachers, were in a formidable period in their careers, a time when their need for reflection and understanding of events in their classrooms was as great as at any other time in their careers. The vehicle for developing this understanding was teaching portfolios. For these teachers, portfolios were not simply collections of artifacts, but rather were opportunities to explore their own teaching.

The study was based in California, and the seminars in which portfolios were developed and analyzed were based on California's standards for teachers, thus providing a direct link to licensure requirements. Teachers were expected to reflect in writing on each piece of evidence in the portfolio. The perceptions and practices of teachers tended to be strengthened in the areas emphasized in the professional development experiences. Novice teachers collected evidence about their teaching, reflected on it, and made changes in their teaching as a result.

Inquiry and Reflection: Lauded by All, Effectively Used by Few

Other inquiry approaches include action research, curriculum analysis, focused observations, journal writing, interpersonal recall (IPR), simulations and gaming, readings, peer coaching, dialogues, experiments, mentoring, or combinations of these. The purpose of such data-based inquiry is not to collect information, but to draw on such information for in-depth reflection on professional practice.

Providing structures and venues for prospective and in-service teachers to reflect on their professional judgments and actions *permeates teacher education as a concept but not as a general practice.* Progress in science, industry, and business in the 20th century was based on the examination of thought and action. It is a mark of Western civilization. Education espouses this stance, but it remains an elusive target; teachers tend to continue to draw on expository forms of instruction, and their preparation and professional development continue to have inquiry and reflection as major voids. The rhetoric of inquiry and reflection reflects a deep commitment to these twin concepts, but actual practice by teachers and teacher educators continues outmoded methods.

Dewey's and later Schön's theories on inquiry and reflection have been translated into models for teacher education (e.g., Clift, Houston, & Pugach, 1990; Cruickshank, 1987; Goodlad, 1990, 1994; Grimmett & Erickson, 1988; Zeichner & Liston, 1987). Schön's contributions to educational thought and action have been largely ignored in practice. The emphasis on standards and "knowledge and skills" has diminished the emphasis on reflection and actions based on reflection.

Reformation of teacher education requires more than an emphasis on cognition, teaching skills, and standards. Practices such as the three described herein that focus primarily on identifying and strengthening knowledge and skills belie the more fundamental attitudes and values that undergird such knowledge and skills. Britzman's (1998) seminal work challenges the more traditional view of reflection, reminding teacher educators that change is not completely rational, that it involves psychic and personal dimensions that shape ultimate conclusions and actions resulting from reflection. Carl Rogers reminded us for decades that the only truly meaningful learning is self-appropriated learning—the learning in which we choose to engage and that we choose to incorporate into our behavior.

Research in teacher education can be no better than the theories and conceptualizations that undergird it, the precision and validity of the tools used to describe actions and outcomes, the tentativeness of conclusions drawn from research, and the quality of teacher education programs in which such research is conducted. As Mortimer Adler (1965) pointed out, focusing questions to be investigated is at least as important as empirically seeking answers. Empirical findings depend on nothing so much as they do on the quality of the questions asked in scientific inquiry. It is a challenge worthy of educators in the 21st century. Drawing on inquiry and reflection and combining them with a professional commitment to increase the effectiveness of professional education are challenges that must be faced to ensure teachers for future generations who are willing and equipped to continue to grow and to learn.

References

Adler, M. (1965). *A liberal education* [Audiotape of Zulauf Lecture]. DeKalb: Northern Illinois University.

Britzman, D. P. (1998). *Lost subjects, contested objects: Toward a psychoanalytic inquiry of learning.* Albany: State University of New York Press.

Clift, R. T., Houston, W. R., & Pugach, M. C. (Eds.). (1990). *Encouraging reflective practice in education.* New York: Teachers College Press.

Cruickshank, D. R. (1987). *Reflective teaching: The preparation of students of teaching.* Reston, VA: Association of Teacher Educators.

Goodlad, J. I. (1990). *Teachers for our nation's schools.* San Francisco: Jossey-Bass.

Goodlad, J. I. (1994). *Educational renewal: Better teachers, better schools.* San Francisco: Jossey-Bass.

Grimmett, P., & Erickson, G. (Eds.). (1988). *Reflection in teacher education.* New York: Teachers College Press.

Zeichner, K. M., & Liston, D. P. (1987). Teaching student teachers to reflect. *Harvard Educational Review, 57*(1), 23-48.

DIVISION III

Mentoring, Social Interaction, and Transformations

OVERVIEW AND FRAMEWORK

Porter Lee Troutman, Jr.

Porter Lee Troutman, Jr., is Professor in the Instructional and Curriculum Department in the College of Education at the University of Nevada, Las Vegas. He teaches courses in multicultural education and elementary education. One of the original founders of the National Association of Multicultural Education (NAME), he has served as Director of Teacher Corps and Director of Student Teaching and has chaired the College of Education's Diversity Committee. He has also received a Fulbright-Hayes Fellowship to study diversity and culture in Singapore.

Mentoring has become a significant part of teacher education programs at all levels, taking the form of peer mentoring in formal cohort groups or informal support groups or as one-on-one mentoring roles often encountered in student teaching situations. The reasons for a significant growth in mentoring programs include the retention of new teachers, the rewards available to experienced teachers by placing them in the energizing role of mentor, and the possibilities for the improvement in the quality of professional development and teacher education in general (Sprinthall, Reiman, & Thies-Sprinthall, 1996). The reasons for mentoring programs abound, the educational settings are complex, and the challenges of mentoring are many, but more active and prolonged engagement in diverse field experiences with some kind of support for new teachers seems essential for the challenges of the 21st century.

The notion of *mentoring* has a long history originating with the character Mentor from Homer's *Odyssey*. Mentor was an old man who watched over and taught Telemachus, the son of Odysseus, while Odysseus was away fighting the Trojan War (Gold, 1996). In *Webster's Encyclopedic Unabridged Dictionary of the English Language* (1996), *mentor* is defined right above the listing of Mentor from the *Odyssey*. The primary and secondary definitions listed for *mentor* are (a) "a wise and trusted counselor or teacher" and (b) "an influential senior sponsor or supporter" (p. 1201). Gold (1996) acknowledges the difficulty of supplying an appropriate definition for mentoring, but in the spirit of recognizing the humanistic side of the concept of mentoring and in keeping a cautious eye on the past as we hurtle into the next millennium, the historical and social origins of the term may be more appropriate for the discussions in the three chapters to follow.

In a recent column from *Duke Magazine* (Bliwise, 1999) that discussed the relationships university scholars establish outside their immediate academic community, the topic of mentoring came up. The importance of student-initiated collaboration was mentioned, along with the importance of demonstrating a commitment to mentoring relationships. Moreover, this commitment to mentoring relationships is demonstrated by a willingness to be open and vulnerable. Many themes involving the emotional complexities of mentoring discussed informally in this *Duke Magazine* column are examined with more rigor and depth in the three chapters that follow.

In a recent critical review on mentoring, Feiman-Nemser (1999) called for more research into the mentoring process, particularly because this strategy is being embraced so extensively. Among the issues needing more research, Feiman-Nemser discussed the personal nature of developing mentor relationships, how this might be difficult to formalize in a program, and the need for self-reflection on the part of mentors as they engage in the process of mentoring. Another significant item discussed in this critical review and mentioned in the chapters presented here is the assessment versus assistance issue. When mentors are placed in the position of grading their protégés, this can interfere with the potential nurturing qualities of the mentoring relationship. Besides these areas for more research, Feiman-Nemser sums up her review by pointing out that mentoring can help in creating tools for improvement and can contribute to reform. The studies in these three chapters address reform issues and programs aimed at creating tools for improvement of curriculum and practice.

The studies that follow are also linked by their emphasizing, to one degree or another, the social and historical nature of the interactions in educational settings. Koeppen, Huey, and Conner, in Chapter 7, report on mentoring as a socialization process and compare the perceived benefits of students participating in different configurations of cohort groups with those who are part of a special project examining the effects of more field experiences. Gomez, Page, and Walker, in Chapter 8, provide a rich study linking elements of Bakhtin's (1986) descriptions of the background of a preservice teacher providing tension in relation to the multicultural social reconstructionist view of the curriculum. Finally, in Chapter 9, Williams and Bowman introduce an assessment instrument that scaffolds mentors who are paired with first-year teachers.

The common strand found in these chapters indicates that teachers must examine and understand their own assumptions, values, and beliefs before fully understanding students' profiles. Understanding mentoring, cohort relationships, and prospective teachers' personal experiences is an invaluable component within teacher education programs. I concur with Gomez et al. in their citing of Bakhtin (1986): All thought is developed. We must continue our effort in understanding the authoritative and internally persuasive discourses with which students struggle.

References

Bakhtin, M. M. (1986). *Speech genres and other late essays.* Austin: University of Texas Press.

Bliwise, R. (1999, March-April). Rules of engagement. *Duke Magazine,* *85*(3), 20.

Feiman-Nemser, S. (1999). *Teaching mentoring: A critical review* [On-line]. Available: http://www.ericsp.org/95-2.html

Gold, Y. (1996). Beginning teacher support: Attrition, mentoring, and introduction. In S. Sikula, T. Buttery, & E. Guyton (Eds.), *Handbook of research in teacher education* (2nd ed., pp. 548-594). New York: Simon & Schuster.

Sprinthall, N., Reiman, A., & Thies-Sprinthall, L. (1996). Teacher profes-sional development. In S. Sikula, T. Buttery, & E. Guyton (Eds.), *Hand-book of research in teacher education* (2nd ed., pp. 666-703). New York: Simon & Schuster.

Webster's encyclopedic unabridged dictionary of the English language (rev. ed.). (1996). New York: Grammercy Books.

7 Cohort Groups

An Effective Model in a Restructured Teacher Education Program

Kim E. Koeppen

Gayle L. Huey

Kathy R. Connor

Kim E. Koeppen is Assistant Professor, Department of Curriculum and Instruction, Iowa State University, Ames. Her research addresses issues of teacher socialization and social studies education.

Gayle L. Huey is Practicum Placement and Project Opportunity Site Coordinator, Department of Curriculum and Instruction, Iowa State University, Ames. Her research focuses on cohort groups and teacher preparation.

Kathy R. Connor is Project Opportunity Director and Coordinator of Elementary Supervisors, Department of Curriculum and Instruction, Iowa State University, Ames. Her research focuses on teacher preparation and cooperating teacher effectiveness.

ABSTRACT

Teacher preparation is a key component in quality education. This chapter examines students' perceptions regarding
their participation in Project Opportunity (PrO), a teacher education program based on a cohort model. Findings indicate that
students perceived membership in cohorts as significant to
their teacher education experiences. Evidence is also strong
that PrO successfully promotes formal and effective cohort
groups. As a result, PrO provides an effective model for universities that want to include cohorts when restructuring teacher
education programs.

Education is a highly analyzed phenomenon drawing numerous recommendations for restructuring the institutions of PK-12 schools and teacher
education programs. These institutions are closely intertwined; however,
this chapter focuses specifically on teacher education because consider-
ations of change in education will be only rhetorical if incoming teachers
lack well-developed visions about successful school practices. Colleges of
education must provide preservice teachers with opportunities to gain
theoretical and practical understandings of schools as organizations, to
debate options for change, and to develop, test, and revise their subsequent ideas (Holmes Group, 1986; U.S. Office of Elementary and Secondary Education, 1991).

The Holmes Group is in the forefront in making recommendations for
school change, especially regarding teacher education. An examination of
the Holmes Group's and others' recommendations produces common
issues: (a) collaborative K-12 school-university settings; (b) revised university course work; (c) earlier and increased field experiences; and
(d) opportunities for students to participate more actively in their teacher
socialization process.

In an effort to improve teacher education, Iowa State University (ISU)
developed Project Opportunity (PrO) to promote (a) integration of content, pedagogy, and practice; (b) development of new learning roles;
(c) infusion of technology; (d) appreciation and understanding of diversity; and (e) practice of democracy in education (Owen, 1993). Each fall, a
new group of 30 elementary and secondary education undergraduate

students is identified. PrO differs from ISU's existing program in five substantial ways. First, students complete three new professional courses (Popular Culture Analysis, Educational Inquiry, and Capstone) designed to foster development as reflective practitioners. Second, they complete their professional courses as a cohort. Third, they take four content methods courses presented in an integrated fashion. Fourth, they complete more than 200 hours of field experiences prior to student teaching (students in the existing program complete 50 hours of field experiences). Fifth, all field experiences are completed in one partner school district.

This chapter describes the perceptions of ISU teacher education students regarding their participation in PrO. The chapter begins with a theoretical framework that examines teacher socialization and cohort groups. Next a study designed to compare the perceptions of students participating in PrO with those of students participating in ISU's existing teacher education program is presented. Finally, findings and their implications for effecting change in teacher education are discussed.

Theoretical Framework

At ISU, communication and human interaction were central concerns when PrO was designed. Cohort groups provide one means for restructuring that appears to influence communication and human interactions among students in teacher education and, in turn, teacher socialization. Consequently, our theoretical framework highlights research concerning the process of teacher socialization and research pertaining to cohort groups.

Teacher Socialization

Teacher socialization is the complex process people go through to become members of the teaching profession (Friebus, 1977). Staton and Hunt (1992) suggest that teacher socialization takes place in two contexts: the university and the field experience site. They also believe that socialization continues through the teachers' careers. Several groups have the potential to act as socializing agents during a teacher's career. Included among these are their peers (Ross, 1988; Su, 1992).

Su's (1992) study revealed contradictory perceptions regarding peers' influence as socializing agents. Faculty working with cohorts in Su's study perceived peer groups as strongly influencing members' educational values and beliefs. The preservice teachers placed much less importance on peer influence. Su's examination of this dichotomy produced no evidence of a strong peer culture, no sense of community, and no feeling among preservice teachers of going through a shared ordeal. In addition, preservice teachers had few collegial interactions, formal or informal. PrO was designed specifically to promote group bonds; therefore, these students' perceptions of their peers' influence may differ from those in Su's study.

Field experience sites also play a role in the teacher socialization process (McDiarmid, 1990; Ross, 1988). Here, preservice teachers incorporate the variety of information gleaned from their university courses with practice. Unfortunately, in traditionally structured teacher education programs, university course work has little influence on preservice teachers' beliefs and perceptions (Lortie, 1975; Ross, 1988). Earlier and extended field experiences can create an environment whereby preservice teachers can apply their theoretical, content, and pedagogical knowledge in classrooms on a regular basis. As Goodman (1986) points out, however, "just placing students in practicum sites will [not] automatically provide valuable experiences" (p. 351).

Teacher educators must design courses that make better connections between university course work and classrooms (Head, 1992) and that strengthen the connections between the various field experiences (Hall, Johnson, & Bownam, 1995). Staton and Hunt (1992) recognize that the ultimate value of early field experience may lie in the contextual awareness it develops in prospective teachers that facilitates subsequent study of teaching techniques and learning processes. The fact that PrO students complete 200+ hours of field experiences in one school district increases their chances of developing such contextual awareness.

Cohort Groups

Cohorts in teacher education consist of small numbers of students selected to participate in the program. Once organized, group members interact and become interdependent (Miles, 1959; Milstein & Associates, 1991; Shaw, 1976) as they work to (a) maintain themselves as a formal versus accidental group, (b) accomplish group goals, and (c) develop and change to improve group effectiveness—that is, meet group goals.

Colleges of education that are considering cohorts should clarify their existing program design and goals (Basom, Yerkes, Norris, & Barnett, 1994; Blankenship, Humphreys, Dobson, Gamble, & Kind, 1989). From there, they can choose from at least three cohort models: closed, open, and fluid (Basom et al., 1994). In a *closed* cohort model, selected students take all their course work together in a prearranged sequence. In the *open* cohort model, selected students enroll in a core set of classes but take additional course work on an individual basis to fulfill their personal needs and university requirements. PrO closely resembles the open cohort model, which is most frequently adopted by programs moving toward cohorts. The *fluid* cohort model is the most flexible of the three, allowing students to join at different stages rather than at a single entry point. From these specific definitions of cohort models, we move to an examination of research on groups and group processing.

Definite themes related to cohort groups emerged from our extensive review of groups and group processing. We organized these themes into what we label "dimensions of cohort groups." The presumption is not that these eight dimensions exist separate from one another; in fact, they are closely entwined. We teased them apart to examine each more closely.

Dimension 1: Social Interaction

A key characteristic of effective groups is active participation by its members. This participation, however, does not automatically accompany the group's formation. In the early stages of cohort development, teacher education faculty can initiate activities to stimulate social interaction. This interaction should foster an appreciation of diversity in backgrounds and in expectations among individual cohort members that ultimately leads to a sense of community (Basom et al., 1994; Kasten, 1992; Schlechty, 1985).

Social interaction can be influenced by cohort size and frequency of contact. Shaw (1976) reported that groups of up to 30 may function as a small group if the members relate closely to one another and are highly motivated to achieve a common goal. Further, the literature on adult learning indicates that "adults learn best when they can build strong relationships and affiliations with their peers" (Basom et al., 1994, p. 6).

Dimension 2: Interdependence

Feelings of isolation are prevalent among preservice and beginning teachers as they enter classrooms. Lortie (1975) argues that a shared rather than a private ordeal helps forge common bonds, solidarity, and a "collegial feeling found in established professions" (p. 74). Groups built on social interaction and interdependency can diminish the effects of isolation. Preservice teachers accustomed to collegial relationships may find "new teacher isolation" less threatening and more quickly become active members of school communities.

Dimension 3: Common Purpose

Preservice teachers can and should participate in setting group goals, determining activities, and evaluating group and individual progress. Once a cohort is formed and its members are given an opportunity for social interaction, faculty members can clarify program expectations and facilitate development of a common purpose. This shared decision making helps members develop a sense of commitment to the common purpose (Stover, 1990; Yerkes, Norris, Basom, & Barnett, 1994).

Dimension 4: Group and Individual Learning

Cultivating both group and individual learning is directly connected to achieving the group's common purpose (Dimension 3) and to promoting members' interdependence (Dimension 2). As the group evolves, the members must be attentive not only to the larger group goals but also to individuals' goals.

The achievement of group goals can be facilitated through collaborative projects, commuting to practicum sites, and reflective seminars (Huey, 1996). Basom et al. (1994) state that individual growth is nurtured through activities that encourage self-evaluation, self-initiation, self-confidence, and risk taking and experimentation, all of which can be built into group activities. Over time, group members come to rely on each other for feedback.

Dimension 5: Cohesiveness

One strength of cohort groups is their cohesiveness (e.g., Hebert & Reynolds, n.d.; Kasten, 1992). *Cohesiveness* is defined as members believing that they are in a special group with common goals and purposes and is fostered by encouraging a sense of belonging and providing support and encouragement (Basom et al., 1994; Blankenship et al., 1989). Anderson (1985) reports that all groups naturally evolve toward cohesiveness but that groups with early structured interactive experiences arrive sooner. Uniformity is one outcome of group cohesiveness. Often, members perceive that group purposes will be served by this uniformity (Festinger, 1950). Such uniformity, however, may impede individual academic performance.

Dimension 6: Interaction With Faculty

Effective facilitators help groups evolve (Anderson, 1985; Norris & Barnett, 1994). Faculty explain the nature of a cohort, facilitate development of group goals, initiate socialization processes, and facilitate group members' growing interdependence (Anderson, 1985; Basom et al., 1994). This group evolution is enhanced by faculty assistance in the development of group processing skills by providing a cognitive framework for change, a regular schedule for reflection and feedback, and a model of leadership that creates change. In the process, faculty often reexamine their classroom roles, course content, and coordination with field experiences to make their university courses more meaningful within the cohort model.

Informal interactions with faculty are as important to preservice teachers' development of educational beliefs and values as formal ones (Su, 1992). This increased time with faculty improves the perception of accessibility that may encourage students to seek out assistance on a more regular basis. The increased interactions provide faculty with greater insights into students' individual needs, which lead to more individualized academic and professional guidance (Barnett & Muse, 1983, p. 407).

Although increased interaction between cohort members and faculty has benefits, challenges also arise. Increased familiarity can make it difficult for faculty to evaluate cohort members. Faculty also report time constraints and instances of feeling like an "outsider" within the cohort model (Barnett & Muse, 1983; Hebert & Reynolds, n.d.).

Dimension 7: Academic Performance

Given the previous six dimensions, we concluded that students' academic achievement may be enhanced by cohort membership. When students feel intellectually and socially connected, they learn better. The cohesiveness that emerges through collaboration may encourage higher level performance. It will be important to test this hypothesis and to examine whether cohesiveness relates to learning styles and teaching methods.

Dimension 8: Student Retention

Social networking processes are strongly associated with higher rates of retention (Tinto, Russo, & Kadel, 1994). Informal student-faculty contact also plays a crucial role in promoting retention (Tinto et al., 1994). College students report higher degrees of satisfaction with courses that allow them to engage in group discussion, and students are more likely to stay in college if they are satisfied with their learning experiences (Cooper, 1990). Cohort groups provide a structure that promotes positive learning experiences and reflection. Participation in cohort groups at the outset of their teacher education program may assist students in clarifying their professional choice. This, in turn, may lead to greater commitment from those who choose to remain and subsequently greater retention rates among beginning teachers.

These eight dimensions of cohort groups culled from the research literature work together to influence students' experiences in teacher education programs. As such, they have the potential to influence teacher socialization processes, which begin formally with teacher education. PrO centered around cohort groups, in part, to offer preservice teachers a peer support group with which to enter a profession noted for perpetuating the status quo through socialization processes. The purpose of our study was to compare perceptions of students in PrO with those of students in ISU's existing teacher education program.

Method

Research Question

The study was guided by this question: To what extent do students participating in PrO perceive benefits to being in a cohort group? Students' perceptions were examined through their responses to a survey designed by Huey (1996).

Participants

Cohort participants included 20 elementary and secondary preservice teachers in PrO's Cohort I and 24 elementary and secondary preservice teachers in Cohort II. Cohort I students (P-1) were juniors, at the end of their second year in PrO. All Cohort I students had completed 44 hours of field experiences in their rural midwestern partner school district when they completed the survey. Cohort II students (P-2) were sophomores at the end of their first year in PrO. Cohort II students had completed 75 hours (secondary) or 285 hours (elementary) of field experiences in their urban midwestern partner school district when they responded to the survey.

Comparison group participants were students taking classes in ISU's existing teacher preparation program. Comparison groups were chosen for their similarity in age and the cohortlike atmosphere that existed within the classrooms. The comparison groups' instructors used discussions, group projects, papers, and presentations, as well as field experience reflections to promote group cohesiveness. Because students were together only for this one course, however, the long-term development of a common purpose and social activities to develop a sense of community were not present.

Comparison Group I (C-1) consisted of preservice teachers in secondary education methods ($N = 39$); Comparison Group II (C-2), of teachers in elementary education methods ($N = 59$). Not all students in the comparison groups were placed in field experiences concurrently with the methods course. Those comparison group students who were in a concurrent field experience had fewer total hours in school sites and were placed in a multitude of school districts. Students in Comparison Groups I and II were primarily juniors at a similar point in their educational programs as those students in Cohort I.

In Cohort I, 16 of 20 (80%) students responded to the survey. In Cohort II, all 24 (100%) students responded. In the comparison groups, 34 of 39 (87%) students in Comparison Group I and 41 of 59 (69%) in Comparison Group II responded. The voluntary nature of participation and class absences account for the less than 100% response rate.

Survey and Implementation

The instrument used was a 67-item survey designed by Huey to ascertain students' attitudes toward cohort group membership. Previous

TABLE 7.1 Factors and Corresponding Sample Survey Items

Factor	n	Sample Survey Questions
Factor 1: Importance of being in a group	26	When our cohort group is together, we frequently talk about class projects and assignments.
Factor 2: Collaboration: student, teacher, faculty	6	When I need advice about a project, I consult a faculty person.
Factor 3: Significance of field experiences	4	Sharing field experiences creates opportunities for worthwhile discussion.
Factor 4: Influence on academic performance	3	I have a sense of pride when praised or singled-out for an assignment well done.
Factor 5: Effect on student retention	4	I would not have stayed in the teacher education program without the support of my cohort members.
Factor 6: Unique experience in PrO	4	Having been a member of PrO, I would apply to the program if I had the decision to make again.
Factor 7: Cohesiveness	3	Some students in my cohort group feel left out.

NOTE: Fifteen items from the survey were not used in analyses because they did not load into meaningful factors.

research (Huey, 1996) identified seven factors within the survey: (a) importance of being a group, (b) collaboration among students, teachers, and faculty, (c) significance of field experience, (d) academic performance, (e) student retention, (f) unique experience in PrO, and (g) cohesiveness. A Cronbach alpha coefficient was computed to determine survey reliability. The result was an alpha of .9213 (a number greater than .5 denotes high reliability). Content validity was established by having external reviewers examine survey questions as they related to research on cohort groups. The factors closely aligned with the dimensions of cohort groups discussed earlier. Analyses were made easier because of this match with the literature. The factors, number of survey items contributing to each, and sample survey items are presented in Table 7.1.

TABLE 7.2 Descriptive Data on Survey Responses by Factors

Factor	Cohort Ia (P-1)		Cohort IIb (P-2)		Comparison Group Ic (C-1)		Comparison Group IId (C-2)	
	M	SD	M	SD	M	SD	M	SD
1	2.1	.66	2.34	.58	2.84	.69	2.87	.80
2	2.7	1.02	2.78	.80	2.84	.80	2.55	.74
3	1.58	.50	1.81	.77	2.94	.70	2.42	.87
4	2.98	.78	2.51	.75	2.27	.77	2.57	1.00
5	5.09	.75	4.84	.93	4.44	.93	4.09	.98

NOTE: The lower the mean, the more positive the perceptions.
an = 16; bn = 24; cn = 34; dn = 41.

Faculty teaching the cohort and comparison groups administered the survey during the last week of classes. The surveys were numbered to ensure confidentiality of responses. The survey used a 6-point Likert scale that ranged from 1 (*strongly agree*) to 6 (*strongly disagree*). Because Huey (1996) found relatively low factor loadings for unique experience in PrO (Factor 6) and cohesiveness (Factor 7), these factors were not included in analyses for the current study.

Results

The Likert scale survey contained 67 items. Responses from items with negative wording were inverted before running statistical tests. The factor scores for each participant were calculated by computing the mean of the responses of the items that contributed to each factor. Smaller scores represented more positive attitudes about the importance of the factor. Descriptive data for these four groups are presented in Table 7.2.

The research question that guided this study was this: To what extent do students participating in PrO perceive benefits to being a member in a cohort? The data collected were analyzed by using analyses of variance (ANOVA) to compare responses from all four groups. The ANOVA was used to compare the four groups' means for the five factors that warranted

TABLE 7.3 Results of ANOVA

Factor	df	F	p	Group Comparison
1. Being in a group	3	6.9120	.0003*	P-1 = P-2 < C-1 = C-2
2. Collaboration	3	.7634	.5170	
3. Field experiences	3	16.3026	.0000*	P-2 < P-1 = C-1 = C-2
4. Academic	3	2.0120	.0631	
5. Retention	3	5.9425	.0009*	P-2 = C-1 = C-2 < P-1

NOTE: $*p < .05$.

analysis based on Huey's (1996) study. These were Factor 1, the importance of being in a group; Factor 2, the importance of collaboration among students, teachers, and university faculty; Factor 3, the significance of field experiences; Factor 4, the influence on academic performance; and Factor 5, the effect on student retention. Table 7.3 provides a summary of the ANOVA scores. Because a significant difference was found on Factors 1, 3, and 5, a Duncan test of least significant differences was conducted.

The results of Factor 1 indicated a significant difference between cohort groups and comparison groups on their perceptions of the importance of being a member of a group. The difference was that cohort group students perceived group membership as being of greater importance than did comparison group students. Cohort groups and comparison groups did not align themselves on Factor 3 as they did on Factor 1. For Factor 3, students in Cohort II viewed the field orientation and unique experiences in PrO as more significant than did students in Cohort I and both comparison groups. On Factor 5, a significant difference was found between one cohort group and the other three groups: Students in Cohort I viewed their membership in a group as less important to their retention in the teacher education program than did students in Cohort II and both comparison groups.

Discussion

Results showed significant differences regarding students' perceptions on Factors 1, 3, and 5. It appears that the cohort structure of PrO provided valuable unique experiences to preservice teachers within the school contexts.

Factor 1 (importance of being in a group) included items regarding students' perceptions relative to group interaction and the development of a group purpose. Data showed a significant difference between the cohort and comparison groups: Students in the cohort groups perceived being in a group as more important than did students in the comparison groups. These data support previous research regarding the advantages to cohort group membership (Hebert & Reynolds, n.d.; Kasten, 1992; Norris & Barnett, 1994). Students' perceptions of cohort group membership suggest that PrO was successful in creating formal cohort groups based on the open cohort model (Basom et al., 1994). Findings also suggest that PrO cohort groups met the requirements of effective groups as outlined by Shaw (1976).

Factor 3 focused on students' perceptions of field experiences. Data showed a significant difference between Cohort II and the other three groups; students in Cohort II perceived field experiences as more significant than did students in Cohort I and both comparison groups. Several circumstances might account for this difference: Students in Cohort II were sophomores and therefore new to teacher education and PrO. As such, students may have been imbued by the initial enthusiasm of choosing teaching as a career. They also might have equated being in classrooms with learning to teach and so were anxious to spend as much time in the field as possible.

Although it may confound the issue regarding cohortness, expanded field experiences are an essential component of PrO. These field experiences offer a greater opportunity for cohort members to strengthen their group bonds. On the one hand, commuting in university vehicles to participating sites gave preservice teachers additional unstructured time to interact socially, to collaborate, and to promote a sense of cohesiveness. On the other hand, the expense of, and time in, transit may be considered disadvantages.

Factor 5 asked whether students perceived that they were more likely to remain in the teacher education program because of their membership in a cohort group. Data on student retention showed a significant difference between Cohort I and the other three groups: Students in Cohort I perceived their membership in the group as less influential on their retention in teacher education than did students in Cohort II and both comparison groups. Students in Cohort I had just finished their four integrated methods courses with extensive field experiences, which demand a great deal of time and energy. Such intensity may account for Cohort I's perceptions that their group had less influence on their retention in the program. In addition, this semester might have revealed teaching as truly hard work, causing students to reconsider their career choice. Sustained contact with fellow cohort members may also cause students to grow weary of one another near the end of the semester.

Tinto's (1993) description of the principles of effective retention includes an institutional and educational commitment to students:

> Effective programs see active involvement of students in the life of the classroom to be a key element. Among other things, they have looked to the construction of supportive learning settings in which students, individually and in groups, can become actively involved in the learning process. (p. 148)

Given the findings of this study, when students' interactions reach a high level for a sustained period of time, the influence of the group might diminish. PrO faculty need to be alert to such situations and willing to make adjustments when necessary

Implications

The report of the National Commission on Teaching and America's Future (1996) sets forth an action agenda that includes "reinvent[ing] teacher preparation" (p. 64). Given the findings from this study, cohort groups may play an influential role in this process.

ISU's PrO was designed to include an open cohort model, earlier and more extensive field experiences. These characteristics were intended to promote new learning roles for all participants and the integration of content and pedagogy, thus improving teacher preparation. On the basis of the data collected for this study, PrO students perceived cohort group membership as an advantage over the existing teacher education model.

Further research about the influence of the cohort group model should include program costs and possible tensions within cohorts. Because the cohorts in this study did not align with respect to the issues of field experiences and student retention, further research in these areas is also warranted. Research should include both quantitative and qualitative studies to provide a well-rounded picture of the impact of cohort groups on teacher education programs. Whereas teacher educators continue to research the influence of cohort groups, PrO offers an effective model from which universities can begin to change teacher education programs.

References

Anderson, J. D. (1985). Working with groups: Little-known facts that challenge well-known myths. *Small Group Behavior, 16*(3), 267-283.

Barnett, B. G., & Muse, I. D. (1983). Cohort groups in educational administration: Promises and challenges. *Journal of School Leadership, 3,* 400-415.

Basom, M., Yerkes, D., Norris, C., & Barnett, B. (1994). *Exploring cohorts: Effects on principal preparation and leadership practice.* Unpublished manuscript.

Blankenship, C., Humphreys, S., Dobson, H. F., Gamble, P., & Kind, W. R., III. (1989, November). *A shared experiential program for principals and teachers at East Tennessee State University.* Paper presented at the annual conference of the National Council of States on In-Service Education, San Antonio, TX.

Cooper, J. L. (1990, May). Cooperative learning and college teaching: Tips from the trenches. *Teaching Professor,* pp. 1-2.

Festinger, L. (1950). Informal social communication. *Psychological Review, 57*(5), 271-282.

Friebus, R. (1977). Agents of socialization involved in student teaching. *Journal of Educational Research, 70*(5), 263-268.

Goodman, J. (1986). University education courses and the professional preparation of teachers: A descriptive analysis. *Teaching and Teacher Education, 2*(4), 341-353.

Hall, J. L., Johnson, B., & Bownam, A. C. (1995). Teacher socialization: A spiral process. *Teacher Educator, 30*(4), 25-36.

Head, F. A. (1992). Student teaching as initiation into the teaching profession. *Anthropology & Education Quarterly, 23*(2), 89-107.

Hebert, F. T., & Reynolds, K. C. (n.d.). *Cohort groups and intensive schedules: Does familiarity breed learning?* Unpublished manuscript.

Holmes Group. (1986). *Tomorrow's teachers.* East Lansing, MI: Author.

Huey, G. L. (1996). *The impact of cohort group membership on preservice teachers.* Unpublished master's thesis, Iowa State University, Ames.

Kasten, K. L. (1992). *Students' perceptions of the cohort model of instructional delivery.* Paper presented at the annual convention of the University Council of Educational Administration, Minneapolis, MN.

Lortie, D. C. (1975). *Schoolteacher: A sociological study.* Chicago: University of Chicago Press.

McDiarmid, G. W. (1990). Challenging prospective teachers' beliefs during early field experience: A quixotic undertaking? *Journal of Teacher Education, 41*(3), 12-20.

Miles, M. B. (1959). *Learning to work in groups: A program guide for educational leaders.* New York: Teachers College Press.

Milstein, M. M., & Associates. (1991). *Internship programs in educational administration: A guide to preparing educational leaders.* New York: Teachers College Press.

National Commission on Teaching and America's Future. (1996). *What matters most: Teaching for America's future.* New York: Author.

Norris, C. J., & Barnett, B. (1994). *Cultivating a new leadership paradigm: From cohorts to communities.* Paper presented at the annual meeting of the University Council of Educational Administration, Philadelphia, PA.

Owen, D. (1993). *An experimental teacher education program.* Unpublished report of the Curriculum & Instruction Committee, College of Education, Iowa State University, Ames.

Ross, E. W. (1988). Becoming a teacher: The development of preservice teacher perspectives. *Action in Teacher Education, 10*(2), 101-109.

Schlechty, P. C. (1985). A framework for evaluating induction into teaching. *Journal of Teacher Education, 36*(1), 37-41.

Shaw, M. E. (1976). *Group dynamics: The psychology of small-group behavior.* New York: McGraw-Hill.

Staton, A. Q., & Hunt, S. L. (1992). Teacher socialization: Review and conceptualization. *Communication Education, 41*(2), 109-137.

Stover, L. T. (1990). Modeling a student-centered approach in the secondary teacher education program. *Action in Teacher Education, 12*(1), 35-46.

Su, J. Z. X. (1992). Sources of influence in preservice teacher socialization. *Journal of Education for Teaching, 18*(3), 239-258.

Tinto, V. (1993). *Leaving college: Rethinking the causes and cures of student attrition.* Chicago: University of Chicago Press.

Tinto, V., Russo, P., & Kadel, S. (1994). Constructing educational commu-
    nities: Increasing retention in challenging circumstances. *Community
    College Journal, 64*(4), 26-29.
U.S. Office of Elementary and Secondary Education. (1991). America 2000:
    An education strategy. *Outlook, 1*(4), 1-6.
Yerkes, D., Norris, C., Basom, M., & Barnett, B. (1994). Exploring cohorts:
    Effects on principal preparation and leadership practice. *Connections!
    2*(3), 1, 5-8.

8 Returning to Learn

A Second-Career Prospective Teacher
Struggles With Personal Experience
as a Guide for Teaching

Mary Louise Gomez

Michelle L. Page

Anne Burda Walker

Mary Louise Gomez is Associate Professor in the Department of Curriculum and Instruction at the University of Wisconsin-Madison. Her research focuses on how to prepare prospective teachers to work effectively with diverse populations of students. Her publications include articles in *Teaching and Teacher Education*, *Language Arts*, and *Journal of Education for Teaching*. She is the coeditor of two books: *Currents of Reform in Preservice Teacher Education* (with Ken Zeichner & Susan Melnick) and *Making Schooling Multicultural: Campus and Classroom* (with Carl Grant).

Michelle L. Page is a doctoral student in literacy education at the University of Wisconsin-Madison. Her dissertation focuses on teachers'

AUTHORS' NOTE: A draft of this chapter was presented at the annual meeting of the American Educational Research Association in April 1998.

understandings and practices of teaching multicultural children's literature.

Anne Burda Walker is a doctoral student in literacy education at the University of Wisconsin-Madison. Her dissertation is a study of how alternative secondary education programs construct and enact what it means to be literate.

ABSTRACT

This chapter addresses the role that personal experience plays in informing understandings about teaching by a second-career prospective elementary teacher. It describes employing the telling of narratives to assist teacher candidates in critiquing their practices via a multicultural social reconstructionist perspective on schooling. The chapter explores how one prospective teacher negotiated her own beliefs about appropriate practices—gleaned from years of success as a student and as a financial analyst—with those ideas offered as guides for practice by her teacher education program. Drawing on the work of Russian theorist M. M. Bakhtin, the chapter concludes with a program critique and implications for teacher education programs using narratives as tools for critically reflective practice.

Introduction

Over the past two decades, teacher educators have become increasingly interested in recruiting second-career teachers into their profession. In part, this interest stems from a desire to draft into the teaching profession adults who are more representative of the diverse current school population than is the contemporary cohort of prospective teachers enrolled in teacher education programs around the United States. Indeed, a goal of providing a more diverse teacher population grounded the development of Teach for Diversity, a master's degree with teacher certification program at the University of Wisconsin-Madison (1994-1997).

Teach for Diversity, initiated in 1994, was a 15-month-long master's degree with teacher certification program grounded in multicultural and social reconstructionist principles. The program emphasized promotion of social and structural equality and cultural pluralism; construction of curriculum organized around social issues involving race, class, gender, disability, and sexual orientation; and development of classroom climates that support collaboration among peers and respect for one another's differences. Further, the program encouraged prospective teachers to draw on students' lives and interests as starting points for development of their skills of analyzing oppression and becoming critical thinkers and social activists. (See Sleeter & Grant, 1988, for elaboration on this approach to teaching and teacher education.)

The program, developed by the elementary education area faculty at the University of Wisconsin-Madison and our colleagues in four elementary schools, aimed to attract (a) people of color, (b) people whose prior work and life experiences provided them with the desire and drive to work successfully with diverse populations of elementary and middle school students, and (c) people who were self-reflexive and desired dialogic interactions with others aimed at understanding the intersections of schooling and the issues of race, class, language background, and sexual orientation. Each year, we enrolled 25 program participants who were then divided into three smaller cohort groups led by a university faculty member; each group was situated for all classroom practice at one school site. This chapter focuses on one school site, Marvin Street Elementary and Middle School, and the learning-to-teach experience of one member of the cohort group. We have chosen to discuss the learning-to-teach experience of Lorena Draper as she is representative in age (mid- to late 20s), race (Caucasian/European American), sexual orientation (heterosexual), prior work experiences (professional work—in her case, banking), and social class (from a low- to middle-income background, now a middle-class person) of the prospective teachers in the 1997-98 program group at-large and, in particular, representative of those whom we educated at the Marvin Street site.

In this chapter, we explore three questions regarding the learning-to-teach experience of Lorena Draper:

1. What life experiences and understandings about schools, schooling, and teaching did Lorena bring to teacher education?

2. How were these understandings manifested in her telling about her teaching and in her classroom practices?
3. How were these understandings examined and affected during participation in a program in which she was educated about multicultural and social reconstructionist theory and practices?

Methodology

Methods of narrative inquiry (see Bruner, 1990; Rosenwald & Ochberg, 1992) were used for data collection and data "production." That is, stories of prospective teachers' classroom practices and their critically reflective stands on these (see Zeichner, 1992, and Zeichner & Tabachnick, 1991, for discussion of critical reflection; and Gomez, 1996, for discussion of stories of teaching as vehicles for critical reflection) were solicited with a goal of telling these to peers who would both support the struggles in which these were produced and critique these in relation to multicultural and social reconstructionist theories.

In nearly every seminar (conducted each Wednesday afternoon for 2 hours) throughout the year, prospective teachers were asked to bring a story that related to a particular topic, to tell each other the story, and to respond to the questions and comments of peers and teacher educators. Topics were designed to coincide with various concerns highlighted in on-campus courses, as well as with issues of practice that emerged in the school site. The teacher educators made a concerted effort to make each seminar a place conducive to the development of a community of mutual support and critique. During the seminars, the teacher educators took field notes of the telling of the stories and the conversations that ensued. Written copies of the stories were collected from participants at the close of each seminar.

Formal, structured interviews were conducted and audiotaped with the prospective teachers following completion of the classroom teaching portion of the school year. Interviews included requests for participants' reflections on their reasons for enrolling in the program; their lived experiences of program course work, seminar experiences, and classroom teaching; and their stories of trying to craft teaching that was multicultural and social reconstructionist. Participants' reflections on telling and critiquing stories in the seminars were also solicited in the interviews.

Collaborative work among the teacher educators and prospective teachers occurred in multiple ways across occasions and time. For example, as stories were told in seminar, prospective teachers and teacher educators jointly considered these—their stated meanings and possible other viewpoints from which teachers' actions and students' responses could be viewed. Also, as teacher educators visited Marvin Street School classrooms to "supervise" prospective teachers' work, a collaborative ethos was purposefully developed. That is, rather than the "supervisor" coming from campus to make an evaluative classroom visit, the "supervisor" and teacher candidate continuously worked together to develop lessons that would respond to children's needs, strategize about meeting particular learning challenges of students, and rethink and improve on pedagogical approaches. Often, questions of how to devise curriculum and instruction oriented to a multicultural and social reconstructionist focus were addressed. Relationships established among participants were collegial in nature; a feeling of community was established and lived out over the course of the year.

Learning to Teach Multiculturally

In this section, we explore ideas that Lorena Draper brought to teaching and how she struggled to incorporate ideas promulgated by the teacher education program into her practices over the course of 1 year. We also draw on interpretive lenses about the relations among talk, thinking, and the social contexts in which these occur, provided by the work of Russian literary theorist M. M. Bakhtin.

In his work, Bakhtin considered how individuals sort through and come to understand what they know. As Bakhtin has written, "The social environment is what has given a person words and what has joined words with specific meanings and value judgments; the same environment continues ceaselessly to determine and control a person's verbal reactions throughout his life" (as quoted in Morris, 1994, p. 44). With this, Bakhtin is not saying that people are without volition in determining what they say and how they act. Rather, he highlights the role that the places in which people live and speak play in what people can say and how they interpret their responsibilities and actions.

We draw on Bakhtin's ideas about the role of contexts and how, as individuals, people develop a self-consciousness about their talk and actions in differing places and times, to show how prospective teachers look simultaneously through their own interpretive lenses and the eyes of others as they craft their practices. We argue that dialogic interactions among the inner speech of individuals—those ideas they bring with them to teacher education—and the new speech/ideas of their teacher educators and teacher education program are in continual tension in prospective teachers. Such tension often leads prospective teachers to engage in what appears to be an amalgam of practices that are at once driven by their prior beliefs about teaching and learning and also beginning to be informed by the ideas of the teacher education program. We show in what follows how Lorena Draper's teaching in one third-grade classroom was influenced both by what she brought to teaching and by a struggle to understand and practice what she was being taught in her teacher education program.

At the time of her program application, Lorena was living in Chicago and working as a financial analyst at a large bank. As a young adult, she had not moved geographically far from her family home in another midwestern state. She was living materially in far different circumstances than she had as a child, however. Then, she was teased by other children because of her discount store clothing and barbered hair that made her "look like a boy." Lorena explained in her program application that her parents were immigrants from Yugoslavia who had struggled financially throughout her childhood and teenage years to raise three daughters in a small midwestern community. Lorena's first language was Serbo-Croatian, and she did not speak English until entering school, where learning to read was difficult.

Lorena learned then that working hard paid off as she became so proficient at her schoolwork that by the second grade she was asked to tutor other children in the school. She wrote in her program application essay:

> Since my school did not give individualized attention to me and classes were structured toward children who already knew English, I was forced to work extremely hard to keep up with my classmates. Through hard work and perseverance, I learned to read and school became much easier for me. As a result, I grew to love school. (1/96)

The importance of persevering in the face of challenge to learn and do
what was expected of you was a cornerstone of Lorena's belief system.
As a child, she learned English and how to read by working hard, eventually surpassing her peers to become a tutor of other children. As a teenager, Lorena also found academic challenges to meet in the advanced
placement social studies courses in which she enrolled. All were taught by
one teacher in her 123-student high school. She admired this teacher both
because he was openly gay in a small midwestern town and because he
held such high expectations for his students. Lorena explained:

> He was just incredible. He had such an impact on so many stu-
> dents' lives in that entire city. Almost every student that he's
> counseled has gone on and become very successful—not just like
> career-wise but as far as what they think about themselves and
> how confident they are about themselves. He made us think. He
> lectured every day for 3 years. Sophomore year we did American
> history; junior year we did world history; senior year was govern-
> ment. He lectured every single day, and then our test for 3 years,
> every single time, was 20 identifications, then we had 2, 3, some-
> times 4 essay questions. . . . It was the first time I had to think like
> that. I didn't do that well in the beginning, I did end up getting all
> A's. On the first test, I got a D. He really wanted to tell us—"You
> have to use the material." I remember him saying that. I remember
> him saying, "Why do we study history? And, when I ask you these
> questions, you just can't write shit." He taught us in high school
> you can't just write any b.s.; you have to use the material. (Inter-
> view, 5/19/97)

Lorena went on to use the skills this teacher taught her at the University of
Michigan, where she earned excellent grades. As an adult, Lorena applied
these same lessons—listening carefully to what was expected and learning new systems of analysis—to her work at a bank. There, she began as an
administrative assistant and was continually promoted until she was a
financial analyst in charge of a unit when she resigned to study teaching.
    Meeting others' expectations through hard work also provided
Lorena with personal confidence. Lorena found that, as a tutor, she could

help her peers develop that same confidence when they were able to perform required school tasks. She explained:

> I continued my role as a tutor to several children throughout grade school and high school. One of my students was a little girl labeled as being "slow" and who was failing math. When I began to help her with her homework, I realized that she knew most of the mathematical concepts but was having problems applying them. I began to convey to her that I believed in her and that I felt she would pass her next exam. She did pass and subsequently was not held back from the second grade. This experience would later help me realize that one of the key ingredients to being a successful teacher was reaffirming a student's self-confidence. (Application essay, 1/96)

Lorena had considered preparing to be a teacher as an undergraduate at the university, but her father—a dental student forced to become a dental technician after fleeing Yugoslavia—urged her to gain a degree with the prospects of higher earnings. So, she majored in economics but continued tutoring children at a local Montessori school. There, she worked effectively with Spanish-speaking children, with whom she identified as they were in a similar position to that which she had experienced as a child. Later, as a banker, Lorena became involved in a group called Chicago Cares, wherein corporations encouraged employees to work in service activities for children and youths from low-income families. Again she tutored, this time children from a large housing project. She found there not only that children were having problems learning mathematics or learning how to read but also that

> there were real problems they were dealing with. . . . I won't even go into the problems the children who lived in the projects had to deal with—not living with parents, drugs, and just everything. And here I am trying to teach them how to read. And it's a struggle just to get them to sit down for half an hour to open a book. So, I think that really solidified it for me, especially since I was doing that when I read the [teacher education] program brochure. People say, "I can't do anything on my own. I can't do anything by myself. I can't change these children's situations on my own." But,

you know if every single person said that, nothing would get done. But if I said it—I can make a change—and somebody else said it, now you've got 26 people in the program who are going to try and go out and help and do something about why some children aren't succeeding in school. Then it can work. So at that point I decided I wanted to go into teaching and help those children who really need help. (Interview, 5/19/97)

Once enrolled in the program, Lorena chose as her summer volunteer option work in a neighborhood center where African American and European American children from neighborhood low-income families enjoyed crafts, cooking, swimming, and games. At summer's close, she requested assignment to the school serving this neighborhood. Lorena worked in one third-grade class for the entire year. There, she struggled with questions of what knowledge to teach and how to involve students in their own learning.

Like her peers, Lorena brought memories of her own school experiences to the program and drew on them for cues regarding how best to teach. Her own experiences as a child with a language background differing from English and as a child from a family struggling economically drew her to the program and to working with children she saw as needing help to succeed in school and in life. As a child, Lorena had not received special help in learning to read. Rather, she had worked very hard and mastered what was expected. As a teenager, she had been challenged by her history teacher's curriculum and at first had not understood how to answer the questions he posed. As a young adult, she had mastered the "curriculum" of banking and financial analysis. Her hard work was rewarded with promotions and pay increases. In each of these instances— in elementary school, in high school, and in her job—Lorena studied the required material and mastered it, often exceeding the skills and knowledge of her peers. Each time, she was rewarded—with the prestige of tutoring her peers, with A grades in advanced placement courses, and with financial incentives.

Theory Into Practice

It was difficult, then, as a teacher, for Lorena to accept that a course of action suggested as a good one by her teacher education program—to tailor curriculum to students' needs and interests and to encourage students to take social action based on what they learned about the world around them—was a good one. Lorena had succeeded, not because she had learned what she thought she needed, but because she had done what was asked of her and learned an existing curriculum deemed important by her teachers and employers. It was difficult for Lorena to accept that teaching everyone in the same way would not be the best course. After all, it had worked for her.

In a story Lorena told in autumn of 1996 about her literacy teaching, she explained that she had read her class a fable with the intent that the text would "teach them something important." Lorena read a story in which a cat with magical powers helps a poor priest win a prize from a wealthy lord. The cat is dismayed when the priest asks the lord for only three pieces of gold, yet later the cat understands that the priest asked for only what he and the cat needed. As Lorena explained it, the moral of the story was "You don't have to be rich to be happy."

Lorena told us that, after reading the book to the class, she had asked the children to write about whether it was "fair" that the cat had helped the priest and what they would have done if they had had the opportunity to ask for anything they desired. Initially, she was disappointed that the children did not seem to understand the moral of the story. Although the children interpreted the cat's assistance as ethical because the priest had been kind to the animal, all but one child found the priest foolish not to have requested more riches. Lorena said:

> Only one child wrote that he wouldn't want to have all of the gold in the world because he didn't want to be wealthy. I was really surprised that the rest of the class did not respond in a way that I expected. Therefore, at the very end of the lesson I thought that I would ask them to tell me what they thought. This time, they were able to tell me exactly what I was hoping to hear. They told me that three gold pieces was enough because all you really need is a home and food to take care of your family. I asked the children if they could tell me what the moral of the story was and why they think I read the story to them. Their answer was, "You don't have to be rich to be happy." I had accomplished my objective.

Lorena was pleased. Although they initially appeared not to understand the book's message, the children were able to demonstrate that they had acquired the information when she asked that they tell, rather than write, their interpretations.

Here, Lorena fails to see the irony of the message she communicates from the text as juxtaposed against her own and many of the children's economic situations. In her own life, Lorena can be viewed as having made a decision similar to that of the priest in living only on what she needed to survive. Just months earlier, she had given up her job, many material possessions, and disposable income to go back to school and learn to teach. Yet, numerous children whom she taught lived in low-income families with poor job prospects, few possessions, and little or no disposable income. Acquiring even modest material means may have seemed a tantalizing prospect to them as they wrote how silly the priest seemed to be by rejecting potential riches. When it was clear that a particular answer was sought from them, however, they told it to their teacher. From Lorena's viewpoint, she had held high expectations for all and also had offered another way for the children to demonstrate what they knew—telling rather than writing. Lorena seemed certain that the lesson had been a good one despite questioning by a peer about why she had pursued oral explanations from the children when they had already written responses to the story.

A few months later, however, Lorena appeared to question her assumptions about what role children should take in a teaching-learning relationship. She also tried to make her mathematics lessons more "student centered" by connecting "what we had learned to students' everyday lives." She tells a story (3/12/97) about a series of lessons on graphing and how she had, in the final lesson, asked children to determine which of the three graphs she had taught them (bar, line, and picture) would best represent particular data:

After we finished discussing what we had done, I wanted to take our discussion of graphing one step further. . . . Therefore, I asked students how we could use graphs in our everyday lives. I asked students to give me examples of how graphs are used for practical purposes and in our everyday experiences.

I was quite pleased that students were able to come up with concrete answers. One student said that a zoo could use a bar graph to see how many people liked each animal so they could get those animals for the zoo. Another student told the class how companies could use bar or line graphs to see which toy was the popular one or which one they sold the most so they could make more of that toy. Others said that we could take a survey of people's "favorites" and make bar graphs of that information. One student even mentioned that a weatherman could make a line graph of temperatures to see how the temperature changed.

I was very surprised that students were able to contribute this much to the discussion. What this lesson confirmed for me is the notion that students come to school possessing much more knowledge than we believe them to have and that students are not passive recipients of knowledge. As a teacher, I do not simply have to pass on information to students. I have learned that, by asking students to apply what they have learned about graphing, they were able to do so without my telling them exactly how. I have learned that it is worthwhile to "extract" as much information as possible out of the students in my class because they know much more than what I thought they did, and they also know how to apply what I have taught them much better than I thought they would.

Her peers' responses to Lorena's story were supportive of her efforts. One classmate wondered why Lorena had not asked students at the beginning of the lesson, rather than at its end, what they knew about graphs and how they might be used. Lorena responded that she had not thought of that. Her goal had been to teach them information about graphs that she assumed the students had not known.

Lorena appears to have made a powerful insight about her teaching, and one might expect that she would then apply that insight to her next lessons. As our next example illustrates, however, learning to teach is not a simple and linear process, and the ideologies grounding prospective teachers' practices are not easily disrupted. Throughout the winter and spring, Lorena's stories of teaching returned to questions of who knowledge makers in school should be, what knowledge is important to know, and how best to help students acquire that knowledge. Lorena asked,

"Should I be a 'skills-based' teacher or not?" and, "If I chose to ground my teaching in 'basic skills,' what ones would I teach?" In another story about her literacy teaching (told 4/23/97), she asked, "How do I teach literacy, and do I focus more on teaching skills in literacy, or do I use the 'whole language' approach to teach literacy in a more holistic manner? I realize that I believe in doing both." In the lesson she describes, Lorena tells how she tried to implement both what she saw as a "skills-based" and a "whole language-based" approach to literacy teaching.

In the story, Lorena tells how she asked the class to examine gender and racial stereotypes in fairy tales such as "The Princess and the Pea" and "Cinderella." She said:

> At first, some of the children were a little bit defensive. I understand how difficult it is to hear that some of the stories one holds dear to their heart may be racist or prejudiced. However, eventually children came to realize they could still enjoy these fairy tales, but they have to really take a look at and think about what it is they're reading. I tried to teach the children in my class that it was important to be aware of some of these elements in all literature and that this does not mean that they cannot enjoy what they read.

Lorena sees this activity as grounded in a more whole language approach. She then explains how she integrated her concerns for teaching skills into the same set of lessons:

> The entire class had just read "The Princess and the Pea" by Hans Christian Andersen. We had already discussed the story in depth. I gave the children a typed three-page copy of the story, and I asked them to go through and identify the nouns, the verbs, and the adjectives. After they had done this, I asked them to go back and cross out as many nouns, verbs, and adjectives as they could and then change those particular nouns, verbs, and adjectives. I asked them to change as many words as they could in order to change the story. I told them to keep in mind using adjectives that they would want characters to possess and to change the story in a way that would make it less racist, elitist, materialistic, and prejudiced.

Lorena does teach skills to her students in the lesson described. She teaches recognition of the parts of speech and asks that children take into account her lessons about race, class, and gender when replacing one word with another, potentially altering which characters take certain roles—hero, fool, and distressed person—and how these characters are portrayed. She did not ask children to write their own fairy tales grounded in different ideas about how relations among people might be constructed.

In October 1996, when she taught the fable of the cat and the priest, Lorena knew what she needed to do and how to do it, and she rebuffed questions from her peers about her lesson. In March 1997, Lorena recognizes that children do bring to school knowledge and experiences on which teachers can draw to enhance student learning and interest. She does not, however, talk about students as knowledge constructors. Rather, she sees how they can apply what she has taught them about graphs and use it in talking about the world they know. A month later, Lorena is asking herself questions about what is important to teach and how to integrate concerns for issues of justice and equity into the existing school curriculum. Yet, as with her lesson about the fable, Lorena remains most comfortable telling that which seems certain—in this case, that fairy tales are "racist, elitist, materialistic, and prejudiced," as well as teaching the names and functions of particular parts of speech.

Not long after she teaches her fairy tale lessons, Lorena conducts her "lead teaching," in which she is the major instructor of the children for 2 weeks. During their lead teaching, we had asked that members of the cohort group teach a unit that integrated various content areas and that demonstrated their understanding of social reconstructionist multicultural education. Lorena chose to teach a series of lessons about nutrition to her third graders.

In stories she told about her nutrition unit (told 5/7/97), Lorena asks how she is taking her students into account in her teaching:

> I was doing a unit on nutrition, and on this particular day I planned to teach about the five different nutrients: carbohydrates, protein, fats, water, and vitamins and minerals. I planned on having five different learning stations and having foods at each sta-

tion that would list all the reasons that these nutrients were important. I then wanted to divide the class into groups of four and have each group visit each of the different learning stations to learn about the five nutrients.

Then, I stopped myself and asked, What was student-centered about this? I realized that I was giving them all of the information and that they weren't really taking an active part in their learning. I decided to find as many books for children about the different nutrients as I could find and have them available for children to look at. I then decided to have each group of students do a study on one nutrient. Each group would be required to create a poster that listed the most important purposes that each nutrient served and also to paste or draw pictures on that poster of major foods that contained that nutrient. This group project required the students to decide which role each person would play. Each group needed at least two researchers/readers, one writer, and two drawers/pasters. I decided to let each group assign roles to each person. I also suggested that students switch roles throughout the project.

Not only were students producers of knowledge that I was trying to teach them, but each student found a role that was most responsive to their learning needs in each group. This is the main reason that this activity was multicultural. It catered to many students' different abilities and allowed each student to learn the material in a different manner, whether it was drawing or reading or writing. . . . They created their own learning stations; they didn't need me to do it for them. I was the facilitator. They were the teachers. They took responsibility for teaching the rest of the class about each of the nutrients.

Lorena was proud of recognizing her inattention to students as knowledge makers and of reconstructing her lessons so that students could work together and find out the information she had requested. Her peers applauded these efforts, pointing out that her teaching had made possible the inclusion of students in her class with various special needs, including two boys with autism.

Discussion

Lorena taught her nutrition unit near the close of her teacher educa-tion program. Her ideas about what constituted good multicultural teach-ing appeared to be changing as she began to see how students could link their current interests and understandings to new ideas and, in so doing, also learn that which their teachers valued. Over the course of a year in which she had opportunities to tell stories about her teaching and to hear her peers' and teacher educators' responses to them, Lorena negotiated tensions between key ideas that had guided her life and new notions that slowly disrupted those. Just as Bakhtin (1986) suggests that all thought is developed, Lorena was considering new ways to think about teaching in "a process of interaction and struggles with others' thought[s]" (p. 92).

The social context in which Lorena told her stories seems central to her changing ideas. When Lorena planned the stories she would tell, she also was taking into account her listeners and our responses to her stories. In planning her stories, she was telling herself what she had taught and how and why she had done so—just as she would later tell us. Or as Bakhtin (1986) has said: ". . . from the very beginning, the speaker expects a response from [those addressed], an active responsive understanding. The entire utterance is constructed, as it were, in anticipation of encounter-ing this response" (p. 94).

This does not mean that speakers tell another only what they antici-pate the other wishes to hear. Rather, speakers take into account their understandings of their listeners' positions and anticipate questions and comments they might have, as well as potential points of conflict and mis-understanding. Over time, Lorena began to anticipate the kinds of ques-tions her peers might ask about her lessons. Recalling her peers' questions about why she had asked students to tell what they knew about graphs *after* she had taught her unit rather than ascertaining what they knew *before* she planned to teach it, Lorena reconsidered how to teach her nutri-tion unit. She told us that she interrupted her "teaching as telling" plans for the unit and asked herself, What is student centered about this? We argue that such self-inquiry occurred in a context where Lorena began to draw on her peers' questions as resources for her teaching.

Near the close of her teacher education program, Lorena began to incorporate into her teaching the ideas she had heard about in her courses and in the voices of her peers in the seminar. Why did it take so long for this to occur? And what implications does the resiliency of Lorena's personal experiences for informing her teaching have for teacher education reform and for the use of personal narrative in accomplishing such reform?

We believe there are several reasons that it took nearly a year for Lorena to initiate incorporation of program ideals and strategies into her practice. First is the power of the personal narrative itself, which as a genre impels the narrator to place her- or himself at the center of the tale. For a teacher, locating oneself at the center of stories means that one's viewpoint is the predominant lens through which classroom experiences are constructed and understood. This is contradictory to our understanding of key tenets of a multicultural and social reconstructionist position, which calls for teachers to reimagine their curriculum and instruction from diverse social, cultural, and historical viewpoints. In retrospect, we see how our emphasis on the telling of personal narratives did not open possibilities for critique of transferring one's own experiences to templates for teaching others. Rather, it reinscribed the sanctity of personal experiences as guides for teaching. It is not surprising, then, that Lorena and her peers consistently turned to their own lives to inform their pedagogy.

Second, the selection criteria employed for program enrollment resulted in our cohort group's composition of young people who had led brief but successful careers in, for example, banking, insurance, securities, and health care. Although these careers had not been as satisfying as they had first imagined, disrupting notions that had grounded their challenging yet fruitful negotiation of their jobs was likely more than could be accomplished in a program packed with activity and lasting only one academic year and two summers. As these prospective teachers encountered new challenges in unfamiliar settings, it was natural for them to return to ways of speaking and thinking that had worked for them in other settings.

What implications does our story of one second-career teacher's learning to teach have for teacher education reform and for the use of personal narrative as a tool to accomplish such reform? One way to think about our intentions and their outcomes is to draw again on ideas from Bakhtin (1981), who wrote about authoritative and internally persuasive discourses. Of the former, he wrote:

> The authoritative word demands that we acknowledge it, that we make it our own; it binds us, quite independent of any power it

might have to persuade us internally; we encounter it with its authority already fused to it. The authoritative word is located in a distanced zone, organically connected with a past that is felt to be hierarchically higher. It is, so to speak, the word of the fathers. . . . It is not a free appropriation and assimilation of the word itself that authoritative discourse seeks to elicit from us; rather, it demands our unconditional allegiance. Therefore authoritative discourse permits no play with the context framing it, no play with its borders, no gradual and flexible transitions, no spontaneously creative stylizing variants on it. It enters our verbal consciousness as a compact and indivisible mass; one must either totally affirm it, or totally reject it. (pp. 342-343)

Bakhtin believed that internally persuasive discourse is more like retelling something in one's own words, rather than reciting an authoritative discourse. The internally persuasive discourse in this case is that which Lorena and her peers brought to the teacher education program about how the world works. For Lorena, this meant allegiance to ways of teaching that emphasized mastery of a canon of information and activities recognized as important by the world at large. The authoritative discourse is that which we, as teacher educators, attempted to impose on our students—that of a multicultural social reconstructionist view of curriculum and instruction.

We see now that the authority we invested in this particular view of multiculturalism remained closed to questioning by ourselves or our students. In saying so, we do not deny its power for transforming teaching and learning. We do, however, see that our failure both to make critique of this message possible in the seminar and to juxtapose it explicitly against the internally persuasive ideals brought to the program by our students resulted in continual yet often unexplored tensions between these varied ideals. Our message for other teacher educators is both to make explicit what grounds your program and practices and to enable students to tangle openly and freely with how such authoritative discourse bumps up against, is congruent with, or denies those internally persuasive discourses they bring to you.

Even though this may sound like common sense, our experiences in this program and in others where we have both taught and been students enable our knowing that those discourses that students bring to their programs are often tacitly dismissed, denied, or suppressed. Our recent experiences tell us that imposition of an authoritative discourse, however lively and engaging, will slow and/or deny prospective teachers' dialogue with its principles.

Finally, with respect for what telling stories about one's teaching offers for reforming teacher education, we remain intrigued by the possibilities offered by narrative as a means for understanding and critiquing one's practices and their outcomes for prospective teachers. We acknowledge our deficiencies in not explicitly supporting and enabling dialogue among the competing ideas present in our students' thinking and our program philosophy. We wonder what the outcome might have been for Lorena and her peers had we encouraged storytelling that would have viewed their teaching from the viewpoint of an omniscient narrator who interpreted practice from her own internally persuasive discourse *and* from that of the program. We wonder whether offering opportunities for the writing of fictional narratives from the viewpoints of various "actors" in schools—students, family members, and teachers—might enable viewing of curriculum and instruction from the various social, cultural, and institutional resources that must be mobilized if schools and schooling are to become more equitable and just places for all learners. For us, telling and listening to stories is a compelling, life-enhancing, and potentially life-altering experience, and we will continue to explore ways to draw on this power for teacher education.

References

Bakhtin, M. M. (1981). *The dialogic imagination: Four essays.* Austin: University of Texas Press.

Bakhtin, M. M. (1986). *Speech genres and other late essays.* Austin: University of Texas Press.

Bruner, J. (1990). *Acts of meaning.* Cambridge, MA: Harvard University Press.

Gomez, M. L. (1996). Telling stories of our teaching, reflecting on our practices. *Action in Teacher Education, XVIII*(3), 1-12.

Morris, P. (Ed.). (1994). *The Bakhtin reader: Selected writings of Bakhtin, Medvedev, Voloshinov.* London: Edward Arnold.

Rosenwald, G. C., & Ochberg, R. L. (1992). *Storied lives: The cultural politics of self-understanding.* New Haven, CT: Yale University Press.

Sleeter, C. E., & Grant, C. A. (1988). *Making choices for multicultural education: Five approaches to race, class, and gender.* New York: Macmillan.

Zeichner, K. M. (1992). *Educating teachers for cultural diversity.* East Lansing, MI: National Center for Research on Teacher Education.

Zeichner, K. M., & Tabachnick, B. R. (1991). Reflections on reflective teaching. In B. R. Tabachnick & K. M. Zeichner (Eds.), *Issues and practices in inquiry-oriented education* (pp. 1-21). London: Falmer.

◨

9 Reshaping the Profession One Teacher at a Time

Collaborative Mentoring of Entry-Year Teachers

Donald A. Williams

Connie L. Bowman

Donald A. Williams is Associate Professor of Education at Trinity International University. His research has focused on professional development in the context of teacher induction, in-service education, and collaborative partnerships.

Connie L. Bowman is Assistant Professor of Education in the Department of Teacher Education at the University of Dayton. Her research interests include the mentoring of beginning teachers, peer coaching, and teacher reflection.

ABSTRACT

This chapter explores the impact of a clinical approach to mentoring on the professional development of a group of entry-year teachers and their school-based mentors with respect to (a) perceptions of support from mentoring, (b) reflection on teaching, and (c) a clinical focus on teaching and learning. The induction program provided 15 teams of entry-year teachers and their mentors with training in mentoring and the application of the Pathwise criteria of the Educational Testing Service (ETS), along with the collaborative support of university professors and a network of teachers participating in the study. Data were obtained through regular reflective summaries of discussions between mentors and mentees and through interviews conducted with these teachers. The results provide evidence that mentoring in the context of teacher induction can go beyond structures that ensure "survival" and encourage beginning teachers to focus on developing competence in professional practice.

Introduction

Mentoring beginning teachers has become a crucial focus in the induction of novice teachers. Beginning in the early 1980s, interest in mentoring burgeoned as part of a larger initiative focused on improving education. The phenomenon of mentoring gained momentum in a survey conducted by the American Association of Teacher Educators in which mentoring was established as the most crucial issue confronting teacher educators in the 1990s (Buttery, Haberman, & Houston, 1990). In the context of educational reform, interest in mentoring has been stimulated by a desire to reform the teaching profession in conjunction with a concern over the dramatic rates of attrition among teachers during their first 3 years of service.

During the past two decades, conceptions of induction have developed from an emerging understanding of the needs of beginning teachers. As Wilkinson (1994, p. 52) notes, early attempts at supportive induction were little more than an orientation to the school building and an indoctrination into bureaucracy by the building principal. Subsequent research efforts disclosed an array of problems frequently encountered by beginning teachers that focused on relational, cultural, logistical, and organizational dilemmas (Veenman, 1984). As a result, induction programs were structured to assist beginning teachers in solving common first-year problems, and where beginning teachers received support during their first years in teaching, attrition was dramatically arrested (Colbert & Wolf,

1992; Odell & Ferraro, 1992). Therefore, these early efforts at induction focused largely on the care of beginning teachers.

In the mid-1980s, several reports recommended programs of teacher induction. Among these were *NCATE Redesign* (National Council for Accreditation of Teacher Education [NCATE], 1985), the Holmes Group report *Tomorrow's Teachers* (1986), and the report by the Association of Teacher Educators (ATE), *Visions of Reform: Implication for the Education Profession* (1986). These recommendations were intended to stimulate reform of the teaching profession and thus affect the nature of education in U.S. schools. According to the ATE report, induction programs should (a) serve to bridge the gap between preservice and in-service experience, (b) be collaboratively developed and implemented by higher education and local school units, (c) afford beginning teachers a protracted period of internship prior to certification, (d) allow for a gradual and sequential assumption of responsibilities based on readiness, (e) provide a program of clinical practice and professional development, and (f) provide ongoing assistance and feedback for each inductee.

Visions of Reform (ATE, 1986) advances a view of induction that is undergirded by the care and feeding of novice teachers. It is a vision in which beginning teachers learn in an environment of support with challenge and in which inductees are given appropriate doses of assistance and feedback. Consequently, this vision of induction reaches beyond the goal of merely helping beginning teachers survive during their first year; it is a conception focused on the continuing professional development of novice teachers. Moreover, this view of induction extends to mentoring as a supporting mechanism in the induction of beginning teachers. In this regard, Little (1990) has drawn a distinction between the social support that ameliorates the demands and stresses experienced by beginning teachers and the professional support needed to advance their knowledge and practice. Similarly, Daloz (1986) contends that beginning teachers need support and challenge to nurture and stimulate their professional development. Therefore, the necessity of supportive agents, structures, and environments in concert with professional support that affords challenging expectations within the induction year serves as a reasonable basis for a model of mentoring that projects a comprehensive approach to the development of beginning teachers.

A foundational element of mentoring is the collaborative nature of such relationships, which are based on a conception of socially constructed knowledge. Researchers have demonstrated that people master new skills best when placed in coaching situations (Joyce & Showers, 1983; Little, 1982). As collaborators talk, they in turn are reflecting on what they are doing. Therefore, the social setting of collaboration provides the opportunity for beginning teachers to think aloud and examine their intentions. In addition, as beginning teachers confront problems, their mentors provide assistance in solving problems that might otherwise remain insoluble. A crucial notion of mentoring is that the coaching or facilitative role of the mentor is never tied to evaluation and thus fosters a collegial relationship in a supportive, nonthreatening partnership (Joyce & Showers, 1983).

Collaboration among teachers in mentoring relationships is intended to promote inquiry into curriculum, instruction, and assessment, with the goal of providing more meaningful educational outcomes for children. As teachers collaborate to develop and enhance curriculum or to pursue solutions to cultural and social problems in their classrooms, inquiry assumes a central role in professional development (Darling-Hammond & McLaughlin, 1994). Such mentoring relationships may be further enhanced by creating a network of similar relationships in which teachers' inquiries regarding their practice are both validated and challenged by others engaged in similar journeys. Therefore, what emerges from the literature on teacher induction and mentoring is a conception of nurturing beginning teachers that recognizes the importance of a clinical focus on teaching and learning so as to provide a meaningful direction for beginning teachers as they find their way in a confusing and sometimes intimidating first year of teaching.

Purpose

In response to emerging conceptions of teacher induction, states and educational communities have begun to develop and assess models of induction that focus on developing professional competencies and dispositions in beginning teachers (e.g., Meister, 1990; Stansbury & Long, 1992). This investigation examined the efficacy of an induction model based on ATE's recommendations on teacher induction and current knowledge and conceptions of mentoring. The two foci of this program were (a) a research-based beginning-teacher assessment instrument focused on student learning and (b) a collaborative mentoring community of university and school-based educators focused on the needs of beginning teachers.

In this study, our conception of beginning-teacher induction was grounded in a human development perspective and a focus on professional development. We contend that teacher development is a uniquely personal journey in which one's professional knowledge and competence are individually constructed and that induction programs should be responsive to individuals. The model of mentoring employed provided sufficient structures to ensure that beginning teachers were supported while allowing individuals to grow in a unique manner.

We also drew a distinction between relational support and clinical support in mentoring relationships. We defined *relational support* as those activities or interactions that pertain to the emotional structures in a mentoring relationship that foster healthy attitudes and perceptions about one's self in relation to teaching. *Clinical support* was characterized by assistance in curricular and instructional processes that promote professional competence and efficacy.

Specifically, we contend that mentoring should be (a) grounded in a vision of good teaching, (b) separated from evaluation, (c) guided by assessment and critical examination of teaching, (d) collaboratively developed and implemented by university and local school personnel, and (e) focused on the needs of individual inductees.

The purpose of this study was to investigate the impact of a clinical approach to mentoring on the professional development of a group of beginning teachers and mentors with respect to their (a) perception of support from mentoring, (b) reflection on teaching and decision making, and (c) focus on teaching and learning. Specifically, we sought to determine whether the structures established in this mentoring initiative would promote a focus on clinical support in the relationship between mentors and entry-year teachers.

Method

This study examined the first-year experience of 15 beginning teachers and their school-based mentors in a suburban school district in central Ohio. The subjects included seven teams of elementary teachers, all female, and eight teams of middle and high school teachers composed of three male and five female entry-year teachers and one male and seven female mentors. The mentees were selected solely on the basis of their status as entry-year teachers, whereas the mentors were selected on the basis of their experience, leadership, and desire to serve as mentors.

Mentoring Program

University and school district coordinators for this program worked together to establish the goals and direction of mentoring. This led to the development of a shared conception of mentoring and related strategies to train, support, and network with mentoring teams. A crucial element in this collaboration between university and school personnel concerned the development of a shared conception of good teaching. Pathwise, developed by the Educational Testing Service (ETS, 1995), served as the programmatic model of effective beginning teaching and consequently as an organizing construct for mentoring beginning teachers.

The Pathwise instrument was developed by ETS through an examination of the research and theory on teaching and learning. Pathwise focuses on 19 criteria organized around four domains of teaching: (a) organizing content knowledge for student learning, (b) creating an environment for student learning, (c) teaching for student learning, and (d) teacher professionalism. The Pathwise criteria were designed to provide a clinical focus in one's teaching and were conceived to encompass the range of teaching competencies expected of a beginning teacher. Consequently, this instrument served as a reflective focus for beginning teachers and their mentors and afforded a common language within which to think and dialogue about teaching and learning.

All the teachers in the mentoring teams were given training in mentoring related to its relational aspects, as well as the development of participants' skills in supervision and coaching by using Pathwise. The formal training was conducted in three half-day workshops: The first provided an overview of mentoring relationships and an introduction to the Pathwise criteria; the second included training in the observational domains of Pathwise and strategies for mentoring; and the third addressed the application of Pathwise to mentoring and additional mentor training, with special emphasis on the relational aspects of mentoring.

In addition to the workshop sessions, the project coordinators met with groups of teachers in discussion groups during December and February to monitor the progress of participants and to discuss their application of the Pathwise criteria to their mentoring. These breakout sessions were also intended to promote networking between teams and to maintain linkages between the university and local school personnel.

Data Sources

Mentor teams (entry-year teachers and their school-based mentors) were asked to meet on a weekly basis to review and discuss their recent teaching experience. Following their conversations, individuals were asked to write a summary and reflection of the issues addressed during their discussion. These journal entries served as a source of descriptive data concerning each team's mentoring activities and important issues discussed in their conversations.

During the beginning teachers' induction year, data were collected through interviews with mentoring teams in addition to the data collected from journal entries. Interviews conducted in January and May were semi-structured, including questions relating to (a) descriptions of mentoring activities and perceptions of the value of mentoring and (b) the impact of using Pathwise as a focus for mentoring and professional growth.

Data Analysis

Journal entries and interview data were analyzed by using (a) content analysis (Krippendorf, 1980) to determine the relative level of discussion concerning relational and clinical support and (b) qualitative research methods to infer the categories and themes of participants' conversations and responses (Patton, 1990). The content of teachers' perceptions regarding their mentoring experience was analyzed initially by using the construct of relational versus clinical support. From this analysis, participants' statements were coded into two major categories—those that pertained to relational support and those that pertained to clinical support—based on the definitions of those terms adopted in this study. Within these two major categories, the data were analyzed qualitatively to determine the categories and themes expressed by participants.

Results

Although it was clear that the emotional support provided by the mentoring relationships was of considerable importance, in the text of their journal entries and during taped interviews, beginning teachers consistently focused on the clinical support they received from their mentors. A content analysis of journal data indicated that 78% of individual topics discussed during team conferences focused on clinical support, whereas 22% pertained to relational support. Similarly, in a content analysis of interview transcripts, 74% of responses offered by beginning teachers and their mentors related to the category of clinical support, whereas 26% pertained to relational support. The following discussion details the study's findings, organized around the dimensions of relational and clinical support.

Relational Support in Mentoring

Themes emerged from an analysis of the data with respect to the relational dimensions of mentoring, or what Ganzer (1996) refers to as mentor "helping roles." Participants emphasized affirmation, commitment, and collegiality as the key attributes of the support received from their mentoring relationship.

In a variety of ways, beginning teachers described being affirmed by their mentors. Moreover, mentoring teams provided evidence of mutual respect and esteem. Beginning teachers consistently reported that their mentoring relationships had grown into friendships in which they were valued personally and professionally. One teacher expressed this idea in the following statement: "My mentor is a friend who is always there to help and encourage." Another mentee observed that she was bolstered by knowing, "Someone is there who believes in me and really cares that I succeed." The affirmation afforded to beginning teachers by mentors brought a sense of validation of their professional status. One beginning teacher expressed this idea in saying, "Having my mentor's support—I have grown as a person and know that I am affecting these students the way I want to. I have a sense that I am doing a good job and feel secure and confident."

The relationships established between beginning teachers and their mentors were characterized by a strong sense of commitment of the mentors' emotional and intellectual resources. That is, mentors invested themselves significantly in the success of their mentees. Mentors reflected this commitment in the pride they expressed in their mentees' growth as teachers. For example, one mentor spoke admiringly of her mentee's teaching: "It has been valuable for me to watch. Her teaching is so relaxed. She makes the students feel that they are really important to her—almost kind of motherly." Another beginning teacher reflected on the commitment of her mentor in recalling, "We seem to do everything together. That's the way [our relationship] started out. She came into my room [at the beginning of the year] and gave me a hug and said, 'And don't you worry, we're a team and we'll make it to June together.' "

Finally, participants described their mentoring relationships in ways that focused on collegiality. In general, as beginning teachers and mentors talked about their mentoring relationships, they described them in terms of collaborative activity and other characteristics indicative of a collegial relationship. Over half of the teams spoke of collaborative planning in cases where either they taught the same grade and developed units together or taught the same subject and shared in planning. For example, one beginning teacher recalled, "I worked with my mentor to combine classes in order to develop a unit on the solar system. The students have really learned, and I can't believe how much they have enjoyed the unit. It's been one of the best things we have done." This teacher's mentor also observed, "People can say that they are teaming, but just because they say that doesn't mean that it is really a team effort. I felt like ours was a different kind of a team situation because we really did work together."

Collegiality was also evidenced by comments that indicated mentors and mentees enjoyed equal status in the relationships. For example, participants focused on what they were learning, talking about "we" in reference to planning and professional growth in their collaboration. For example, one teacher commented, "We're coaching each other and growing together." And another said, "During our weekly meetings, we take a domain [of the Pathwise criteria] and say, 'Let's focus on one thing.' " Three fourths of the mentor teachers offered comments to the effect that they had learned as much in the relationships as the beginning teachers. Indeed, mentor teachers talked nearly as much as beginning teachers about how much their teaching had been affected by their focus on the Pathwise criteria. Therefore, participants came to define their interaction more as peer-mentoring relationships than traditional hierarchical relationships typically found in mentoring.

Clinical Support in Mentoring

In addition to vital supports derived from the relational component of mentoring, participants described ways in which mentoring afforded them clinical support. Beginning teachers and mentors attributed the clinical support received in mentoring to two primary factors: (a) the scaffolding of their partner in the mentoring relationship and (b) the organizing construct of Pathwise in promoting inquiry into one's teaching. Both factors interacted to promote the professional development of beginning teachers. Furthermore, it is important to note that although the participants focused on the professional development of beginning teachers, mentors also reported that their thinking about their own teaching had been significantly provoked through their mentoring activities.

The beginning teachers in this study reported that their mentors served to help them solve, through reflection, problems that at the time were beyond their reach. Typical problems involved such issues as developing clear and meaningful goals for instruction and difficulties in management and discipline. Mentors apparently brought needed clarity and perspective to the problems faced by their mentees. One beginning teacher observed: "My mentor served as a sounding board—allowing me to talk aloud and define my problems and then work on solutions. She helped me focus on what's important in solving problems."

Mentors also scaffolded their mentees by assisting them in reflecting on their teaching. With the exception of one team, the exchange of ideas about teaching and related reflection on teaching practice occurred in an atmosphere of openness and trust. Beginning teachers and their mentors displayed a willingness to be vulnerable with one another in mutually evaluating their teaching. One mentor said, "It's not that I am the one who knows everything. I am learning with my mentee—(our mentoring)—it helps me focus on my own teaching. It has given me an avenue to help and be helped." Another noted, "When we talk about her [mentee's] teaching, not only do we look at her [teaching]—I reflect on my own teaching."

Whereas mentors provided resources of expert knowledge borne of experience, the Pathwise criteria furnished the mentoring teams with a rich organizational construct for thinking about teaching. In general, participants described Pathwise as a metacognitive tool that stimulated a keen awareness of important elements of teaching. Several representative comments from beginning teachers support this finding. One teacher said, "I'm more aware of things that I need to be doing, and when I'm doing my lessons, I think more about my students and my strategies to meet students' needs." Another commented, "It [Pathwise criteria] forces me to look intently at my teaching—at issues I would not have considered." A third teacher observed, "[Pathwise is] . . . helping me think more about my goals in teaching and asking, Why am I doing what I am doing; what exactly the children are learning, and how do I know?"

These criteria also served as a reflective focus in conversations between beginning teachers and their mentors. One beginning teacher noted: ". . . we get together and talk about [my teaching]. [Pathwise] gives me a way to think about what I did and to explain what I did. It also allows me to see other ways of approaching the same situation." Another beginning teacher shared that the Pathwise criteria served as a focus and an organizer for her conversations with her mentor, noting that "otherwise it is just a gab session."

It is telling that, in the one team that reported consistently negative results (beginning teacher felt low relational and clinical support), the mentor did not exhibit a strong commitment to the entry-year teacher. This lack of commitment was evidenced by an inconsistency in meeting with the beginning teacher and a lack of initiative in pursuing mentoring activities (e.g., meetings, class observations). Indeed, this is the one team in which the entry-year teacher and the mentor did not develop as colleagues. That is, they did not work together on any curricular projects, did not work together on classroom problems, and did not use Pathwise as a reflective focus to examine their teaching. Therefore, this case suggests that the absence of relational attachment in this team apparently foreclosed the pursuit of pedagogical goals in their mentoring relationship.

Discussion

The most significant finding of this study is that participants were able to develop a rich conception and practice in mentoring distinguished by a clinical focus on professional growth in teaching and learning. This is especially significant in view of recent studies of more traditional mentoring programs that were found to focus more narrowly on emotional support and assistance with paperwork and institutional procedures (Ganzer, 1996; Head, Reiman, & Thies-Sprinthall, 1992). Moreover, the tendency of participants in this study to focus on their clinical interactions regarding teaching and learning is encouraging because these outcomes are both desired and expected in an environment that fosters professional development.

The rich conception of mentoring and the strong commitment to mentoring developed by mentors and beginning teachers could be attributed, in part, to the emotional support they received and, in part, to the clinical support structures established in their mentoring program. It seems more fruitful, however, to consider the interaction between relational and clinical support structures.

Other researchers have pursued a similar line of thinking in conceptualizing the interaction of support and challenge (Daloz, 1986; McNally & Martin, 1997). Daloz (1986) describes support as an act of affirmation in which the novice feels cared for and characterizes challenge as actions that "open a gap that creates tension in the (mentee), calling for closure" (p. 213). Daloz conceptualizes the impact of various amounts of support and challenge on the development of novices. For example, Daloz contends that high support and low challenge tend to affirm but not provoke the beginning teacher to further development. In contrast, when support and challenge are both high, the novice will grow and progress professionally. In our work with beginning teachers in this study, we maintain that their progress was facilitated by the challenge implicitly and explicitly held in their shared vision of teaching. To use the language of Daloz, the goals embedded in the Pathwise criteria "opened a gap" between the current level of action and decision making of the beginning teachers and the standards held before them in Pathwise.

Research on mentoring has demonstrated that relational elements of trust, commitment, and mutual respect serve as a crucial foundation for mentoring (Butler, 1987). Without an organizational structure within which professional development goals can be established, however, there is little reason to believe that mentoring will go beyond providing emotional support and assistance with school routines for the inductee. Therefore, we maintain that reform-based mentoring is realized through an interaction between relational and clinical supports in which mentoring is focused on the professional development of both the beginning teacher and the mentor and is undergirded by the emotional support of a truly collaborative relationship.

The results of this investigation indicate that beginning teachers can be engaged in an ongoing, focused examination of their teaching and that mentoring can be expanded to include a reflective orientation and critical examination of an entry-year teacher's instructional practice. Induction programs have typically focused on providing relational support to entry-year teachers. Although it is certainly necessary—even foundational—we argue that relational support is not a sufficient stimulus to prompt beginning teachers to develop instructional competence in their professional practice. Therefore, we contend that, as beginning teachers are engaged in a reflective examination and development of their instructional practice with veteran colleagues, they will more likely develop confidence and satisfaction in their teaching, teaching that is rooted in professional competence.

Implications

As policymakers develop mentoring initiatives, consideration should be given to the nature of mentoring. The results of this study suggest that, in addition to providing novices with strong relational supports, mentoring should be grounded in a meaningful, reform-minded vision of teaching and learning. Mentoring that is not so grounded will not significantly contribute to the restructuring of education. In the context of conventional thinking about schooling, mentoring may indeed tend to preserve existing educational structures and ideologies. Mentoring that is fused with reform-minded conceptions of teaching and learning, however, can serve as a powerful tool for reform.

Furthermore, mentoring should be considered for its potential to serve as a career-long professional development tool; the benefit of mentoring to veteran teachers and school cultures may be as important to reform efforts as the benefit derived by beginning teachers. Therefore, restructuring the profession one teacher at a time refers not only to beginning teachers but also to veteran teachers. While veteran mentors guide and provoke beginning teachers to develop as autonomous, growing, and reflective practitioners, these same veterans are obliged to reconsider their own teaching practice. These collegial partnerships can lead individuals to relate in new ways, forging the substance of deeper professional relationships and stimulating new conceptions of "what it means to learn, and what it means to be educated" (Little, 1993, p. 129).

References

Association of Teacher Educators (ATE). (1986). *Visions of reform: Implications for the education profession*. Reston, VA: Author.

Butler, E. D. (1987). *Lessons learned about mentoring in two fifth-year teacher preparation-induction programs*. Paper presented at the annual meeting of the Association of Teacher Educators, Houston.

Buttery, T. J., Haberman, M., & Houston, W. R. (1990). First annual ATE survey of critical issues in teacher education. *Action in Teacher Education, 12*(2), 1-7.

Colbert, J. A., & Wolf, D. E. (1992). Surviving in urban schools: A collaborative model for a beginning teacher support system. *Journal of Teacher Education, 43*(3), 193-199.

Daloz, L. A. (1986). *Effective teaching and mentoring*. San Francisco: Jossey-Bass.

Darling-Hammond, L., & McLaughlin, M. W. (1994). Policies that support professional development in an era of reform. *Phi Delta Kappan, 74*(10), 752-761.

Educational Testing Service (ETS). (1995). *Pathwise: Orientation guide*. Princeton, NJ: Author.

Ganzer, T. (1996). Mentor roles: Views of participants in a state-mandated program. *Mid-Western Educational Researcher, 9*(2), 15-20.

Head, F. A., Reiman, A. J., & Thies-Sprinthall, L. (1992). The reality of mentoring: Complexity in its process and function. In T. M. Bey & C. T. Holmes (Eds.), *Mentoring: Contemporary principles and practices*. Reston, VA: Association of Teacher Educators.

Holmes Group. (1986). *Tomorrow's teachers*. East Lansing, MI: Author.

Joyce, B., & Showers, B. (1983). *Power in staff development through research on training*. Alexandria, VA: Association for Supervision and Curriculum Development.

Krippendorf, K. (1980). *Content analysis: An introduction to its methodology*. Beverly Hills, CA: Sage.

Little, J. W. (1982). Norms of collegiality and experimentation: Workplace conditions of school success. *American Educational Research Journal, 19*(3), 325-340.

Little, J. W. (1990). The mentoring phenomenon and the social organization of teaching. *Review of Research in Education, 16,* 297-351.

Little, J. W. (1993). Teachers' professional development in a climate of educational reform. *Educational Evaluation and Policy Analysis, 15*(2), 129-151.

McNally, P., & Martin, S. (1997). *Support and challenge in learning to teach: The role of the mentor.* Unpublished manuscript.

Meister, G. (1990). *Help for new teachers: Developmental practices that work.* Philadelphia: Research for Better Schools.

National Council for Accreditation of Teacher Education (NCATE). (1985). *NCATE redesign.* Washington, DC: Author.

Odell, S. J., & Ferraro, D. P. (1992). Teacher mentoring and teacher retention. *Journal of Teacher Education, 43*(3), 200-204.

Patton, M. Q. (1990). *Qualitative evaluation and research methods.* Newbury Park, CA: Sage.

Stansbury, K., & Long, C. (1992). *Assessment component of California new teacher project: Framework of knowledge, skills, and abilities for beginning teachers in California. A work in progress.* (ERIC Documents Reproduction Service No. ED 355 192)

Veenman, S. (1984). Perceived problems of beginning teachers. *Review of Educational Research, 54*(2), 143-178.

Wilkinson, G. A. (1994). Support for individualizing teacher induction. *Action in Teacher Education, 16*(2), 52-61.

DIVISION III

Summary

MENTORING, SOCIAL INTERACTION, AND TRANSFORMATIONS: REFLECTIONS AND IMPLICATIONS

Porter Lee Troutman, Jr.

Cohorts as Supports

The Koeppen, Huey, and Connor study, in Chapter 7, compared perceptions of students in a special cohort group with students participating in an existing teacher education program, which also had varied cohort arrangements. In this study, as in the Williams and Bowman study (Chapter 9), human communication and interactions were central concerns; mentoring was viewed as a socialization process. A set of criteria was developed from a review of the literature to use as a tool for reflecting on the interactions of members of the cohort groups. This set of criteria included engagement with individual and group goals, strength gained from a feeling of cohesiveness, formal and informal activities with faculty, and academic content of their courses. These parameters provided a framework for examining cohort-group features that can have positive or negative effects on preservice teachers in a cohort program.

Results showed that preservice teachers participating in the special cohort program significantly benefited from being members of the cohort group with regard to perceptions of field experiences. These benefits were discussed in terms of retention in the teacher program because of feelings of "membership" to the group. These positive reactions to group membership in the special cohort group were acknowledged by the authors as possibly occurring because of the increased amount of field experience required of those in Project Opportunity (PrO) when compared with those in the existing teacher education model.

Koeppen et al. illustrated the positive influences from social interaction. In the Koeppen et al. study, the focus is more on group membership as a feature of mentoring. Group bonds were strengthened during extensive field experiences. The results from this study imply the need for more investigation in extending field experiences beyond the parameters currently followed. The increased intensity of social interaction and mentoring as a result of more frequent field or lengthened field experiences might be related in further research as providing stronger foundations and overall competence in teaching, particularly in diverse settings.

Prospective teachers must spend time in their students' community environments to understand fully the perspectives brought to schools. Troutman, Powell, Jarchow, Fussell, and Imatt (1999) state that "the potential for overcoming instructional racism is limited unless teachers are willing to view themselves in alternative roles" (p. 121). Social interaction is an essential component of understanding alternative roles.

Dialogic Tensions

In Chapter 8, Gomez, Page, and Walker investigated interactions from a Bakhtinian perspective, wherein meaning is seen as constructed from and with others in a dialogic (Bakhtin, 1986). This study focused on a first-year teacher (Lorena) entering education as a major career change from her position as a financial analyst. Gomez et al. reveal Bakhtin's notions of moving within and between speech genre groups and how this is related to the tension that exists between what the preservice teacher brings to the classroom and the framework from the teacher education program. This tension between the preservice teacher's beliefs about teaching and the multicultural social reconstructionist view of curriculum and instruction presented to this teacher emerged as a central feature of the study. Narratives became the central focus of the data analysis.

From a perspective following a related line of inquiry as Gomez et al., Wertsch (1998) discusses the narrative as a *mediational means* and explores situations that express the tension between the agent and the mediational means. One example is the "quest for freedom" narrative that most high school students in the United States were taught about early settlers as a part of the public school history curriculum. This view that European settlers colonized the United States in search of freedom from persecution or constraints on freedom creates a foundation to the narrative. This narrative foundation significantly influences discussion of the events surrounding the treatment of Native Americans and the use of slaves in colonial times and afterward and influences the discussion and perception of events affecting Native Americans and African Americans throughout the country's history (Wertsch, 1998).

In the Gomez et al. study, Lorena's having a "mastery of a cannon of information" as the dominant narrative and having the multicultural social reconstructionist view as an opposing narrative presented to her by the teacher education curriculum is comparable to Wertsch's (1998) example of the quest-for-freedom narrative providing the tension between agent and mediational means, particularly when the agent knows that some of the information is false (e.g., settlers were aggressively stealing land, many of the founding fathers were connected in one way or another to slavery).

As Gomez et al. pointed out, Lorena's early beliefs about teaching and learning express Bakhtin's notion of an internally persuasive discourse changing and challenging authoritative discourse, thus creating a tension. Bakhtin's (1996) perspectives are cited by Wertsch (1998) to support Wertsch's description of tensions created by this quest-for-freedom narrative. Wertsch elaborates further on tensions between agents and narratives as mediational means in his description of the tension created between the official histories of Soviet-dominated cultures and nations and local histories existing simultaneously as two distinct narratives during the Cold War.

In their discussions, Gomez et al. emphasized that assumptions about the learning that preservice teachers bring with them to the program need to be acknowledged more openly. They suggested that the narrative might be useful for the preservice teachers in becoming more aware of the internally persuasive ideas they bring with them to the program.

In conclusion, this promotion of self-reflection through social interaction to become aware of the internally persuasive, authoritative dialogues that we all carry is essential to any teacher education program.

Collaborative Mentoring

In Chapter 9, Williams and Bowman demonstrated how a programmatic model, Pathwise, worked as a scaffolding tool for building and reflecting on relationships between mentors and beginning first-year teachers. Moreover, their notions that knowledge is socially constructed and that new skills are learned in coachlike situations emphasize the transformational nature of social interaction. Their philosophy of recognizing the value of the unique nature of each beginning teacher in the mentoring relationship supports symmetry between mentor and students. Within this perspective of promoting equitable nurturing relationships, mentors and their beginning first-year teachers used the domains from the Pathwise instrument to reflect on their interactions.

The types of support provided by the 15 participants in the study were distinguished in terms of clinical and relational supports. Clinical supports revolve around advice on instructional strategies. Relational supports are more concerned with self-perceptions and other emotional elements. Results from this study shed some light on what may be more effective directions in understanding how to research and improve mentoring relationships in teacher education.

From a content analysis (Krippendorf, 1980) of interviews, discussions, and journal entries, the first-year teachers in the Williams and Bowman study emphasized affirmation, commitment, and collegiality as significant relational supports. Mentors affirmed the first-year teachers' position by encouraging them and providing friendship. Mentors also showed a commitment by speaking with pride of their mentees' teaching, and one mentee spoke of the mentor's motherly qualities. Furthermore, mentors promoted collegiality by collaboratively planning lessons, in some cases developing new and creative units such as one on the solar system, which the first-year teacher involved said her students really enjoyed. The Pathwise criteria were used as a tool for continuous reflection on interactions for the mentor and first-year teacher, providing them with a common reference point.

Regarding the clinical support themes revealed in the analysis of the data, participants emphasized scaffolding partners in their mentoring relationships and using the Pathwise criteria for organizing their inquiries into each other's teaching techniques and strategies. Self-reflection is pointed out as being an important part of mentoring, and one mentor added that mentoring provided an "avenue to help and be helped." As mentioned above, this supports the idea that the Pathwise instrument was essential in providing participants with a common focus to prompt and follow transformations. Participants in the study mentioned clinical supports more often than relational supports in their journals and interviews; however, the data revealed the interwoven nature of clinical and relational supports and how these are related to truly collaborative relationships focused on joint inquiry and reflection.

This positive report on the possibilities of growth through the use of a reflective tool along with a promotion of equitable, collaborative relationships in teaching and learning provides an example of the powerful transformations possible from social interactions. Mentoring and open dialogue, supported by a philosophy of equity in collaboration and self-reflection, seem to be essential elements to the challenges in preparing teachers for the diverse educational settings and populations of the 21st century.

In conclusion, the Pathwise criteria provide a prerequisite framework for effective teaching by emphasizing relevant aspects of students' background knowledge and experience. Domain A is crucial in teacher preparation. Also noted by Troutman (1998), administrators and teachers must understand their own culture, values, and attitudes to unlock the future at diverse students.

Implications and Conclusions

Suggestions from the Gomez, Page, and Walker study (Chapter 8) of finding the means to highlight and discuss more of the assumptions and beliefs, in a Bakhtinian sense (Bakhtin, 1986), of what preservice teachers bring to the educational setting can provide a starting point for discussing the implications from all three chapters. Williams and Bowman (Chapter 9) and Koeppen, Huey, and Connor (Chapter 7) support the recognition of the importance of more equitable relationships and the potential of equitable relationships becoming enriched by the establishment of a common focus. In the Williams and Bowman study, the Pathwise instrument provided a common focus for reflection, and in the Koeppen et al. study, the cohort group provided peer support and dialogue to understand how the participants were situating themselves in relation to the educational settings and the pedagogical transformations taking place. The importance of this type of open, equitable dialogue and support that emerge in the Williams and Bowman and Koeppen et al. studies is demonstrated in the Gomez et al. study by Lorena's struggle with the persuasive internal dialogue (the mediational means) she brings to the educational setting. The interactions with her cohorts were reported to have mentored her into becoming more reflective on her pedagogy in relation to her audience. These positive transformations occurred despite the tensions created between the mediational properties of the narrative used from her previous perspective on learning and the diverse narratives she encountered in her new role as teacher.

From all the mentoring relationships described, this tension between agent and mediational means described by Wertsch (1998) and Bakhtin (1986) emerges as a significant feature for further research. With mentoring in teacher education providing some of the most promising changes and challenges in education today, it seems important to consider what participants are bringing to an educational setting and how they are involved in coconstructing interactions and meaning.

As a prerequisite for effective teaching in an ongoing increasingly diverse setting, teachers are compelled to examine their own values, attitudes, and culture before understanding their students' profiles. This concept of social interaction is carried through in all three chapters.

References

Bakhtin, M. M. (1986). In C. Emerson & C. Holquist (Eds.), *Speech genres and other late essays* (V. Mcgee, Trans.). Austin: University of Texas Press.

Krippendorf, K. (1980). *Content analysis: An introduction to its methodology.* Beverly Hills, CA: Sage.

Troutman, P. (1998). The key role of school administrators in multicultural education: Unlocking the future of diverse students. *National Forum of Educational Administration and Supervision Journal, 15*(1), 9-18.

Troutman, P., Powell, R., Jarchow, E., Fussell, L., & Imatt, D. (1999). *Educators healing racism.* Reston, VA: Association of Teacher Educators.

Wertsch, J. (1998). *Mind as action.* New York: Oxford University Press.

DIVISION IV

Effective Models for Alternative Programs in Teacher Education

OVERVIEW

R. Keith Hillkirk

R. Keith Hillkirk is Dean of the College of Education, Southern Illinois University, Carbondale. He earned his PhD in curriculum and instruction at Penn State University, University Park. He has taught at Penn State and Ohio University, where he also served as Assistant Dean for Teacher Education and Partnerships. His research interests include teacher mentoring and professional development, as well as school-university partnership development.

Alternative Certification

In the past 15 years, alternative certification has blossomed as a public policy initiative. In 1982, Virginia became the first state to implement a statewide alternative certification program (Cornett, 1990). Since then,

40 additional states and the District of Columbia have initiated a variety of alternative routes to teacher certification (Feistritzer, 1999). According to Feistritzer (1998), estimates indicate that more than 75,000 teachers have gained state-run certification through alternative routes, with thousands of additional teachers having graduated from university-sponsored alternative programs.

A review of the alternative certification literature reveals several key issues and trends:

- The term itself has multiple and sometimes contradictory meanings and applications.
- Motives and purposes for alternative certification initiatives vary and often reflect particular ideological beliefs about the nature of teaching and teacher education.
- Earlier alternative certification initiatives have been followed by a variety of responses by state boards and legislatures, regional collaboratives, local school districts, schools and colleges of education, as well as partnerships of these various players.
- Research findings on alternative certification are predictably mixed, given the complexities of comparing disparate teacher education programs with varying entry and exit requirements and the competing ideologies noted above.
- Contradictions aside, support for alternative certification is likely to continue into the foreseeable future, alongside growing efforts to professionalize teaching. These competing agendas will continue to fuel ongoing experimentation, study, and debate.

Defining Alternative Certification

Feistritzer (1994) distinguishes nine classifications of state-approved alternative certification programs, ranging from comprehensive programs that focus on attracting high-quality entrants and incorporate extensive mentoring and support, through programs with quick and easy entry, to states that rely solely on traditional 4-year college-based programs. Several other authors (Darling-Hammond, 1990; Tozer & Miretzky, 1999; Zumwalt, 1996) rely on the term *alternative routes to cer-*

tification to place emphasis where program differences lie—in the route the prospective teacher follows to gain certification.

Motives and Purposes for Alternative Certification

Fenstermacher (1990) suggests six plausible reasons for interest in alternative certification:

1. Recruiting bright and promising college graduates into teaching who for a variety of reasons do not follow traditional certification routes
2. Addressing teacher shortages and lessening reliance on emergency certifications
3. Breaking the monopoly of traditional teacher certification programs
4. Allowing politicians to make "political hay" with teacher preparation
5. Providing a mechanism for various outsiders, such as foundations and corporations, to become players in formulating teacher certification policy
6. Encouraging choice during an era of marketplace deregulation

Although some early calls for alternative certification routes during the 1980s were based on projections of widespread teacher shortages, broad shortages have not occurred (Feistritzer, 1998). What has followed are calls and support for alternative certification that derive from one or more of the above motives.

Haberman (1994) posits an additional rationale for alternative certification in contending that traditional teacher certification programs continue to fail urban schools and students. Citing the unique characteristics and needs of urban students, he argues for specially designed teacher preparation that screens, selects, and prepares candidates who can and will be successful in urban contexts.

These various motives and goals reflect the competing ideologies that continue to foster debate over other educational issues, such as school choice, vouchers, and testing, and increase the likelihood that alternative certification will be a hot topic for years to come.

Alternatives to Alternative Certification

Given the competing motives and goals of alternative certification routes, it is not surprising that a wide variety of programs has been developed. As Darling-Hammond (1990) points out, program requirements vary widely, from a handful of credits to the completion of a master's degree. In 1986, Wisniewski described a University of Tennessee, Knoxville, alternative program that focuses on selective admission by both university and public school partners and that emphasizes extensive mentoring by both partners as well. In contrast are programs like Teach for America that provide 8 weeks of intensive instruction prior to placing novice teachers full-time into their own classrooms.

Zumwalt (1991), who compares and contrasts the approaches taken by Los Angeles Unified School District, New Jersey, and Connecticut, which vary markedly in their entry requirements and expectations, concludes that the variety of alternative routes that have emerged places significant responsibility on teacher educators:

> If our aim is to prepare teachers better and to improve the education all students receive, then it is up to us as professionals to make the most of these experiments in teacher education—to use what we can from their experiences and to help shape future attempts to strengthen and diversify the teaching pool. (p. 92)

Zumwalt's call for scrutiny and ongoing search for best practice is echoed by other researchers, including Wisniewski (1986), Darling-Hammond (1990), and Cornett (1990).

Research on Alternative Certification

Researchers continue to explore diverse facets of alternative certification policy and practice. As noted above, Zumwalt (1991) has contrasted the varying approaches taken by different states and districts by analyzing the underlying motives that prompt different levels of reform and commitment. Darling-Hammond's (1990, 1994) analytical and comparative work uncovers the contradictions of continuing efforts to create quick and easy entry routes to teaching concurrent to professionalization efforts such as the National Board for Professional Teaching Standards. In particular, her critique of the Teach for America program (Darling-

Hammond, 1994) notes our tendencies as a nation to discount urban students and to disparage both the concept of a teaching knowledge base and the professionalization of teaching.

Other researchers have focused efforts on exploring particular assumptions that support either alternative or traditional approaches to teacher preparation. As noted above, Haberman (1994) argues that traditional programs have failed urban schools and students by overlooking the particular demands and needs of urban children and calls for specially designed recruitment, selection, and support mechanisms to ensure qualified teachers for urban schools. While pointing out that alternative routes have increased the numbers of minorities and males who enter teaching, Zumwalt (1996) notes that research findings on the quantity and quality of alternatively certified teachers continue to be mixed, with alternative routes proving to be neither "the panacea nor the disaster some predicted" (p. 41).

McDiarmid and Wilson (1991) examine the subject matter knowledge of alternative-route teachers and find reason to question the assumption underlying some alternative programs that an academic major in a discipline provides sufficient preparation for teaching.

Other studies that have compared traditionally and alternatively prepared teachers (Jelmberg, 1996; Miller, McKenna, & McKenna, 1998; Norton & Andersen, 1997) reflect the mixed results that Zumwalt (1996) has cited. Jelmberg's (1996) comparison of New Hampshire's traditional programs and the state's Alternative 4 certification program notes that 26 of 27 significant differences in his study favor the traditional programs reviewed, whereas Norton and Andersen's (1997) study of first-year teachers in 11 western states indicates that alternative-route teachers studied have a significant retention edge, compared with teachers from traditional programs. Miller, McKenna, and McKenna (1998) compared 70 alternatively prepared middle school teachers with an equal number of traditionally certified teachers and found no discernible differences in teaching behavior, student outcomes, or teacher self-perceptions.

The Future

If, as demographer Harold Hodgkinson has suggested, the best way to predict the future is to take a really close look at the present, alternative certification is going to be with us for a while. A recent issue of *Education*

Week (Bradley, 1999) reports that Minnesota has joined the ranks of states that allow public schools "to train teachers as they see fit" (p. 15).

A decade ago, Schlechty (1990) suggested that if teacher educators did not heed the demand to improve the quality of teacher preparation and effectiveness, two alternatives were likely: Either policymakers would "simply abandon the teacher education enterprise altogether or schools would be compelled to invent their own teacher education agencies and bypass institutions of higher education" (p. 63). During the 1990s, concrete examples of either of Schlechty's alternative paths continued or came to fruition through programs like Teach for America and district-based training models in Texas, California, New Jersey, and, most recently, Minnesota.

A third option continues to gain support and grows out of the work of groups like the Holmes Partnership and Goodlad's National Network for Educational Renewal. Certainly, these programs are diverse, but what they share in common is the belief that teachers and public schools, as well as teacher educators and schools and colleges of education, can and should bring complementary strengths to the challenging and complex task of preparing competent teachers for the nation's schools. School-university partnership models have been described by several authors, including Wisniewski (1986), Zumwalt (1991), and Darling-Hammond (1994). Although distinct from one another, quality partnership programs typically share several characteristics, including emphasis on sustained fieldwork with ongoing mentoring by skilled practitioners, integration of theory and practice, shared ownership and selection by public school and university faculty, and performance-based feedback and assessment.

Unclear as the future may be, Fenstermacher (1990) concludes his review of current and future trends in alternative certification with a prescient observation:

> Given that both traditional teacher education and alternative certification have some distance to travel in meeting the profound ends of teacher education, there may be value in ceasing to think of them as oppositional to one another. Perhaps the best course of action lies in blending these ideas, wherein the benefits of being close to practice are maintained, but so are the advantages of reflective and critical approaches to pedagogy. This blending of the best from both approaches to teacher preparation would require new models of teacher education. The invention and im-

plementation of such models may be one of the lasting benefits of alternative certification's challenge to traditional teacher education. (p. 182)

The three upcoming chapters provide additional examples of the ongoing research that is so important in enabling us to sort through the competing agendas and outcomes of alternative certification and teacher education reform. Stone and Mata's study (Chapter 10) focuses on California's class-size reduction mandate, which led to the creation of "fast-track" alternative certification routes. Implemented in 1996, the class-size initiative challenged districts to hire nearly 20,000 new teachers in a state that typically certifies 5,000 new teachers each year. Through questionnaires and interviews of both newly certified teachers and university supervisors, Stone and Mata examine the experiences of these novice teachers and describe steps that must be taken to provide the support and resources needed if class-size reduction is to be as effective as intended.

Examining the 10-year history of Project Promise, an alternative teacher education program at Colorado State University, Paccione, McWhorter, and Richburg (Chapter 11) compare Project Promise graduates with both traditional route and professional development school graduates. Their analysis lends credence to program characteristics like rigorous selection, cohort design, and heavy emphasis on coaching and mentoring.

Shen's review of alternative certification policy (Chapter 12) is derived from the 1993-94 Schools and Staffing Survey by the National Center for Education Statistics. Particularly noteworthy about Shen's analysis of demographics and trends in alternative and traditional teacher education is the large size of the sample examined—nearly 15,000 teachers.

References

Bradley, A. (1999). K-12 settings get chance to train future teachers in Minnesota. *Education Week, XVIII*(38), 15.

Cornett, L. M. (1990). Alternative certification: State policies in the SREB states. *Peabody Journal of Education, 67*(3), 55-83.

Darling-Hammond, L. (1990). Teaching and knowledge: Policy issues posed by alternative certification for teachers. *Peabody Journal of Education, 67*(3), 123-154.

202 RESEARCH ON MODELS FOR TEACHER EDUCATION

Darling-Hammond, L. (1994). Who will speak for the children? How Teach for America hurts urban schools and students. *Phi Delta Kappan, 76*(1), 21-34.

Feistritzer, C. E. (1994). The evolution of alternative teacher certification. *Educational Forum, 58*(2), 132-138.

Feistritzer, C. E. (1998). *Alternative teacher certification: An overview* [On-line]. Available: HYPERLINK http://www.ncei.com/Alt.Teacher.Cert.htm

Feistritzer, C. E. (1999, May 13). *Teacher quality and alternative certification programs.* Prepared statement before the House Education and the Workforce Committee Postsecondary Education, Training, and Life-Long Learning Subcommittee, Washington, DC.

Fenstermacher, G. D. (1990). The place of alternative certification in the education of teachers. *Peabody Journal of Education, 67*(3), 155-185.

Haberman, M. (1994). Preparing teachers for the real world of urban schools. *Educational Forum, 58*(2), 162-168.

Jelmberg, J. (1996). College-based teacher education versus state-sponsored alternative programs. *Journal of Teacher Education, 47*(1), 60-66.

McDiarmid, G. W., & Wilson, S. M. (1991). *Journal of Teacher Education, 42*(2), 93-103.

Miller, J. W., McKenna, M. C., & McKenna, B. A. (1998). A comparison of alternatively and traditionally prepared teachers. *Journal of Teacher Education, 49*(3), 165-176.

Norton, M. S., & Andersen, M. (1997). Alternative teacher certification: A study of first-year personnel in 11 western states. *Planning and Changing, 28*(4), 240-245.

Schlechty, P. C. (1990). *Reform in teacher education: A sociological view.* Washington, DC: American Association of Colleges for Teacher Education.

Tozer, S., & Miretzky, D. (1999). *Alternative routes: Teacher certification in Illinois.* Prepared for the Council of Chicago Area Deans of Education.

Wisniewski, R. (1986). Alternative programs and the reform of teacher education. *Action in Teacher Education, VIII*(2), 37-44.

Zumwalt, K. (1991). Alternative routes to teaching: Three alternative approaches. *Journal of Teacher Education, 42*(2), 83-92.

Zumwalt, K. (1996). Simple answers: Alternative teacher certification. *Educational Researcher, 25*(8), 40-42.

10 Fast-Track Teacher Education

Are We Adequately Preparing Teachers
for California's Class-Size Reduction?

Bernice Stone

Susana Mata

Bernice Stone is a Professor in the Department of Curriculum, Teaching, and Educational Technology at California State University, Fresno. Her current research interests include portfolio assessment for preservice and in-service teachers, portfolio evaluation in higher education, preservice teacher education, and beginning teacher support and assistance.

Susana Mata is an Associate Professor in the Department of Curriculum, Teaching, and Educational Technology at California State University, Fresno (CSUF). Her current research interests include sociology of education, preservice teacher education, and educational program evaluation. She directs the Center for Complex Instruction at CSUF.

ABSTRACT

Forced to hire 20,000 teachers as a result of California's sudden class-size reduction, school districts pressured universities for "fast track" certification. First-year teachers prepared in California State University, Fresno's alternative certification

203

program during 1996-97 completed questionnaires and participated in structured interviews. University supervisors were
interviewed. Results indicated that first-year teachers, particularly from fast-track preparation programs, needed a great deal
of support and assistance. Support was not uniformly supplied, however, by either the school districts or the university
supervisors. Support and assistance were most often supplied
by uncompensated classroom teachers at the school sites,
rather than by mentor teachers who were compensated and
assigned by the districts. If legislatively mandated political
decisions are imposed on school districts, then the state must
provide the necessary organizational support and resources.
Class-size reduction alone will not improve achievement but
should be only one part of a total effort to improve education.

Introduction

The California state-initiated Class-Size Reduction Program, which
occurred suddenly during the summer of 1996, caused school district
administrators to panic and found teacher educators unprepared for the
demand for teachers. To implement fully the K-3 Class-Size Reduction,
California's schools would need to add nearly 20,000 teachers. Only 5,000
are typically credentialed by the state each year. District recruiters lured
teachers from other districts, other states, and even Mexico, as well as
from the ranks of temporaries, retirees, and substitutes.

Large urban districts with poor minority populations quickly ran out
of qualified applicants and were forced to fill the gap with novices, students, and other trainees. Legislation was rushed through the state legislature in late summer to make it easier for districts to start their own
internship programs. College graduates who had passed the state's
teacher qualifying examination, CBEST (a test of basic reading, writing,
and mathematics skills), earned emergency credentials after 120 hours,
or roughly 3 weeks, of "on-the-job" training.

To accommodate school districts in the Fresno area of California's
large central valley, California State University, Fresno (CSUF), provided
alternative certification by increasing the numbers in its intern program.
Interns were interviewed and carefully screened to ensure that they had

passed the appropriate tests, had some classroom experience, were mature, and had good interpersonal skills. Armed with emergency credentials, students entered classrooms as new teachers while the university hastily provided course work and supervision for them during the summer months and the fall semester. In addition, students who had completed their course work and initial student teaching during the fall semester obtained emergency credentials and began as first-year teachers in January, following only 6 weeks of "fast track" final student teaching instead of the usual 15 weeks. University faculty supervised and offered workshops and seminars for these two groups of beginning teachers, interns, and fast-track student teachers. School districts agreed that these beginning teachers would also receive assistance and support from districts and schools where they were teaching.

At the end of the spring semester, June 1997, a questionnaire was distributed to a representative group of novice teachers who had been part of the CSUF alternative certification program (interns and fast-track student teachers) to gather information on their beginning teaching experience. Interviews were held with a sample of both beginning teachers and university supervisors.

This study had four major purposes: (a) to identify the concerns, problems, and specific needs of these first-year teachers from alternative preparation programs; (b) to gather information on the assistance and support provided for them by the university and school districts; (c) to help prevent new teacher attrition; and (d) to help improve the teaching knowledge and skills of new teachers, which directly affect student achievement.

The Research Questions

1. What were the specific needs of these beginning teachers?
2. What kinds of assistance and support were provided for them by the university, the schools, and the school districts?
3. What kinds of assistance and support did they think they needed that were not provided?
4. Which services, in-service workshops, and personnel did the teachers find most helpful during their beginning teaching experience?

5. What kinds of course work, assistance, and supervision provided by the university did the new teachers believe would have contributed positively to their beginning teaching experience?

Literature Review

Class-Size Reduction and the Demand for New Teachers

The California Legislative Analyst's Office in 1997 estimated that the Class-Size Reduction Program resulted in the hiring of 18,400 additional teachers in the 1996-97 school year. The program could require about 7,800 more teachers in 1997-98 if it operated under the same provisions in its second year and approached full implementation. Even without class-size reduction, the state would need an additional 41,500 teachers in the next decade, or about 4,150 teachers per year just to accommodate enrollment growth. An even greater long-term demand for teachers could come as a result of retirements and attrition. In 1995 alone, 7,100 certificated employees retired. With half of California's teachers now over age 45—and one out of every six teachers over age 55—it is logical to assume that retirements will increase. In addition, data indicate that about half of all new teachers leave the profession after less than a year. In California, attrition is estimated at between 11,000 and 15,000 teachers annually.

Complicating the problem even further is the increase in the use of noncredentialed teachers because of these shortages. The benefits of reducing class size can be lost if not implemented properly (Mitchell & Beach, 1990). In reducing class size, California might be lowering the quality of teaching. Nearly two thirds of the new hires have little or no teaching experience, and nearly one fourth of all teachers in California public schools are teaching without proper credentials. Michael Kirst, Stanford University professor, believes that the quality of many new hires is suspect and that the schools may be stuck with bad teachers for many years. Urban schools are suffering most because it is difficult to lure new teachers to these schools, and many of their best veterans are leaving to teach in higher paying and less stressful suburbs (Toch & Streisand, 1997).

Although students are getting more attention, new teachers are getting less. The California State University System, which trains 60% of the state's teachers, may be offering courses to credential teachers over the

Internet through a plan for a virtual university. If this proposal is accepted, teachers-in-training will be able to earn a semester's course credit by using a textbook and a 4 ½-hour video of classroom techniques.

Research on Class-Size Reduction

The California Research Bureau (Illig, 1996) examined the research literature on the relationship between class size and student achievement and the Tennessee class-size demonstration project, Project STAR (Egelson, Harmon, & Achilles, 1996). It found that classes must be smaller than 15 students and that class size should be reduced in kindergarten and first grade to have the greatest effect. It is questionable whether reduction in class size without other education reforms will produce consistent improvements.

Analysts have concerns about whether other reforms, such as curriculum and teaching style changes and quality improvement mechanisms, should accompany smaller classes to ensure consistent achievement gains. In addition, the money is wasted if classes get smaller but teachers do not adjust their styles and continue to use large-class techniques such as relying on textbooks instead of working directly with students. Most researchers believe that training in small-class teaching techniques is an important component of reducing class size. A study of 15 poorly performing elementary schools in Austin, Texas, found that only two schools showed improvement with class-size reduction (Sadowski, 1995). They adopted new curricula; changed to teaching methods focused on individual attention; mainstreamed students with disabilities into the regular classroom; and increased parental involvement and initiated health services that allowed many students their first trip to a physician. Harvard economist Richard Murnane (Murnane & Levy, 1996) stated that class-size reduction does help, but only in schools able to use the resources effectively. Illig (1996) suggested that the state legislature may wish to give schools flexibility to use their class-size reduction funds to test other strategies, such as individual tutoring programs.

If the objective is to improve student achievement, then other strategies must be included, such as professional development, along with class-size reduction. Slavin (1990) suggested that "evidence does exist that smaller is better. . . . [I]t's important to emphasize, additionally, the need to choose effective professional development strategies for teachers who take on these new assignments." Star Project researcher Achilles (1996) stated, "The teacher is important. Each pupil's learning depends upon the teacher." Michael Kirst (California Education Policy Seminar, 1996) stated, "My underlying concern is, if you have poor (teacher) qualifications, what does that do? Are you better off with a poor teacher with 20 students or a really good teacher with 30? The research doesn't tell you that."

Because smaller classes and more teachers require more classrooms than California schools can currently provide, hundreds of schools have given up libraries, science labs, preschool, and parent education programs for lack of space. In addition, many crowded inner-city schools are unable to reduce class sizes fully. The richer suburban school systems, however, are able to reduce class sizes for a greater percentage of their students. RAND Corporation reached a similar conclusion: Smaller classes benefit students from low-income families most, middle-class students less, and those from upper-income backgrounds least of all.

Experts emphasize that it makes more sense and is more cost-effective to reduce class size only for certain subjects, such as reading. Slavin (1990) stated that California could have improved instruction in its elementary schools dramatically for a fraction of the money it has spent simply by hiring and carefully training retired teachers and other part-timers as reading instructors to reduce the size of classes during the time reading is taught. Using smaller classes only for specific subjects allows money to be spent on other reforms that could produce greater increases in student achievement, such as high-quality teacher training and peer tutoring.

Concerns and Problems of Beginning Teachers

Currently, one of the most serious problems of the teaching profession is the lack of a formal induction process, a gradual transition from student teacher to teacher. First-year teachers are expected to do exactly the same job as a 20-year veteran teacher, and administrators expect this new teacher to take on the total responsibility of the classroom without any formal support and assistance. Districts usually provide a brief orientation and a mentor teacher to help. But this is not uniformly provided by all schools. Also, teachers spend the majority of their day isolated from other teachers, so it is not possible for them to receive ongoing assistance from their more experienced peers. Studies of the concerns and problems of beginning teachers (Huling-Austin, 1990) indicate that they are overwhelmed by the realities of their responsibilities, frequently experience panic, often engage in stressful trial-and-error periods, and count survival as their primary goal.

Research has well documented the fact that without support and assistance, many potentially good teachers are discouraged and leave teaching. Schlechty and Vance (1983) estimated that approximately 30% of beginning teachers leave the profession during their first 2 years and that, of all beginning teachers who enter the profession, 40% to 50% leave during the first 7 years.

A synthesis of the research on teacher induction programs and practices by Huling-Austin (1988) reported four significant findings: (a) the need for flexibility in induction programs, personalizing and individualizing the support to meet the needs of specific beginning teachers; (b) the important role of the support teacher, reported by beginning teachers as the most helpful aspect of the program; (c) the importance of placement in promoting beginning teacher success—difficult, challenging, and inappropriate assignments frequently lead to failure for new teachers; and (d) the need to educate the profession and the public about induction, a pressing need for supporting first-year teachers.

Current Induction Programs

By 1995-96, California had implemented 30 Beginning Teacher Support and Assessment (BTSA) programs across the state. Each program offered beginning teachers support from experienced colleagues at their school sites. Formative assessments that helped beginning teachers assess and improve their own teaching were also included. The state's SB 1422 advisory panel and the California Commission on Teacher Credentialing (CTC) proposed that all new teachers participate in an "induction" program. The panel pointed to BTSA as a successful model and urged that sufficient resources be provided for an induction program for all districts.

Methods

The population for this study comprised 37 new teachers, both interns and teachers with limited teacher preparation and teaching experience who began their first full-time teaching assignment during the fall and winter of 1996-97. They were employed in elementary schools, Grades K-6, that had low-income, highly diverse populations and with 25% to 50% of students designated as limited or non-English speaking.

In June 1997, a questionnaire with both closed and open-ended questions was distributed, and structured interviews were conducted with a sample of teachers and university supervisors. Results were analyzed by using both quantitative and qualitative methods. Using ethnographic procedures designed specifically for the analysis of text-based qualitative data, the researchers systematically analyzed the open-ended questions and interviews to determine categories and relevance to the research questions. To ensure validity, standard triangulation procedures were used. Several data sources, two data collectors, and two researchers to analyze data were involved in the project.

Results

Our exploratory study revealed many interesting results. The common understanding is that the majority of fast-track teachers have little or no teacher education preparation before entering the classroom. In our sample, however, 71% of beginning teachers reported they had completed most of their university course work before entering their own classrooms; 12% reported they had no student teaching experience; and 59% reported they had completed course work and 6 weeks of initial student teaching. The majority of students in the study were at the point of completing their credential but had not completed their 15 weeks of full-time student teaching and were lacking some course work. All these students were teaching with only emergency credentials.

Fast-track beginning teachers were placed in schools with highly diverse student populations (94%), low socioeconomic levels (88%), and a high number of limited-English or non-English-proficient students (82%). Only 35% of beginning teachers taught in middle socioeconomic schools. Students in highly diverse, low-income schools require skilled, well-trained teachers to meet their needs. These new teachers were placed in particularly challenging situations, which added to the other typical problems of beginning teachers.

A high level of linguistic heterogeneity existed in each of their classrooms. Over half (59%) of beginning teachers reported that 50% of students in their classrooms were limited- or non-English-speaking; only 18% reported that a quarter (25%) of their students were limited- or non-English-speaking; and almost a third (29%) reported that 10% or less of their students were limited- or non-English-speaking. Developing a specific instructional program that incorporates bilingual/bicultural methodologies and strategies was another problem for these new teachers.

Research Questions/Responses
From Objective Questions

1. *What were the specific needs of these beginning teachers?* Beginning teachers ranked their needs as the following: (1) curriculum development, (2) classroom materials and resources, (3) teaching strategies, (4) dealing with difficult students, and (5) classroom management and feedback on their teaching from an observer.

2. *What kinds of assistance and support were provided for them by the university, the schools, and the school districts?* Our findings suggest that fellow teachers provided the most support for beginning teachers. Most beginning teachers reported that mentor teachers (76%) and grade-level meetings (65%) provided the most support services for them at their school sites. Only 53% reported that they were assigned a grade-level teacher or resource teacher at their schools. Interestingly, only 35% had beginning teacher workshops or in-services to assist them during their first year of teaching. Only 24% had a teacher specifically assigned to them as a helper. Sometimes mentor teachers who were assigned to novices were located at another school site, which prevented them from providing frequent assistance and support. Findings suggest that fast-track teachers did not receive adequate support and assistance at school sites.

3. *What kinds of assistance and support did they believe they needed that were not provided?* New teachers stated that the following areas of support and assistance were needed but not provided:

(a) *Record keeping, paperwork, and assessment,* such as grading and report card documentation, reading inventories, and student portfolios

(b) *Curriculum development and materials,* such as clear definitions of expectations of what to teach, how to deal with the wide range of linguistic and academic abilities of students, how to remediate and provide services to varied abilities without appropriate materials or textbooks, help with curriculum development and materials, types of supplies needed to be purchased by first-year teacher, time to find resources and prepare materials, and preparing for class field trips

(c) *Teaching strategies,* such as team teaching with another experienced teacher to share lesson plans and curriculum materials, short cuts, real-world methods, more feedback and constructive criticism from university supervisors

(d) *Classroom management strategies,* such as support from school administration regarding discipline, training in conflict management

(e) *Mentoring,* such as identifying cooperating teacher at the beginning of the year who knows and is willing to assist, more classroom visits from principal with feedback, more contact with mentor teacher

Beginning teachers need many different types of assistance and support. Although most teachers had covered these areas in their university course work, they still needed reinforcement and application of concepts and theories to the real world of teaching. These findings suggest the need for more and better integration of theory and practice at the university.

4. *Which services, in-service workshops, and personnel did the teachers find most helpful during their beginning teaching experience?* Other teachers in the school were ranked as the most helpful for the beginning teacher. Ranked second were university supervisors, and third were other teachers at the same grade level. Other teachers were ranked above resource teachers, mentor teachers, principals, workshops, in-services, and conferences as being most helpful. This finding suggests that other sources of support are not providing the kind of help that beginning teachers need during the crucial first year. More workshops and in-service training do not provide the kind of practical, "day-to-day" help these teachers need.

5. *What kinds of course work, assistance, and supervision provided by the university did the new teachers believe would have contributed positively to their beginning teaching experience?* Beginning teachers do not always value their theoretical university course work. At this point in their careers, they feel strongly the need for practical and applicable information and strategies. Classroom management course work, more help on teaching reading and phonics, more exposure to the classroom, hands-on training and expectations for teachers, materials development, record keeping, assessment, daily planning using district curriculum and grade-level requirements, more observations and feedback, time management, developing centers, and observations of other teachers were all mentioned as needs by new teachers. Most important, they identified the need for a rich, realistic teaching experience in the classroom. More classroom experience, along with course work, can provide the opportunity to bridge theory and practice and to apply new teaching concepts. They seem to need a more hands-on orientation to the real world of teaching during their final student teaching experience. Unfortunately, many fast-track teachers did not experience final student teaching at all.

Analysis of Open-Ended Questions and Interviews

Analysis of the open-ended questions and structured interviews generally supported the responses to the objective questions. The major categories addressed and the typical teacher comments that represent these categories are listed below:

1. *Lack of mentor teacher support on-site.*
   - "I would have liked to have contact with a mentor teacher. The mentor teacher assigned to me was not on my campus, and there was zero contact."
   - "My mentor was supposed to be there for questions and support, but that didn't happen."
   - "Mentor teacher lost my name and number . . . mentor teachers need to be monitored and held accountable."
   - "Need a mentor teacher on site to help with curriculum development and materials."

2. *Support from fellow teachers at the school and on-site mentors provided most valuable assistance and support.*
   - "My fellow teachers on campus have contributed most to my professional development."
   - "The teacher next door was very patient and thorough in telling me what I need to know. . . . [H]owever, this was not always well planned or organized."
   - "We had no formal time to meet or prepare . . . could have been improved."

3. *Needed more information on specific procedures, paperwork, issues in running a classroom.*
   - "Frustrating because she [mentor teacher] was late in passing on information she thought I would know, i.e., protocol for field trip supervision . . . many ideas and activities were not passed on so I could use them in the classroom."
   - "I think the staff and administration assumed that I knew more than I did . . . until I made a mistake."
   - "How to handle the immense amount of paperwork."

4. *University needs to provide a more realistic preparation for teachers with more hands-on field experience.*
   - "Teach about the 'little' things that teachers don't know until they start teaching, i.e., field trip procedures, cum folders, etc."
   - "Paperwork 101 would have helped a lot."
   - "More daily planning. . . . [I]t was really challenging to devise a daily plan on my own."
   - "We learned about how students learn but little about how teachers teach."

Supervisors reported that they were aware the new teachers were not getting the assistance and support they needed or the feedback they required. Unfortunately, the university is limited by a specific supervisory load, which requires supervisors to carry a large number of students who are often situated in schools quite a distance apart. Because beginning teachers were weighted the same as student teachers, supervisors did not have the time to provide *quality* assistance for them, although their needs were much greater than those of student teachers. Despite these university-imposed restrictions, some supervisors spent a great deal of extra time and effort, without compensation, to help beginning teachers who were struggling.

Implications and Conclusions

The results of this study indicate that beginning teachers, particularly from fast-track preparation programs, need a great deal of support and assistance during their first year of teaching. Unfortunately, this support is not uniform throughout the schools and is often supplied by patient, overworked classroom teachers at the school site, rather than by mentor teachers who are compensated by the state and assigned to beginning teachers by the district. Novice teachers need on-site support persons who are specifically assigned by the principal to the new teachers to provide the essential information they need to be successful. In addition, a formal time should be set aside to deal with all the questions and problems that arise and not relegated to the lunch table or while passing in the hall.

Although districts often provide district orientations, schools need in-depth orientation at the site for the new teachers, and a beginning teacher's handbook would be invaluable. University supervisors should have more time to work with beginning teachers. Universities also need to provide hands-on, realistic preparation programs more relevant to current classrooms. Students should be working in classrooms beginning in their freshman year.

Implementation of California's Class-Size Reduction Program occurred with no formal support provided for the large numbers of beginning teachers who were hired. Our results indicate that uncompensated teachers at the school sites provided the majority of support and assistance identified as most helpful and needed by the beginning teachers in our study. It appears that the onus of responsibility for supporting this class-size reduction may have fallen on the overburdened shoulders of classroom teachers. Legislatively mandated political decisions should not be unfairly imposed on school sites without careful consideration for the necessary organizational support and resources. If veteran teachers are called on to support new teachers, then administrators must provide the time and the resources.

If California plans to use fast-track alternative preparation programs to relieve the severe teacher shortage, the state must strengthen district and school support through the Beginning Teacher Support and Assistance (BTSA) program for all new teachers. In addition, principals must take a stronger role in the support process to ensure that beginning teachers are actually getting the help they need.

Class-size reduction and teacher support must go together. Simply putting students into smaller classes does not ensure achievement. Instruction must be conducted differently, and schools must support teachers to do this. All new teachers, but especially those with emergency credentials, require help. The BTSA program can provide constructive assistance to beginning teachers. New teachers need to be paired with strong veterans. First-year teachers consider mentors and support teachers to be the most helpful aspect of new teacher support. Schools need to plan creatively and comprehensively, making small class size only part of a bigger effort to improve instruction in the classroom.

Universities must also take a stronger role in providing appropriate support and assistance for novice teachers by integrating theory and practice and earlier field experiences. Students who are selected to enter fast-track alternative preparation programs must also meet specific criteria and eligibility requirements. Careful selection of candidates might help avoid ineffective, marginal teachers as well as attrition. In addition, a smaller ratio of interns/beginning teachers to supervisors would allow for more time with new teachers to provide needed support.

Most important is the political climate of the state. As a result of the class-size reduction, the then Republican Governor Wilson's approval ratings were the highest he had enjoyed. Even the Democrats were highly supportive, and the teachers' unions were silenced by the fact that 90% of their members believed that the class cuts had improved instruction. Parents are highly supportive because they believe that its funding is money that will go directly into the classroom. Class-size reduction may be inefficient and not cost-effective in terms of student achievement, but politically it is extremely popular. If California's current governor and legislature are truly dedicated to education, as they claim, then they need to take into consideration the complex problems facing education today. Professional development, beginning teacher support, and a variety of educational reforms are also needed. It is not enough to reduce class size. An understanding and willingness on the part of politicians to support

California education *totally* is needed to make a substantial impact on the achievement of California's children.

References

Achilles, C. (1996, February). Response: Students achieve more in smaller classes. *Educational Leadership.*

California Education Policy Seminar & California State University Institute for Education Reform. (1996, November). *Is less more? Exploring California's class-size reduction initiative.* Sacramento: Authors.

Egelson, P., Harmon, P., & Achilles, C. M. (1996). Does class size make a difference? *South Eastern Regional Vision for Education.* Greensboro: University of North Carolina School of Education.

Huling-Austin, L. (1988). A synthesis of research on teacher induction programs and practices. *Centering Teacher Education, 6*(1), 19-28.

Huling-Austin, L. (1990). Teacher induction programs and internships. In W. R. Houston (Ed.), *Handbook of research on teacher education* (pp. 535-548). New York: Macmillan.

Illig, D. C. (1996, June). *Reducing class size: A review of the literature and options for consideration.* Sacramento: California Research Bureau, California State Library.

Mitchell, D. E., & Beach, S. A. (1990). *How changing class size affects classrooms and students.* San Francisco: Far West Laboratory for Educational Research and Development.

Murnane, R. J., & Levy, F. (1996, September 11). Why money matters sometimes. *Education Week, 48,* 36-37.

Sadowski, M. (1995, March/April). The numbers game yields simplistic answers on the link between spending and outcomes. *Harvard Education Letter.*

Schlechty, P., & Vance, V. (1983). Recruitment, selection, and retention: The shape of the teaching force. *Elementary School Journal, 83*(4), 469-487.

Slavin, R. (1990, Fall). Class size and student achievement: Is smaller better? *Contemporary Education.*

Toch, T., & Streisand, B. (1997, October 13). Does class size matter? *U.S. News & World Report.*

11 Ten Years on the Fast Track

*Effective Teacher Preparation for
Nontraditional Candidates*

Angela V. Paccione

Barbara A. McWhorter

Robert W. Richburg

Angela V. Paccione is Assistant Professor in the School of Education
at Colorado State University, Fort Collins, and Associate Director of
Project Promise.

Barbara A. McWhorter is Assistant Professor at Colorado State University, Fort Collins, and Director of Project Promise.

Robert W. Richburg is Professor at Colorado State University, Fort
Collins, and Founder of Project Promise.

ABSTRACT

This chapter describes an experimental teacher preparation program for nontraditional, postbaccalaureate students.
The program, Project Promise, is compared with the traditional
licensure route and with the professional development school
(PDS) model. Data compiled from three studies show that the

experimental model surpasses both the traditional and the PDS approach in nearly all measures of program effectiveness. Students who completed the Project Promise program were working in schools at significantly higher rates than students who completed the traditional program. In addition, Project Promise program completers remained in teaching at significantly higher rates than traditional program completers. On measures of satisfaction in the areas of teaching strategies, diversity, and technology, Project Promise program completers rated their preparation significantly higher than traditional program completers rated their preparation. Finally, principals supervising first-year teachers reported that Project Promise first-year teachers were better prepared than other first-year teachers on all 28 items measured.

Introduction

Current research aimed at improving the condition of teacher education has called for increasing the approaches to teacher preparation (National Commission on Teaching and America's Future, 1996). In particular, reformers have encouraged the development of programs designed specifically for the nontraditional teacher candidate. Still, slightly more than 200 accredited universities within the United States have developed programs that offer postbaccalaureate or alternative routes to becoming an educator (National Commission on Teaching and America's Future, 1996).

For the past 10 years, Project Promise has been preparing nontraditional teacher education candidates in a comprehensive, master's level, fast-track program at Colorado State University. The program has been highly successful in preparing exceptional secondary teachers who are sought after by school districts all over the state. In 1992, Project Promise was recognized as a "Program of Excellence" by the Colorado Commission on Higher Education. This occasion marked the first time that a teacher education program had ever received this distinction. In addition, during a 1996 National Council for Accreditation of Teacher Education (NCATE) review of the teacher licensure programs at Colorado State University, Project Promise was designated an "Exemplary Program" within the School of Education. Recent research has demonstrated that the Project Promise approach excels beyond the traditional approach and the professional development school (PDS) approach to teacher preparation. Additional research and 10 years of experience in preparing nontraditional candidates serve as the foundation for this chapter on the effectiveness of the Project Promise model.

Description of the Program

We are faced with how to begin unimprisoning ourselves from a way of thinking that does not allow us to raise and think through this question: Can we come up with new ways of selecting and preparing educators that, over time, would decrease the incidence of educational problems, reducing thereby the time, energy, and waste attendant on the repair problem (Sarason, 1993, p. 58)?

Project Promise is designed exclusively for secondary teacher licensure. It begins with tremendous attention to the selection of participants. A cohort of 20 teacher candidates are selected through a rigorous process that includes a preliminary interview, a written application, and a series of interviews using a modification of the Teacher Perceiver Instrument developed by Selection Research Incorporated (SRI). The Project Promise applicant pool often exceeds 200 individuals who are post-baccalaureate, nontraditional students intent on making a career change.

Once a cohesive student cohort is established, a comprehensive curriculum is taught in "chunks" interspersed with field experiences. University instructors who deliver the curriculum also supervise the field experiences. A seamless integration of theory and practice is coupled with consistency of instruction and supervision. This establishes a coherent articulation of what it means to be a teacher.

The comprehensive curriculum provides for five field experiences in a variety of social-cultural environments. Students complete a week-long student teaching experience in both rural and urban settings, two long-term (10 weeks each) student-teaching experiences in suburban junior and senior high schools, and a service learning week during which students self-select a special population with which to work. The final 2 weeks of the program culminate with the course Philosophy of Education. Because of their extensive exposure to the different contexts of schooling, students are able to engage in scholarly dialogue about issues of school reform as they develop their own philosophy of education. In addition, students are able to make educated decisions regarding where to take a teaching position. Having worked in a variety of contexts, they are better able to judge in which setting they will be most successful.

Major Program Components

There are several reasons why Project Promise has been able to make such progress in creating a gestalt in teacher preparation for the adult learner: cohort development, innovative curriculum, multiple field experiences, specialized training, teacher/scholars, and intensive supervision and feedback.

Cohort Design

The Project Promise faculty attempts to achieve a culturally diverse cohort that is also gender balanced. The average candidate is 33 years old, has a grade point average of 3.12, and has been in a prior occupation for 7 years. One in three will already have earned an advanced degree. One in three will be married and have children. All will be motivated to become superior teachers after highly successful experiences in their former occupations. Like most adult learners, typical Project Promise students are eager for field experiences in which they are able to implement the instruction and theory they have received in course work. They are pleased that they do not have to wait for a capstone experience at the end of three semesters of instruction before they are student teaching.

Students also recognize the commitment made on the part of the faculty who spend many more contact hours with students than most other professors on campus. A faculty member with a nine-credit teaching load per semester spends approximately 270 contact hours with students over a 9-month teaching contract. In comparison, the Project Promise faculty member spends more than 1,000 contact hours with students in the classroom and many more hours during field experience supervision (Richburg, Knox, Carson, & McWhorter, 1996). The mutual commitment and investment made on the part of students and faculty help create an environment in which everyone is invested in the others' success.

In addition to the emphasis placed on developing a mutually invested cohort, the program encourages students to acquire the skills of being a reflective practitioner. Using the scholarship on reflective practice (Grant & Zeichner, 1984; Schön, 1987), students are required to maintain reflective journals. The journals are used to examine the practices they observe and those they employ. Weekly seminars also assist in developing a reflective perspective and facilitating the synergy of the cohort.

Knowledge Base

Whereas those who call for reform in teacher education identify the lack of subject area expertise as a significant concern (National Commission on Teaching and America's Future, 1996), Project Promise candidates typically have advanced degrees in their content areas. In addition, years of employment in the content areas allow Project Promise candidates to integrate school-to-work principles and practices into their content area specializations. The ability of midcareer teacher candidates to infuse the curriculum with a school-to-work focus is especially valuable for preparing students for the world of work and makes the curriculum relevant and meaningful for secondary students.

The pedagogical knowledge base is a combination of NCATE standards, Colorado state standards for educators, and current research in best pedagogical practice. Program instructors never teach about a strategy without modeling the strategy; for example, cooperative learning is used to teach cooperative learning, and lessons are planned to demonstrate the mastery lesson planning model (Hunter, 1994).

Candidates also receive preparation in multicultural education, exceptionality, and learner characteristics, including learning styles, multiple intelligences, and developmentally appropriate instruction. Students participate in a Diversity Institute during which complete immersion in different cultures is facilitated. Throughout the program, students also receive specialized training in teaching the at-risk student, educational uses of technology, and peer mediation. These specialized trainings result in the increased marketability of program completers.

Theory Into Practice

To accommodate the needs of adult learners, Project Promise students spend 3 to 7 weeks receiving classroom instruction in chunks that are followed by short- or long-term field experiences. The integration of theory and practice affords students the opportunity to apply immediately in the secondary classroom the theories and strategies learned in the Project Promise classroom. Students practice the instruction through a variety of field experiences or "authentic activities" related to teacher decision making. Authentic activity involves situations in which students have to think and act for themselves (Resnick, 1987). For adult learners, experience is the essence of learning; therefore, authentic activity is more instrumental to the adult learning process and more attractive when considering instructional programs. The pattern of theory interspersed with practice creates an optimal learning environment for the adult learner (Wilson, 1993).

Contextual Learning

Immersion in a variety of educational settings is a program feature facilitated through field experiences. Field experiences amount to 23 weeks of hands-on experience in secondary schools. The five field experiences are in five different educational contexts: rural, urban, suburban junior high/middle school, senior high school, and community agencies. Students learn to understand the contextual nature of the teaching profession (Darling-Hammond, 1996; Darling-Hammond & Sclan, 1996). Hopkins (1995) said, "Teaching is a demanding, complex activity that requires deliberate thought based upon careful analyses of situational variables. The only places that can offer preservice teachers the opportunity to develop these analytical skills are field experience sites" (p. 8).

The rural field experience provides teacher candidates with their first teaching experience in an environment that is typically nonthreatening, with students who are typically more respectful of adults, and in a community that is typically highly invested in the school. A 2-week, full-time instructional session follows the rural experience. Based on the faculty assessment of teacher candidates' performance in the rural teaching experience, the curriculum for the 2-week session may include remediation of key pedagogical principles. Following the 2-week session, candidates continue their placement with the master teacher with whom they began the academic school year and the Wednesday experiences in a long-term (10-week) student teaching assignment. Weekly supervision by program faculty, the cooperating teacher, and cohort peers provides approximately four evaluations with written feedback each week.

Coaching and reflective learning are keys to candidate success. The Project Promise faculty supervise all student teaching experiences, creating a connection between classroom instruction and student teaching. In contrast with traditional programs, in which student teachers receive an average of six or seven visits from the university supervisor (Darling-Hammond, 1996), a Project Promise candidate receives 25 to 30 visits over the duration of the program. The importance of these interactions is not lost on those calling for reform in teacher preparation. Schlechty (1990) has stated that "teacher educators seem less aware that the frequency of interaction between supervisor and student teacher is at least as powerful a determinant of the effectiveness of supervision as are the skills and procedures used by the supervisor" (p. 2).

Following the middle school/junior high school student teaching field experience, program students return to the Project Promise classroom for a 3-week Diversity Institute. During this instructional time, students are instructed in the more sophisticated knowledge of multicultural education, inclusion, and exceptionality. In addition, students are immersed in communities that work with exceptional students. The institute culminates in a week-long immersion experience in an urban setting. Teacher candidates live and teach in inner-city Denver for a week in an experience that resembles the rural immersion experience. In addition to teaching in the urban schools, Project Promise students work closely with an after-school antigang intervention program and spend a day interacting with incarcerated students at a youth correctional facility.

A 10-week student teaching placement follows the urban immersion experience. This second long-term student teaching placement is typically in a suburban senior high school. On completion of the senior high student teaching placement, candidates return to the Project Promise classroom for additional instruction that focuses on the nature and practice of integrating service learning activities into the secondary curriculum. Students then engage in a week-long service learning field experience during which each candidate self-selects a special population with which to conduct service learning activities.

The five distinct field experiences provide candidates with exposure to the contextual nature of teaching and learning. In addition, students are made aware of the educational inequities that exist in some communities. A goal of the program is to facilitate the success of the teacher candidate. This is accomplished as candidates are more informed of the context within which they are better suited to teach and succeed as educators.

Evidence of Effectiveness

The Project Promise teacher candidate is significantly better prepared than other licensure approach candidates to assume the duties of a professional educator. In addition to the research indicating that older individuals have the necessary maturity, expertise, and life experience suited for classroom teaching (Eifler & Potthoff, 1998; Haberman, 1992), the comprehensive curriculum and varied field experiences of the Project Promise program contribute to the effectiveness of this model. Anecdotal evidence suggesting the superiority of this model abounds. The following three studies provide empirical evidence of its effectiveness.

Cost-Benefit Study

A cost-benefit analysis was conducted comparing the innovative, experimental Project Promise program with the traditional teacher licensure program at Colorado State University. The enhanced training and extensive faculty-student contact of the Project Promise model requires more faculty time and is more costly than conventional teacher preparation programs. This study sought to determine how much more than a traditional program the Project Promise program costs and whether the expense leads to better outcomes (Richburg, Penna, McWhorter, Paccione, & Knox, 1996).

The year 1993-94 was chosen to explore the costs and benefits of the two programs: Project Promise and the general licensure program at Colorado State University. Using data from both programs, researchers analyzed the employability of the graduates, as well as attrition from the teaching profession for a 2-year period following program completion. A random sample of equivalent size and content area specialization was drawn from seniors in the general licensure program. A second random sample of equivalent size and content area specialization was drawn from postbaccalaureate students in the general licensure program. Both random samples from the general licensure program were combined for cost comparisons with the Project Promise data.

Costs calculated from the random samples and the Project Promise program included (a) faculty costs, (b) travel costs related to student teacher supervision, and (c) facility usage costs. Instructor costs in the general licensure program amounted to $1,445 per student. This figure pales in comparison with the Project Promise instructor costs, which amounted to $6,597 per student. Two factors play major roles in the staggering difference in instructor costs: (a) The general program maintains enrollments of 45 to more than 100 students in sophomore- and junior-level classes, and (b) nearly every section of teacher licensure classes in the general program is taught by an instructor- or assistant professor–level teacher. The Project Promise program, in contrast, enrolls an average of 17 students, and over half of the instructor costs are attributable to the former director's full professor salary. Additional staffing costs are incurred because Project Promise employs a "teacher-scholar" from the public schools to provide a contemporary perspective in curricular instruction while pursuing an advanced degree. The teacher-scholar salary is typically significantly higher than instructor-level salaries at the university.

Project Promise faculty costs were also increased because the program is offered at the graduate level, whereas the general program is offered at the undergraduate level. To account for the credit hour difference, the Project Promise costs should be decreased by 18%, or $1,204. As Table 11.1 shows, each program has benefits and drawbacks. The Project Promise per-student costs are over four times those of the general program. The per-student tuition revenues realized by the university, however, are greater for the Project Promise program at a rate of $1,459 per student.

In addition to the fiscal analysis described above, this study sought to determine the satisfaction rates of program completers. The 1993-94 completers of Project Promise and the random samples drawn from the general program were asked to indicate their level of satisfaction with the preparation received through the respective programs. Satisfaction with the preparation was rated on a 5-point Likert scale from 1 (*not satis-*

TABLE 11.1 Costs and Revenues per Student

Program model	Facility Costs	Student-Teaching Supervision Costs	Instructor Costs	Total Cost (per student)	Tuition Revenue (per student per academic year)	Yearly Revenue Minus Costs
General program	$5.09	$12.50	$1,445.79	$1,463.38	$6,610.08	$5,146.70
Project Promise	$14.50	$18.50	$6,596.87	$6,689.87	$10,377.12	$3,687.25

fied) to 5 *(very satisfied)*. Each of the 15 Project Promise program completers rated their satisfaction a 5, indicating they were very satisfied. The postbaccalaureate sample from the general licensure program rated their satisfaction a 3.72 average, slightly less than *somewhat satisfied.* The undergraduate sample rated their satisfaction a 4.44 average, indicating that about half were *very satisfied* and the remainder *somewhat satisfied.*

Although there is strong competition for initial teaching positions in metropolitan and suburban areas of Colorado, 87% of the 1994 Project Promise program completers secured teaching positions within 4 months of completing the program. This is compared with 60% of the undergraduate sample receiving teaching contracts and only 40% of the postbaccalaureate sample. In addition, attrition from either the teacher preparation program or the teaching profession must be accounted for in a thorough cost-benefit analysis. Of those who completed the Project Promise program (15 out of 17) and secured teaching positions (13 out of 17), 100% were still teaching after 2 years. In comparison, 42% of candidates originally admitted to the general licensure program actually completed the program and were licensed; 46% of those who were licensed became employed within 4 months, and after 2 years 73% were still teaching. Said another way, of the original group of 250 admitted to the general licensure program from the same content area specializations as the Project Promise candidates, only 13% of individuals were actually teaching after 2 years.

This study found that more Project Promise candidates completed their teacher preparation program, more were hired by school districts, and more remained in the teaching profession than those in the general program. Candidate employability, candidate satisfaction, and retention in teaching are evidences of higher quality teacher candidates. The results of this study indicate that although Project Promise is a costlier program on the surface, its program completers are more satisfied with their preparation, are hired more frequently, and remain in the teaching profession more consistently than those completers of the general program (Richburg et al., 1996). Since these data were compiled, the cost of Project Promise has decreased considerably. The current director and associate director are both assistant professors, and the teacher-scholar position was funded by a grant that has since expired.

Does Program Structure Make a Difference?

A follow-up study was conducted after the teacher licensure program at Colorado State University added a professional development school (PDS) model to its licensure programs. This study was conducted to determine whether program structure makes a difference in employment, retention, and program satisfaction of those who complete teacher licensure. The study examined completers of the general program, the new PDS model, and the Project Promise model (Mantle-Bromley, Gould, McWhorter, & Whaley, 1998).

Results of this study with regard to employment and retention did not differ much from results of the cost-benefit study. For instance, significantly more Project Promise program completers (92%) were working for a school system 2 years after completing the program than were completers of the traditional program (71%); 81% of PDS completers were working for a school system. This result indicates that although the Project Promise model still exceeds both approaches to teacher licensure, the PDS model is attempting to bridge the gap. The pattern that emerged in the data analysis consistently indicated that the PDS results exceeded those of the traditional program but still fell well below results of the Project Promise program.

Respondents were asked to rate on a Likert scale from 1 (*poorly*) to 5 (*very well*) how well they were prepared in five areas: classroom management, diversity, lesson planning, technology, and teaching strategies. To determine whether program satisfaction varied by program structure, a one-way analysis of variance (ANOVA) was conducted for each of the five variables. Results of the ANOVA indicated that Project Promise ratings were significantly higher (more positive) than the traditional program and the PDS in the areas of diversity, technology, and teaching strategies. The Bonferroni technique was applied to the data, as was Levene's test of equal variances. The final analysis indicated that the Project Promise ratings were significantly higher than the traditional program ratings in four of the five variables. Only in the area of lesson planning was no statistical difference found. Between the Project Promise program and the PDS program, the final analysis indicated that the Project Promise ratings were significantly higher than the PDS ratings in the areas of diversity preparation and preparation in teaching strategies. In no areas were the

TABLE 11.2 Means and Standard Deviations of Program Satisfaction
Ratings

		Program Structure		
Knowledge Area		Project Promise (n = 36)	PDS (n = 36)	Traditional Program (n = 78)
Classroom management	M	4.09	3.77	3.37
	SD	1.06	.95	1.07
Diversity	M	4.52	3.69	3.51
	SD	.69	1.03	1.05
Technology	M	3.77	3.02	2.70
	SD	1.04	1.20	1.00
Teaching strategies	M	4.47	3.66	3.84
	SD	.65	1.04	.88

PDS ratings significantly different from the traditional program (see
Table 11.2).

Results of this study confirm the sustained excellence of the Project
Promise program in preparing teachers. Project Promise candidates
already bring a strong content area background to the teaching profession; as a result of the program, they are significantly more equipped
than other routes to licensure in the areas of teaching strategies and preparation for student diversity. Since this study was conducted, Project Promise has added an intense component of technology training (Paccione,
McWhorter, & Richburg, 1997). The new technology training is so comprehensive that some Project Promise candidates have been asked to conduct
in-service training while they were still student teachers. In addition,
many Project Promise program completers are asked to become technology resource contacts when they accept a teaching position.

Principal's Satisfaction Study

A study was conducted to determine whether school principals were
satisfied with the preparation of Project Promise program completers as

compared with other program completers (Lauterbach, 1998). A 28-item questionnaire was administered to the 16 principals who were supervising 17 of the 19 completers of the 1995-96 class of Project Promise. Of the 19 program completers, 1 remained in graduate school to complete a master's degree, and another was employed part-time in the Denver Public Schools. Only those who were employed full-time were included in this study.

Principals were asked to compare the Project Promise teacher with the average teacher of equal teaching experience. The survey provided a 5-point Likert scale ranging from 1 *(significantly inferior)* to 5 *(remarkably better)*. Principals received the survey from 1 to 7 months into the school year marking the Project Promise teachers' first year on the job. In each of the 28 survey items, principals rated Project Promise teachers' performance higher than that of an average teacher with similar teaching experience. The 28 items represented domains of professionalism; planning, organizing, and delivering instruction; content knowledge and pedagogy; and learning environment.

Although Project Promise first-year teachers were rated higher than an average teacher on every item on the inventory, Project Promise scored highest in the domain of planning, organizing, and delivering instruction. These are areas in which first-year teachers often have difficulties, yet Project Promise program completers exceeded principals' expectations in this area as well. This study adds to the growing body of evidence that the Project Promise program is an effective model for preparing nontraditional teacher candidates.

Conclusion

Even though this model for postbaccalaureate/midcareer candidates has been extremely successful over the past 10 years, it is not without its problems. As with all human processes, our selection process is not infallible. The program is not for all students. In the course of 10 years, six students have left the program within the first semester. Other students have found the emphasis on affective issues in education to be uncomfortable. Still others have found the accountability to the cohort to be too invasive or too demanding a commitment. For others, the stress and intensity are not a good fit for their personalities or learning styles. In addition, as gatekeepers of the profession, the staff has made ethical and moral decisions to ask two students to leave the program.

Likewise, the amount of time committed by the faculty can be prohibitive for some teacher educators. The 10 ½ months of instruction, supervision, organization, and support require full and focused attention. Because the staff is responsible for all instruction as well as all supervision, members of the staff must be able to model and deliver literally every skill and knowledge component of a teacher education program. In addition, concurrent with this process is the mentoring of the previous class, as well as the intensive recruitment and selection of the future class. The sheer time factor makes it very difficult, if not impossible, to devote time to writing. The "publish or perish" axiom must be given due consideration for faculty members on a tenured track. Program costs are also an area of concern. Candidates must have, or be able to secure, the resources necessary to engage in a full-time, nearly year-long program.

In 1991, a report of the Commission on the Education of Teachers Into the 21st Century stated, "For years teacher preparation has had the image of being accessible and accommodating—that is, easy to enter, relatively brief in nature, convenient to academic programs in the major, lacking in academic challenge, inexpensive, and non-exclusive." Project Promise challenges this image of teacher preparation and demonstrates that a program that is highly selective, academically challenging, intense in nature, and focused on students can produce excellent teachers.

For the past 10 years, Project Promise has prepared approximately 17 teachers each year who are making a difference in the lives of young people and in education across the country. In contrast with national statistics that indicate about 36% of those who complete teacher education programs actually land contracts (National Commission on Teaching and America's Future, 1996), over its 10-year history Project Promise has a placement rate of approximately 92%. Statistics on teacher attrition show that, of all the students who enter a teacher education program, only 27% are still teaching after 3 to 5 years (National Commission on Teaching and America's Future, 1996). Yet, 84% of Project Promise graduates are still in the classroom. Therefore, an investment in the preparation of Project Promise teachers truly becomes a perpetual investment in the future of secondary students in classrooms across America.

References

Darling-Hammond, L. (1996). The changing context of teacher education. In F. B. Murray (Ed.), *The teacher educator's handbook: Building a knowledge base for the preparation of teachers.* San Francisco: Jossey-Bass.

Darling-Hammond, L., & Sclan, E. M. (1996). Who teaches and why: Dilemmas of building a profession for 21st-century schools. In J. Sikula (Ed.), *Handbook of research on teacher education* (2nd ed.). New York: Macmillan.

Eifler, K., & Potthoff, D. E. (1998). Nontraditional teacher education students: A synthesis of the literature. *Journal of Teacher Education, 49*(3), 187-195.

Grant, C., & Zeichner, K. (1984). On becoming a reflective teacher. In C. A. Grant (Ed.), *Preparing for reflective teaching.* New York: Macmillan.

Haberman, M. (1992). Should college youth be prepared for teaching? *Educational Forum, 57*(1), 30-37.

Hopkins, S. (1995). Using the past, guiding the future. In G. A. Slick (Ed.), *Emerging trends in teacher preparation: The future of field experiences.* Thousand Oaks, CA: Corwin.

Hunter, M. (1994). *Mastery teaching* (4th ed.). Thousand Oaks, CA: Sage.

Lauterbach, D. K. (1998). *Principals recognize outstanding new teacher performance in graduates from Project Promise teacher licensure at Colorado State University.* Unpublished master's thesis, Colorado State University.

Mantle-Bromley, C., Gould, L., McWhorter, B. A., & Whaley, D. (1998). *Employment, retention, and program satisfaction: Does program structure make a difference?* Manuscript submitted for publication.

National Commission on Teaching and America's Future. (1996). *What matters most: Teaching for America's future.* New York: Author.

Paccione, A. V., McWhorter, B. A., & Richburg, R. W. (1997). *Coaching preservice teachers in technology: The Project Promise model.* Paper presented at the annual conference of the Society for Information Technology in Teacher Education, Orlando, FL.

Resnick, L. B. (1987). Learning in school and out. *Educational Researcher, 16*(9), 13-20.

Richburg, R. W., Knox, K. A., Carson, S. R., & McWhorter, B. A. (1996). Adding power to our ability to develop outstanding new teachers. *Teacher Educator, 31*(4), 259-270.

Richburg, R. W., Penna, C. J., McWhorter, B. A., Paccione, A. V., & Knox, K. A. (1996). *Can universities afford to train world-class teachers?: A cost-benefit study.* Paper presented at the annual conference of the International Council for Innovation in Higher Education, Vancouver, CA.

Sarason, S. B. (1993). *The case for change: Rethinking the preparation of educators.* San Francisco: Jossey-Bass.

Schlechty, P. C. (1990). *Reform in teacher education: A sociological view.* Washington, DC: AACTE Publications.

Schön, D. A. (1987). *Educating the reflective practitioner: Toward a new design for teaching and learning in the professions.* San Francisco: Jossey-Bass.

Wilson, A. L. (1993). The promise of situated cognition. In S. B. Merriam (Ed.), *An update on adult learning theory* (pp. 71-79). San Francisco: Jossey-Bass.

12 The Impact of the Alternative Certification Policy

Multiple Perspectives

Jianping Shen

Jianping Shen, a recipient of the 1998-99 National Academy of Education/Spencer Postdoctoral Fellowship, is Assistant Professor of Educational Leadership in the College of Education, Western Michigan University, Kalamazoo. His research interests include policy studies, leadership theories, and research methods. His recent articles have appeared in such professional journals as *American Journal of Education, Education Evaluation and Policy Analysis, Journal of Education Policy, School Leadership and Management, Journal of Educational Research, Educational Research Quarterly, Journal of Experimental Education, Journal of Teacher Education,* and *Theory and Research in Social Education.*

AUTHOR'S NOTE: This chapter uses some materials from the following publications: Shen, J. (1997). Has the alternative certification policy materialized its promise? *Educational Evaluation and Policy Analysis, 19,* 276-283; Shen, J. (1998). The impact of the alternative certification policy on the elementary and secondary teaching force in public schools. *Journal of Research and Development in Education, 32,* 9-16; Shen, J. (1998). Alternative certification, minority teacher, and urban education. *Education and Urban Society, 31*(1), 30-41. I thank the publishers for permission to use the materials in these sources.

The research reported here is supported by a fellowship awarded to me by the National Academy of Education/Spencer Foundation Postdoctoral Fellowship Program. I appreciate the support. The opinions expressed here are mine, however, and do not necessarily represent those of the funding agencies.

ABSTRACT

This chapter synthesizes the author's studies on the impact of alternative certification policy from multiple perspectives. It discusses the overall impact of the policy on the public teaching force, the impact at the elementary and secondary levels, and the impact on minority and majority teachers. The alternative certification policy appears to have a mixed effect in terms of fulfilling its promises. The data source for the studies is the Schools and Staffing Survey 1993-94, a large national survey conducted by the National Center for Education Statistics.

Introduction

Recent years have witnessed a continuing debate on alternative teacher certification programs and their impact on the teaching force (e.g., Bombaugh, 1995; Dill, 1996; Imig, 1997; Jelmberg, 1996; Myles-Nixon & Holloway, 1997; Neumann, 1994; Norton & Andersen, 1997; Shen, 1997, 1998a, 1998b; Zumwalt, 1996). Proponents of alternative certification (AC; TC for traditional certification) hold that alternative routes to teaching reduce the teacher shortage and enhance the quality of teachers. Nonetheless, opponents of AC argue that AC lowers the professional status of teaching and is not constructive for the future of the teaching profession. Given that the number of states allowing AC increased from 18 in 1986 to 41 in 1997 (Feistritzer, 1993, 1997; Feistritzer & Chester, 1996; Stoddart & Floden, 1995), it is important to test the arguments for AC against the empirical data. The purpose of this chapter is to synthesize my research (Shen, 1997, 1998a, 1998b) on the multiple impacts of AC based on the national data collected in the Schools and Staffing Survey 1993-94.

Arguments For and Against
Alternative Certification

Several major arguments can be made for alternative certification (AC). First, as summarized by Stoddart and Floden (1995), there has been a shortage of qualified teachers in urban schools and in subject areas such as mathematics and science, and therefore AC should be employed to alleviate the shortage. Second, it has been argued that good teaching is based primarily on subject matter knowledge and an enthusiasm for teaching; hence, opportunities should be provided to those people who are competent in subject matter knowledge and interested in teaching but who would not otherwise have the opportunity to go into teaching (Kearns, 1990; Kerr, 1983; Kramer, 1991). Third, it has been argued that AC teachers are older, more likely to come from minority groups, and more likely to have worked in other jobs than the traditional teacher education population; therefore, the teaching force can be diversified through AC policy (Cornett, 1990; Kirby, Darling-Hammond, & Hudson, 1989; Stoddart, 1990). This is particularly true for urban schools (Natriello & Zumwalt, 1993; Stoddart, 1993). Finally, it has been argued that the traditional university-based teacher education has monopolized preparation of teachers, and AC introduces competition into this area (Bliss, 1990; Cornett, 1990; Fenstermacher, 1990).

The arguments against AC are also multifaceted. First, it has been argued that AC lowers the cost of entering teaching and degrades the professional status of teaching (Darling-Hammond, 1990; Kirby et al., 1989). Ultimately, students (particularly those disadvantaged students in inner-city schools where teacher shortage occurs more frequently) are hurt by AC policy (Darling-Hammond, 1990, 1994). Second, the assumption that AC teachers know the subject matter and can learn to teach by working on the job has been questioned (Feiman-Nemser & Buchman, 1987; Kennedy, 1991; Zeichner, 1986). Research suggests that pedagogical content knowledge plays a very important role in teaching and that teachers without teacher education or certified alternatively have more difficulties learning to teach than those certified traditionally (Darling-Hammond, 1990; Grossman, 1989a, 1989b; McDiarmid & Wilson, 1991; Shulman, 1987; Wilson, Shulman, & Richert, 1987). Third, it has been argued that AC policy fails to materialize the promise of bringing into teaching those who have higher academic qualifications (Natriello, Hansen, Frisch, & Zumwalt, 1990).

What are the limitations in the existing studies on AC policy? First, data sources have been limited to a school district, a state, several states, several programs, or a combination of several school districts and states. Therefore, it has not been possible to generalize findings to the national scene. Second, most empirical studies of AC policy collected data in the mid-1980s; given the history of AC policy, these studies were not able to explore the impact of AC policy on the public teaching force. Finally, previous studies were preoccupied with curricular characteristics of AC programs, and sociological aspects of AC policy, such as the differences between AC and TC teachers, were largely ignored. The synthesis of my studies overcomes some of these limitations and contributes to knowledge of AC policy.

Methods

Data for the studies are extracted from the Schools and Staffing Survey 1993-94 (SASS93). SASS93, a large, national survey conducted by the National Center for Education Statistics, includes, among others, the Public School Teacher Questionnaire, from which the data are drawn. SASS93 has provided the first nationally representative sample to investigate the impact of AC policies.

Because AC policies have been in place on a large scale primarily for the past decade, my studies focus only on those teachers who were certified in the 10 years prior to the 1993-94 survey. TC teachers in this study are those who had the advanced professional certificate or the regular/ standard state certificate, whereas AC teachers are those who had the certificate through, as it is phrased in the questionnaire, "what the state calls an 'alternative certificate program.'" As is explained in the next paragraph, the extracted sample from SASS93-94 is weighted to ensure national representativeness. As a result, the relative weighted sample for the study includes 14,719 subjects—13,601 TC teachers and 1,118 AC teachers (weighted $N = 800,412$).

Because the sample design of SASS93 involves clustered probability sampling, stratification, and disproportionate sampling of certain strata, the resultant SASS93 sample is not a random one. Therefore, a relative sample weight, based on SASS93 teachers' final weight, is used to approximate the population but is adjusted down to the actual sample size of the study. Thus, the sample is a nationally representative sample of teachers certified in the 10 years prior to the 1993-94 survey, and the following findings are generalizable to the national scene.

Overall Impact of Alternative Certification

Geographic Distribution

The sample suggests that, among public school teachers who were certified between the 1984-85 and 1993-94 school years, 6.7% of elementary school teachers and 8.6% of secondary school teachers were AC teachers. The percentages were relatively small. AC teachers, however, were unevenly distributed across the country. At the elementary level, AC teachers consisted of 13.7% of the public teaching force in the Northeast, 8.7% in the Midwest, 5.3% in the South, and 2.3% in the West. At the secondary level, AC teachers constituted 14.3% of the public teaching force in the Northeast, 10.3% in the Midwest, 6.7% in the South, and 5.7% in the West. Therefore, on the national scene, AC policies had a moderate impact on the public teaching force.[1] The impact, however, was greater in the Northeast and Midwest than in the South and West. The pattern of impact at the elementary and secondary levels was similar.

Demographics

Gender. Among the 13,602 TC teachers, 23.7% were male and 76.3% female. As to the 1,119 AC teachers, 25.7% were male and 74.3% female. There was little difference between TC and AC teachers in their gender composition.

Age. The percentage of those younger than 30 years of age was higher among AC teachers (33.4%) than among TC teachers (28.1%), whereas the percentage of teachers age 50 or older was higher for TC teachers (8.7%) than for AC teachers (4.5%). It seems that a higher percentage of young teachers were certified through AC than through TC and that AC policy did not bring more older people into the public teaching force.

Work Experience and Professional Preparation

Main Activities Before Entering Teaching. When "What was your main activity the year before you began teaching at the elementary or secondary level?" was asked, a higher percentage of TC teachers (68.7%) than AC teachers (51.0%) indicated they were studying at college. A higher percentage of AC teachers, however, were holding teaching- or education-related positions (23.8%) and out-of-education jobs (22.2%) than were TC teachers (16.5% and 11.2%, respectively). Given the definitions of TC and AC, these findings were not unanticipated because it was expected that AC teachers would include a higher percentage of people holding positions in fields other than education. The surprise, however, was that, among AC teachers, 51.0% came right out of college, another 23.8% already held teaching- or education-related positions, and only 22.2% came from occupations other than education. This finding suggested that AC policy brought some experienced people into teaching but at the same time allowed many fresh college graduates to circumvent the TC process.

Degrees Earned. A higher percentage of TC teachers (99.0%) had bachelor's degrees than did AC teachers (96.7%). It appears that, as far as possessing a bachelor's degree was concerned, AC teachers had lower academic qualifications. Another way to compare the educational attainment by TC and AC teachers was to examine the highest degrees they earned. Data indicate that a lower percentage of AC teachers (22.2%) had master's degrees than did TC teachers (31.8%). Although the fact that AC teachers were younger might be a factor here, it is particularly disturbing to note that 2.4% of AC teachers had no degrees at all. Data on both bachelor's degree and highest degree suggested that AC failed to attract personnel with higher academic qualifications.

Subject Specialization and Subjects Taught

Subject Specialization. As illustrated in the literature review, one argument for AC was to overcome the shortage of mathematics and science teachers. This seems to be supported by data on subject specialization of respondents' bachelor's degrees. The percentage of teachers with bachelor's degrees in mathematics, science, or engineering was higher among AC teachers (6.5%) than among TC teachers (5.4%).

Subjects Taught. A higher percentage of AC teachers (19.2%) taught mathematics or science than did TC teachers (13.5%). AC policy seems to channel more mathematics and science teachers into the public teaching force. The percentage of AC teachers who had a bachelor's degree in mathematics, science, or engineering (6.5%), however, was much higher than that of those AC teachers who taught mathematics and science (19.2%).

Career Pattern

Becoming a Teacher Again. The respondents were asked, "If you could go back to your college days and start over again, would you become a teacher or not?" and they indicated their answers by using a scale ranging from 1 (*certainly would become a teacher*) to 5 (*certainly would not become a teacher*). The means for TC and AC teachers were 2.057 and 2.062, respectively. Therefore, no difference was found between AC and TC teachers in their plans to become teachers again. But as is illustrated in the next paragraph, this was not the case with their plan to remain in teaching.

How Long They Planned to Remain in Teaching. A difference was found between TC and AC teachers in their plan to remain in teaching. The differences between TC and AC teachers occurred primarily in the categories of "until I am eligible for retirement" and "undecided at this time." A lower percentage of AC teachers (19.7%) than TC teachers (22.7%) chose "until I am eligible for retirement," but a higher percentage of AC teachers (26.0%) than TC teachers (22.3%) responded "undecided at this time." These findings raise a question about AC teachers' intention to treat teaching as a lifelong career.

Impact on Elementary and Secondary Teachers

In the sample of my studies, 54.6% of TC teachers were in elementary schools and 45.4% in secondary schools, whereas 47.9% of AC teachers were in elementary schools and 52.1% in secondary schools. Therefore, a higher percentage of AC teachers were in secondary than elementary schools. The patterns of the comparative characteristics of TC and AC teachers, however, were similar at the elementary and secondary levels, and the patterns were consistent with those reported in the previous section on the overall impact of AC policy. Nevertheless, one significant difference was found between AC elementary and secondary teachers: All AC elementary teachers had bachelor's degrees, whereas 6.3% of AC secondary teachers did not have them. AC policy attracted a higher percentage of those without bachelor's degrees into the secondary than the elementary teaching force.

Impact on Minority and Majority Teachers

In the sample of this study, among TC teachers 87% were white and 13% were minority.[2] In contrast, among AC teachers 79% were white and as many as 21% were minority. Therefore, AC recruited a higher percentage of minority teachers than did TC. It is interesting to note that a very high percentage of minority teachers, and particularly AC minority teachers, worked in urban schools: 67% of TC minority teachers and 87% of AC minority teachers worked in urban schools, whereas the corresponding percentage for white teachers was about 40%. On the other side of the same coin, TC minority teachers, and particularly AC minority teachers, were much less likely to work in suburban and rural areas than their white counterparts.

Because the percentage of minority students in urban schools is higher, another angle to investigate the link among AC, minority teacher, and urban education is to inquire into the distribution of teachers in relation to the types of schools with a different percentage of minority students. For example, 67% of TC minority teachers and 89% of AC minority teachers worked in schools where minority students consisted of 50% to 100% of the student body; in contrast, only 21% and 25% of the TC and AC white teachers, respectively, worked in schools where 50% to 100% of the student body was minority. Thus, AC recruited a higher percentage of minority teachers into schools where minority students were the majority.

The aforementioned results indicate a link among AC, minority teacher, and urban education at the national level. In comparison with TC, AC recruited a higher percentage of minority teachers into urban schools where minority students constituted more than 50% of the student body. When one compares AC minority with AC white teachers, AC policies appear to have differential impact on the two groups. In comparison with AC white teachers, AC policies were able to recruit a higher percentage of older minority teachers who had higher educational qualifications and more experience in business and military service. AC minority teachers, however, in comparison with AC white teachers, had a higher percentage of female teachers, tended to work at the elementary level, were less willing to treat teaching as a lifelong career, and were less likely to have bachelor's degrees in mathematics, science, or engineering.

Conclusion

As my studies on the impact of AC policy indicate, some arguments for AC are not supported by the national data. In comparison with TC, AC fails to recruit a higher percentage of male and mature individuals into teaching, does not reduce the teacher shortage in rural schools, and is unable to recruit individuals with higher educational attainment into teaching.

The following arguments for AC, however, are supported by the national data: AC recruits a higher percentage of minority teachers into the public teaching force than does TC; a higher percentage of AC teachers than TC teachers work in urban schools where minority students are concentrated; a higher percentage of AC than TC teachers teach mathematics and science in public schools; and a higher percentage of AC than TC teachers have experience in business or military service.

The impact of AC on the public teaching force is similar at the elementary and secondary levels. The impact appears to be different, however, on minority and majority teachers. Data suggest a link among AC, minority teacher, and urban education. In comparison with all other three groups of teachers, a higher percentage of minority teachers enter teaching via AC and teach in urban schools where minority students make up more than 50% of the student body. Given the research findings that, generally speaking, minority candidates are less likely to enter teaching (Gordon, 1994) and that the number of certain groups of minority teachers continues to shrink in comparison with the increase of minorities in the study population (Rong & Preissle, 1997), AC appears to be constructive in recruiting more minority teachers. AC policies appear to have more impact on minority teachers than on white teachers, and more on the teaching force in urban than suburban and rural settings.

Therefore, the impact of AC is mixed when we view it from multiple perspectives. Further studies will help us have a more precise picture of the impact of AC. For example, an inquiry into AC and TC teachers' retention and impact on student learning will further our knowledge on AC policies. Furthermore, this study treats AC teachers as a single group.

Given the many kinds of AC programs (Dill, 1996; Feistritzer & Chester, 1996; Zumwalt, 1991, 1996), an effort to associate programmatic characteristics with qualities of their graduates will give us new insights. These two limitations do not negate the findings of this study, however, which focused on the impact of AC policies on the national scene by studying a nationally representative sample.

Notes

1. Because the result of statistical testing depends, in part, on the sample size, the null hypothesis could be easily rejected because of the large sample. Therefore, terms such as *significant difference* and *statistically different* are not used. Readers should pay more attention to the actual difference in percentages.

2. The concept of "minority" includes "American Indian or Alaska Indian Native," "Asian or Pacific Islander," "Black, Not Hispanic," and "Hispanic."

References

Bliss, T. (1990). Alternate certification in Connecticut: Reshaping the profession. *Peabody Journal of Education, 67*(3), 35-54.

Bombaugh, R. (1995). Coping and growing: Peace Corps Fellows in the urban classroom. *Journal of Teacher Education, 46*(1), 35-44.

Cornett, L. M. (1990). Alternate certification: State policies in the SREB states. *Peabody Journal of Education, 67*(3), 55-83.

Darling-Hammond, L. (1990). Teaching and knowledge: Policy issues posed by alternate certification for teachers. *Peabody Journal of Education, 67*(3), 123-154.

Darling-Hammond, L. (1994). Who will speak for the children? How "Teach for America" hurts urban schools and students. *Phi Delta Kappan, 76*(1), 21-34.

Dill, V. S. (1996). Alternative teacher certification. In J. Sikula, T. J. Buttery, & E. Guyton (Eds.), *Handbook of research on teacher education* (2nd ed., pp. 932-960). New York: Macmillan.

Feiman-Nemser, S., & Buchman, M. (1987). When is student teaching teacher education? *Teaching and Teacher Education, 3*(4), 255-273.

Feistritzer, C. E. (1993). National overview of alternative teacher certification. *Education and Urban Society, 26*(1), 18-28.

Feistritzer, C. E., (1997). *Alternative teacher certification: A state-by-state analysis, 1997.* Washington, DC: National Center for Education Information.

Feistritzer, C. E., & Chester, D. T. (1996). *Alternative teacher certification: A state-by-state analysis, 1996.* Washington, DC: National Center for Education Information.

Fenstermacher, G. D. (1990). The place of alternate certification in the education of teachers. *Peabody Journal of Education, 67*(3), 3-34.

Gordon, J. A. (1994). Why students of color are not entering teaching: Reflections from minority teachers. *Journal of Teacher Education, 45,* 346-353.

Grossman, P. L. (1989a). Learning to teach without teacher education. *Teachers College Record, 91*(2), 191-208.

Grossman, P. L. (1989b). A study in contrast: Sources of pedagogical content knowledge for secondary English. *Journal of Teacher Education, 40*(5), 24-31.

Imig, D. (1997). Professionalization or dispersal: A case study of American teacher education. *Peabody Journal of Education, 72*(1), 25-34.

Jelmberg, J. (1996). College-based teacher education versus state-sponsored alternative programs. *Journal of Teacher Education, 47*(1), 60-66.

Kearns, D. (1990, February 28). Do teachers really need licenses? *Wall Street Journal,* p. 14.

Kennedy, M. M. (1991). Some surprising findings on how teachers learn to teach. *Educational Leadership, 49*(3), 14-17.

Kerr, D. H. (1983). Teaching competency and teacher education in the United States. *Teachers College Record, 81*(3), 525-552.

Kirby, S. N., Darling-Hammond, L., & Hudson, L. (1989). Nontraditional recruits to mathematics and science teaching. *Educational Evaluation and Policy Analysis, 11,* 301-323.

Kramer, R. (1991). *Ed school follies: The miseducation of America's teachers.* New York: Free Press.

McDiarmid, G. W., & Wilson, S. M. (1991). An exploration of the subject matter knowledge of alternate route teachers: Can we assume they know their subjects? *Journal of Teacher Education, 42*(2), 93-103.

Myles-Nixon, C., & Holloway, P. (1997). Alternative certification: The good, the bad, and the ugly. *Delta Kappa Gamma Bulletin, 63,* 40-47.

Natriello, G., Hansen, A., Frisch, A., & Zumwalt, K. (1990). *Characteristics of entering teachers in New Jersey.* Unpublished manuscript, Columbia University Teachers College, New York.

Natriello, G., & Zumwalt, K. (1993). New teachers for urban schools? *Education and Urban Society, 26*(1), 49-62.

Neumann, R. A. (1994). Reconsidering emergency teaching certificates and alternative certification programs as responses to teacher shortages. *Urban Education, 29*(1), 89-108.

Norton, M. S., & Andersen, M. (1997). Alternative teacher certification: A study of first-year personnel in 11 western states. *Planning and Changing, 28,* 240-245.

Rong, X. L., & Preissle, J. (1997). The continuing decline in Asian American teachers. *American Educational Research Journal, 34,* 267-293.

Shen, J. (1997). Has the alternative certification policy materialized its promise? *Educational Evaluation and Policy Analysis, 19,* 276-283.

Shen, J. (1998a). Alternative certification, minority teacher, and urban education. *Education and Urban Society, 31*(1), 30-41.

Shen, J. (1998b). The impact of the alternative certification policy on the elementary and secondary teaching force in public schools. *Journal of Research and Development in Education, 32,* 9-16.

Shulman, L. S. (1987). Knowledge and teaching: Foundations of the new reform. *Harvard Educational Review, 57*(1), 1-22.

Stoddart, T. (1990). Los Angeles Unified School District Intern Program: Recruiting and preparing teachers for the urban context. *Peabody Journal of Education, 67*(3), 84-122.

Stoddart, T. (1993). Who is prepared to teach in urban schools? *Education and Urban Society, 26*(1), 29-48.

Stoddart, T., & Floden, R. E. (1995). *Traditional and alternative routes to teacher certification: Issues, assumptions, and misconceptions.* East Lansing, MI: National Center for Research on Teacher Learning.

Wilson, S. M., Shulman, L. S., & Richert, A. E. (1987). "150 different ways" of knowing: Representations of knowledge in teaching. In

J. Calderhead (Ed.), *Exploring teachers' thinking* (pp. 104-124). Eastbourne, UK: Cassell.

Zeichner, K. (1986). The practicum as an occasion for learning to teach. *South Pacific Journal of Teacher Education, 14*(2), 11-28.

Zumwalt, K. (1991). Alternate routes to teaching: Three alternative approaches. *Journal of Teacher Education, 42*(2), 83-92.

Zumwalt, K. (1996). Simple answers: Alternative teacher certification. *Educational Researcher, 25*(8), 40-42.

DIVISION IV

Summary

EFFECTIVE MODELS FOR ALTERNATIVE PROGRAMS IN TEACHER EDUCATION: IMPLICATIONS AND REFLECTIONS

R. Keith Hillkirk

Each of the three preceding chapters provided an example of the types of investigations that will enable us to continue to sort through the competing agendas in teacher certification. As Schlechty (1990) has observed, the fractious tendencies in education parallel that of medicine in its earlier history. Between 1840 and the early 1900s, "schools of medicine often represented specific schools of thought about medicine, and/or various faculty subgroups formed cliques that advocated one approach above others. Such developments were accompanied by monumental battles within and between faculties" (p. 46). Like medical school faculty in the 19th century, teacher educators and others who are concerned about the future of public schools and education are experiencing a watershed moment in the preparation of teachers.

248

Within this context, we need to continue to examine carefully the national trends in teacher certification that are the focus of Shen's study (Chapter 12). Several of Shen's observations need to be highlighted as they challenge underlying assumptions for alternative certification.

In Shen's words, in comparison with TC, "AC fails to recruit a higher percentage of male and mature individuals into teaching, does not reduce the teacher shortage in rural schools, and is unable to recruit individuals with higher educational attainment into teaching." At the same time, it does appear that alternative certification avenues do attract a greater percentage of minority teachers and do place a higher percentage of teachers in urban settings with higher concentrations of minority students. Whether those alternatively prepared teachers meet the qualifications that Haberman (1994) avers for urban teachers is unclear.

Focused on a statewide reform initiative—California's Class-Size Reduction Program—Stone and Mata's study (Chapter 10) reminds us that implementation of a complex, large-scale reform requires equally complex supports to increase the likelihood of its success. As they point out, much of the necessary support and assistance was most often supplied by uncompensated classroom teachers at the school site, rather than by mentor teachers who were compensated and assigned by the district. Echoing Darling-Hammond's (1994) critique of Teach for America, they note that the vast majority of the "fast track" teachers in their study were placed in schools with extreme diversity, low socioeconomic levels, and large numbers of limited- or non-English-speaking students. A reminder of Haberman's (1994) iteration of the ways that teacher preparation has failed urban students, the teachers in Stone and Mata's study were hurriedly prepared and placed in challenging classrooms with minimal structured support. Predictably, what these teachers report they lacked are the skilled coaching and mentoring that inconsistently appear in alternative or traditional programs.

In contrast, Paccione, McWhorter, and Richburg (Chapter 11) describe an alternative program, Project Promise, that has successfully incorporated several exceptional features over its decade-long history. Structured around student cohorts, a carefully defined knowledge base, integration of theory and practice, and intensive coaching, Project Promise provides a prime example of effective collaboration between public school and university-based teacher educators.

Conclusion

In 1986, Wisniewski lamented the lack of innovation and experimentation in teacher education during the 1970s and early 1980s. Well, times have changed.

The proliferation of alternative certification initiatives continues to spark intense debate and competition for resources. The sorting out of which practices and programs will survive remains an uncompleted task.

The pressures of alternative certification present both momentous challenge and wonderful opportunity to teacher educators. If we can muster the necessary courage and collective wisdom, we may yet achieve Fenstermacher's (1990) hope for a synthesis of the best of both the worlds of practice and the worlds of critical scholarship and pedagogy.

References

Darling-Hammond, L. (1994). Who will speak for the children? How Teach for America hurts urban schools and students. *Phi Delta Kappan, 76*(1), 21-34.

Fenstermacher, G. D. (1990). The place of alternative certification in the education of teachers. *Peabody Journal of Education, 67*(3), 155-185.

Haberman, M. (1994). Preparing teachers for the real world of urban schools. *Educational Forum, 58*(2), 162-168.

Schlechty, P. C. (1990). *Reform in teacher education: A sociological view.* Washington, DC: American Association of Colleges for Teacher Education.

Wisniewski, R. (1986). Alternative programs and the reform of teacher education. *Action in Teacher Education, VIII*(2), 37-44.

Index

pre-service teachers, 109
purpose of, 97-98
student engagements, 109
video vs print, 99-100
Certification. *See* Alternative certification
Class-size Reduction Program:
    alternative certification and, 204-205
    origin of, 201-204
    political support and, 216-217
    support lacking in, 215
    teacher shortages and, 204
Class-size reductions:
    classroom space needs from, 208
    primary grades and, 207
    reforms supporting, 207
    research on, 207-208
    student achievement focus in, 207-208
    subject selectivity in, 208
Clinical support:
    defined, 177
    factors primary in, 182
    mentoring problems and, 182
    organizational thinking, 182-183
    teaching reflecting, 182
Cohesiveness:
    as cohort dimension, 141
    defined, 141-142
    uniformity from, 142
Cohort groups:
    benefits of, 189
    characteristics of, 139-140
    college use of, 140
    dimensions of, 140-143
    institution racism, 189
    positive influences from, 189
    teacher preparation reinventing, 149-150
Collaborative mentoring:
    clinical supports, 191-192
    collegiality, 191-192
    rational supports, 191
    self-reflection, 192

social interactions, 191
transformation from, 192
See also Mentoring
Collegiality:
    equal relationship status, 181-182
    mentoring relationships as, 181
Colorado State University, 219
Common purpose:
    as cohort dimension, 141
    decision making sharing, 141
Constructivism:
    adults use of, 46
    effectiveness of, 59-60
    professional development and, 48-49
    reflections and, 74
    teacher evaluation of, 57-58
    theory of, 46

Draper, Lorena:
    background of, 158-161
    multicultural teaching, 158-161
    pre-service beliefs of, 189-191
    program selection criteria, 169-171
    social context for, 168-169
    theory into practice, 161-167
Duke Magazine, 133

Education Week, 200
Educational reform:
    analysis of, 62-66
    characteristics of, 67
    future challenges for, 67-69
    performance-based outcomes, 67
    professional development and, 2-4
    reflection and, 69-70
    school role from, 68-69
    science sustainability, 65-66
    teacher change sustainability, 67-68
    teacher knowledge and, 66
    teacher resources, 69
    teaching portfolios and, 112
Educational Testing Service, 178

CORWIN PRESS